Flight Into Oblivion

BY A·J·HANNA

JOHNSON PUBLISHING COMPANY

Composition and presswork by The William Byrd Press, Inc., Richmond, Virginia; binding by L. H. Jenkins, Inc., Richmond, Virginia; illustrated by John Rae.

This volume is affectionately dedicated
To my mother

SARAH JACKSON HANNA

Born on the Florida frontier on the very day
The tragedy of war was breaking at Fort Sumter

FOREWORD

A HAVANA correspondent, reporting the arrival in Cuba of the Confederate Secretary of War, General John C. Breckinridge, in the *New York Herald* of June 27, 1865, expressed the belief that the manner of his escape from the United States so savored of romance and adventure that it might "yet form the groundwork of an exciting novel or thrilling drama."

This adventurous episode, precipitated by the fall of Richmond on April 3, 1865, was made possible by the clever use of the Southern "underground" passage to elude both the Federal forces in Virginia and North Carolina and Stoneman's cavalry which pursued the Confederate leaders through North Carolina, South Carolina, and Georgia. Other portions of the United States Army and Navy which continued the chase to the tip end of the Florida peninsula were also outwitted. By weathering the storm-torn Gulf Stream in a sloop the size of a lifeboat, Breckinridge, former Vice President of the United States, finally landed safely on

Cuban soil. His narrow escapes formed only a small part of the moving drama created by the retreat of the Confederate Government.

Accused of the "greatest crime of the ages—a crime costing the lives of more than half a million men, and aimed at the overthrow of the best government the world ever saw" by the *New York Times* of May 1, 1865, and other Northern publications and officials, President Jefferson Davis and the Confederate Cabinet were not included in the terms of surrender granted at Appomattox Court House to General Lee and his officers and men, which allowed them to return to their homes and resume their normal existence.

On the contrary, there was a large public sentiment in the North clamoring for the severest punishment of the civil leaders of the South. "The same detestation that is now almost instinctively excited by the name of Catiline or of Arnold, should also," asserted the *Times* editorial, "through all future times be inevitable when the Davises, the Benjamins and the Breckinridges of the rebellion are remembered. . . . The leading traitors should die the most disgraceful death known to our civilization—death on the Gallows." Judah P. Benjamin, Confederate Secretary of State, wrote to his sister that he preferred to risk death in attempting to escape than to endure the "savage cruelty" which he was convinced the Federals would inflict on any Confederate leader who might fall into their hands.

To what extent were the Cabinet members and other Confederate leaders successful in their retreat? What happened to those who did fall into the hands of the Federals? And where did those who escaped go? Who, indeed, were the members of the Confederate Cabinet? Who got the Confederate treasure which wild rumor estimated at the impossible total of $13,000,000? Answers to these questions are known only to those who have made a study of this period. Almost complete oblivion has been visited on all but one member of the Confederate Cabinet, although for many years, preceding the War, their names were household words. An endeavor is made here to answer these questions by relating in a connected narrative the experiences of members of the Cabinet as the Confederate Government retreated south following the fall of Richmond.

Although this period in American history still arouses great interest and strong feeling, yet writers dealing with this sectional conflict have been so engrossed in the tedium of dates and battles and the bitter aspects of the so-called Reconstruction Era, that the official advisers of Jefferson Davis have been virtually overlooked or forgotten. Their flight, made by train, horseback, ambulance, buggy, oxcart, boat, and foot over nearly two thousand miles, ended in oblivion. But its stirring, continuous action surpassed much of the most imaginative fiction. The rare resourcefulness, for instance, of Colonel John Taylor Wood, aide to President Davis, in breaking away from the captors of the Confederate President, and his astonishing ingenuity in providing a safe passage through the wild jungles of Florida for Secretary of War Breckinridge, even to the extremity of temporarily becoming a pirate, are reminiscent of Marco Polo and his travels. A similarly breath-taking series of experiences were achieved by Secretary of State Benjamin, when in quick succession he escaped almost miraculously from one rapidly sinking boat and then was rescued from a ship a part of whose hull had burned to an eighth of an inch of its thickness.

The purpose of this volume is to describe an unique episode in the history of the United States, namely, the flight of the Confederate Cabinet. The reality of this episode has been recreated, it is hoped, by a brief description of conditions during those tempestuous months in 1865 immediately following the War, as they provide background for the hurried exodus from Richmond of the "Rebel Chiefs," as the "Yankees" called them. The reproduction of the bitter denunciations which form a vital part of those tragic times, though unpleasant and even revolting to read today, are, nevertheless, an index to public opinion and, therefore, essential to a true interpretation of the period.

Emphasis has been placed on that part of the narrative about which little or nothing has been hitherto published. Since the Cabinet is the subject, references to Jefferson Davis have been limited to his relations to the Cabinet as the Government retreated. Although he had no connection with the Cabinet, references are made to Alexander H. Stephens because of the position he occupied as Vice President of the Confederate States. More space has been allotted the escape through Florida inasmuch as this, the more dramatic part of the narrative, is least known. In the final chapter will be found a summary of the lives of the seventeen men, who, during the life of the Confederacy, held positions in the Cabinet.

A revival of interest in the Confederate Cabinet and a further study of the lives of its members may yet produce full-length, critical biographies and rescue them from the oblivion that has for so long engulfed them. Many of them were heroic figures whose careers might well "form the groundwork of an exciting novel or thrilling drama."

Rollins College   ALFRED JACKSON HANNA
June 10, 1938

CONTENTS

FLIGHT INTO OBLIVION

CHAPTER I

WHERE, AFTER THE FALL OF RICHMOND?

THE violence of the emotional storm which swept both North and South at the beginning of April, 1865, was bewildering in its intensity, whether produced by whiskey or faith, by despair or hope, by determined energy or helpless exhaustion. The curses it provoked were as ferocious as its prayers were fervent.

Virginia was the focal point of the divided nation. The First Lady of the Confederacy, Mrs. Jefferson Davis, and her four small children left the Confederate capital the last day of March, 1865, to seek refuge south of Richmond. When at parting her husband held her in a farewell embrace it was with the feeling that he might never see her again.

"If you cannot remain undisturbed in our country," President Davis told her, "make for the Florida coast and take a ship there for a foreign country." [1] Colonel Burton

N. Harrison, his private secretary, escorted Mrs. Davis, her sister, Miss Howell, and the Misses Trenholm from Richmond to Charlotte, North Carolina, in a special train that also carried some of the more valuable government records. These had been quietly packed during the previous few weeks.[2] Although President Davis and the Cabinet hung desperately to the hope of victory, they nevertheless made definite preparations for the abandonment of Virginia. The heads of each of the six executive departments and Captain M. H. Clark, Chief Clerk of the President's office, worked feverishly during the day and night of April 1, 1865, assorting papers, destroying the less important ones and packing the documents they deemed it essential to remove.

General Lee's Army of Northern Virginia, after a long year in valiant defence of Richmond and Petersburg, was beginning to yield its thirty-mile line to "overwhelming numbers and resources." General Grant's thrusts were gaining strength as the ill-clad, underfed soldiers in gray gradually weakened. It was the beginning of the end of the government of the Confederate States of America.

On Sunday morning, April 2, 1865, Richmond was outwardly calm despite rumors of impending evacuation emphasized by the booming of cannon in the distance. Many of the Confederate leaders had responded to the invitation of the church bells by the latter part of the morning. The popular Dr. Charles F. E. Minnigerode was conducting services in the aristocratic St. Paul's Church[3] when a telegram from General Lee, "announcing his speedy with-

4

drawal from Petersburg, and the consequent necessity of evacuating Richmond, was handed to me" in the President's pew, wrote Jefferson Davis. "I quietly rose and left the church . . . went to my office . . . assembled the heads of departments . . . and gave the needful instructions for our removal that night." [4] Members of the Confederate Cabinet who had been called to the President's office for this consultation returned immediately to their respective offices and resumed the packing of effects and records. Subsequent events were described by an eyewitness as follows:

"Suddenly, as if by magic, the streets became filled with men, walking as though for a wager, and behind them excited negroes with trunks, bundles and luggage of every description. All over the city it was the same—wagons, trunks, bandboxes and their owners, a mass of hurrying fugitives, filling the streets." [5]

The subdued unrest of the morning had completely vanished. Confusion was everywhere as members of Congress, various underofficials, and dignitaries clamored for places on all available trains of the Richmond & Danville Railroad which began leaving the Confederate capital late in the afternoon. About $500,000 in double eagle gold pieces, in Mexican silver dollars, in copper coins and in silver bricks, gold ingots and nuggets, packed in sacks and boxes—all that remained of the treasure of the Confederacy and the private treasure of the banks of Richmond—had been loaded, during the afternoon, on one train under the supervision of Walter Philbrook, Senior Teller of the Treasury Department, and a group of his assistants. It was guarded by sixty young midshipmen from the Confederate States Naval Academy who were told by their Commandant, Captain William H. Parker, that they had been selected for this dangerous service because they were known to be brave, honest, and discreet young men, and gentlemen. They had been rushed up to Richmond from their school ship, the *Patrick Henry,* on the James River, and had arrived just in time to prevent what might have developed into a serious pillaging of the treasure by a mob.[6] On another train were Brigadier General Josiah Gorgas, Chief of Ordnance, and a large number of employees from the armory which he had established at Richmond with the machinery captured at Harper's Ferry.

As the presidential counselors reached the railroad station, they were forced to push their way through hundreds of excited people seeking ways and means of leaving Richmond. The clear, calm, silvery voice of the West Indian born, Yale trained Secretary of State, Judah P. Benjamin, contrasted sharply with the cries of the hysterical crowd at the station. An Anglo-American lawyer of Jewish descent, he was about five feet ten inches in height, stout and had a pleasant, businesslike manner and a never-ceasing smile. His resolute, square face, animated by piercing black eyes that revealed unusual intelligence, gave confidence to those whose nerves were out of control. He had begun his service for the Confederacy at the outbreak of the War as Attorney General. Later he had acted as Secretary of War. His

6

*"Hundreds of excited people seeking ways and means
of leaving Richmond"*

chief contribution, however, as an adviser to and fellow
worker with President Davis, had been as Secretary of State.
Benjamin's was the most powerful intellect in the Cabinet;
his influence, the most steadying at this time.

7

The heavy-set, handsome Attorney General, George Davis of North Carolina, one of the noted orators of the South, soon joined his colleagues on the train. Having been graduated at the head of his class from the University of North Carolina, he had become a lawyer of distinction. His influence had been dominant in the Provisional Congress that created the Confederacy. From the beginning he had been a Confederate Senator. Only during the last year of the War had he become a member of the Cabinet. He was neither a relative, nor at first a supporter, of the Confederate President, but at this time he was one of the closest advisers and warmest friends of Jefferson Davis.

Intimate also was the relation between President Davis and the Postmaster General, Judge John H. Reagan, known as a "Grand Old Roman." Tennessee farm boy and woodsman, he had moved to Texas while it was still a republic, joined its army, and then had become a surveyor and later a lawyer. As his ability attracted attention, he was elected to Congress. He administered the Confederate Post Office Department so efficiently that it had been self-sustaining throughout the War.[7] Judge Reagan and the Secretary of the Navy, Stephen R. Mallory of Florida, were the only members of the Cabinet who held their positions during the entire life of the Confederacy.

Mallory's life had been as varied as had Reagan's. Born in Trinidad, an island near Venezuela, while his father, a New Englander, was engaged in an engineering project

8

there, the future Confederate Secretary of the Navy grew up by the sea in the island city of Key West, Florida, where his widowed mother kept the principal boarding house. On moonlight nights his flute was often heard in the traditional Spanish serenades he and his friends gave eligible young ladies. Ships became an absorbing interest in his life, an interest which was interrupted when he devoted a few years to formal studies in a Moravian academy in Pennsylvania. After fighting Seminole Indians in Florida, practicing law in Key West and serving as Collector of Customs in that city, he went to Washington in 1851 as United States Senator. Immediately he became active in the naval reform movement. His leadership in maritime activities led to his appointment as Chairman of the Senate Committee on Naval Affairs. As an observer of advanced experiments in this field he was aware that England and France were constructing iron fleets. Mallory realized, therefore, when he became head of the Confederate Navy Department, the futility of attempting to build wooden ships to compete with the superior numbers and greater resources of the Federals. Accordingly he adopted a policy of creating armored vessels and as a result of such pioneer work, he became a factor in revolutionizing naval warfare.

George A. Trenholm of South Carolina, Secretary of the Treasury, was the fifth member of the Confederate Cabinet to board the train about to leave Richmond. By self-training and hard work he had become one of the leading financiers of the country and was regarded as one of the wealthiest men in the South. Before the War his firms had handled fabulous sums in shipping cotton abroad where his credit was more than well-established. Fraser, Trenholm & Co., his Liverpool branch, was, next to the official Confederate agents, the most important representative of Southern interests in Europe and was the authorized depository of Confederate funds abroad. His companies in Liverpool and Charleston were also extensively engaged in blockade-running and similar enterprises on which the Confederate Government was largely dependent.[8] Trenholm's wealth had consisted of steamships, railroads, hotels, cotton presses, real estate, wharves, plantations, and thousands of slaves.

Not present, and probably not particularly wanted in the departing presidential party, was the Vice President of the Confederacy, Alexander H. Stephens, known as "Little Ellick" in his native Georgia. After the election of Lincoln he had endeavored to prevent the dismemberment of the Union but was soon swept into the secession movement. His commanding influence throughout the South was used in organizing support for the new Confederate Government and his leadership was continued as a member of the Provisional Congress. But as Vice President he had no power except to preside over its Senate. This irked a man of his restless and sensitive temperament. To make matters worse he had not been consulted by President Davis in the formation of policies. Consequently, Stephens remained at his Georgia home during much of the War period. Almost from the beginning of hostilities he had become leader of the opposition to the Davis administration. His public and private utterances and writings were constant, scathing, and unrelenting. One of his critics maintained that he would never be entirely satisfied until he had corrected the proof of his own obituary.

Numerous underofficials were helping President Davis, the Cabinet, and General Samuel Cooper, the Adjutant-General of the Confederate Army, move the government from the doomed Richmond on the night of April 2, 1865. Much of the responsibility, however, fell on two aides of the President, Colonel William Preston Johnston of Kentucky and former Governor Francis Richard Lubbock of Texas. Upon the arrival of the Chief Executive of the Confederacy, tall and slim, attired in a Prince Albert coat and trousers and waistcoat of Confederate gray cashmere, the official train finally creaked out of the station and headed for Danville.[9]

All but one member of the Cabinet were spared from seeing the saturnalia that took place in Richmond the night of the evacuation. "About dusk the government commissaries begun the destruction of their immense quantities of stores," according to the *Richmond Times.* "Several hundred soldiers and citizens gathered in front of the building, and contrived to catch most of the liquor in pitchers, bottles and basins, that was poured out. This liquor was not slow in manifesting itself. The crowd became a mob and began to howl. Soon other crowds had collected in front of other government warehouses. At some, attempts were made to distribute supplies, but so frenzied had the mob become, that the officers in charge, in many cases, had to flee for their lives.

"All through the night, crowds of men, women and children traversed the streets, rushing from one store-house to another, loading themselves with all kinds of supplies. . . . This work went on fast and furious until after midnight, about which time large numbers of straggling soldiers made their appearance on the streets and immediately set about robbing the principal stores on Main Street. Drunk with vile liquor, the soldiers roamed from store to store, followed by a reckless crowd, drunk as they." [10] Such was the report of a Virginia newspaper.

The one member of the Cabinet who remained in Richmond, General John Cabell Breckinridge, Secretary of War, was left behind to supervise the evacuation. What he witnessed after the departure of the President and Cabinet was particularly revolting. The restraint previously imposed by martial rule had disappeared. Thieves and deserters, several thousand of them, who had been awaiting just such an opportunity, swarmed out of dark and filthy hiding places and began plundering. Cotton and tobacco warehouses, public stores, and magazines were fired to prevent the Federals from using the supplies they contained. As the blazes spread, the city itself caught fire. Streets were soon blocked with screaming citizens dragging their household furnishings out of the reach of the flames. Throughout the night the mob pillaged stores and private homes.

Early Monday morning, April 3, 1865, Breckinridge, accompanied by a group of high army officials, rode out of this city of Roman-like hills and proceeded toward General Lee's headquarters.[11] As he left this tragic scene on the James River, he had ample opportunity to reflect on the strange turn his own life had so recently taken. Slightly more than one month before the War began, he was the second highest official in the United States—at the age of thirty-six. This unprecedented achievement had climaxed a career that had been advanced by pronounced political ability and rare powers of oratory coupled with an impressive bearing and personal magnetism that dominated through deep-set eyes, large and brilliant. Grandson of Attorney General John Breckinridge of Thomas Jefferson's Cabinet, he was trained at Centre College in Kentucky, at the College of New Jersey (later Princeton), and at Transylvania University. He had been a major in the Mexican War and had been sent to Congress twice by his native Kentucky. As Vice President of the United States he had presided over the Senate for a full month after the Confederate Government had been formed. Even after Lincoln, who had defeated him for the Presidency, took office, Breckinridge became a member of the United States Senate. He remained there until late in the summer of 1861, at least four months after the War had begun. His colleagues from the South had resigned many months before. Alone, he defended the South in its right to secede. He pleaded eloquently for peace and condemned the new administration

13

for initiating a war of subjugation. Convinced at last that war could not be averted, he became a major general in the Confederate Army and was subsequently expelled from the United States Senate.

Breckinridge had been head of the Confederate War Department less than two months. Five others had preceded him, and when he came into office the fortunes of the Confederacy were past saving. His outlook on the spring morning of April 3, 1865, as he left Richmond was none too bright.

His colleagues in the Cabinet, who had left Richmond by train the night before, were even less secure than he was and much less optimistic about the future of the Confederacy and about their own personal safety. Momentarily expecting an attack, their train followed the only available rails southwest from Richmond to Burkeville and then southward. The uncertainty of their situation was intensified by the ever-present threat of an attack by Major General P. H. Sheridan, whose withering devastation had converted the rich Shenandoah Valley into such a barren waste that, according to one description, a crow could not fly over it without carrying his rations with him! Frequent stops of their train, made necessary by the condition of the roadbed, slowed the journey interminably through the night of April 2 and much of the next day.

"As the morning advanced," said Secretary Mallory, "our fugitives recovered their spirits, a process which was doubtless aided somewhat by Mr. Trenholm, the astute Secretary

14

of the Treasury, whose well-filled hampers of 'old peach' seemed inexhaustible." [12] Mrs. Trenholm, the only Cabinet wife present, tenderly cared for her husband, ill with neuralgia, and cheered his Cabinet colleagues. Mrs. Breckinridge had remained in Richmond and later, with the aid of General Lee, returned to Kentucky. Mrs. Mallory had already gone to Georgia, Mrs. Benjamin was abroad, and George Davis and Reagan were then widowers.

The long ride from Richmond southwest to Danville through the sloping Piedmont section, a distance of only 140 miles, was so broken that the latter city was not reached until the middle of the afternoon of April 3. As soon as the people of Danville heard that Richmond was being evacuated and that the Confederate Government was retreating to Danville, a mass meeting was held at the town hall to discuss plans for its proper reception and accommodation. Mayor J. M. Walker presided and arrangements were made to provide quarters for the Government offices and temporary homes for the hundreds of refugees en route to southern Virginia.[13]

"Whether Danville will be made for the time the seat of the Confederate Government, we have no means of knowing," commented the Danville *Weekly Register*, but it inclined to the opinion that it would be. This newspaper was more concerned, however, over the "fate of the people of Richmond under Yankee rule," and uttered the prayer, "May God shield and protect them!" [14]

When President Davis and other ranking officials of the

Confederacy arrived at Danville, they were given an "Old Virginia Welcome," said Davis, by the city officials and a committee of prominent citizens who extended the visitors every hospitality. At the commodious Benedict House on

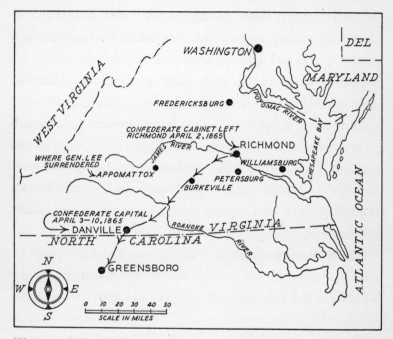

The route followed by the Confederate Cabinet after the evacuation of Richmond. Distances given are in statute miles.

Wilson Street, the offices of the Confederacy were temporarily established and partially reorganized, the presidential headquarters being situated in Major W. T. Sutherlin's mansion on Union Street,[15] now (1938) the public library. Although the future of the Confederate Government was desperately uncertain, the prestige of the head officials lent some stability to conditions surrounding Danville, the temporary capital.

But Danville was far from tranquil and there were many infractions of law and order. Probably with the purpose of instilling new hope in the people of the South and to counteract discouragement over the loss of Richmond, President Davis issued a proclamation on the day following his arrival in Danville. It gave, unmistakably, the impression that the head of the Confederacy had no intention of relinquishing the struggle. "I will never consent to abandon to the enemy one foot of the soil of any of the States of the Confederacy," asserted the proclamation; "let us . . . meet the foe with fresh defiance, with unconquered and unconquerable hearts." [16] Desperation rather than reason obviously produced such a statement.

Since no news of General Lee's army had been received, this overoptimistic proclamation, the last one made by the Confederate President, partially restored confidence in the Confederate Government. Day after day passed without any word, encouraging or otherwise, but when the heavy firing ceased it was inferred that the situation had improved. Rumors intensified the cruel uncertainty.

The fall of Richmond was hailed with jubilation by the North as the beginning of the end of the long and weary war. "It is a natural speculation to wonder what the rebels will do next," stated an editorial in *Harper's Weekly;* and then with reference to the Cabinet it said: "Their leaders are not men who will relinquish the struggle until the defeat and disappearance of their soldiers assure them that there is no alternative. Those soldiers comprise the most desperate men of the insurrection. . . ." [17]

In Philadelphia at Independence Hall on Tuesday, April 4, Phillips Brooks prayed with his accustomed eloquence. He thanked God for the fall of Richmond by the "power of Thy right arm" which has "set the banners of our Union in the central city of treason and rebellion." He prayed also for the continuation of Federal victory "till the great work is done, and there is no longer a rebel or slave in all our land." [18]

While in this manner the Deity was being invoked in the City of Brotherly Love, the President of the United States, Abraham Lincoln, exemplifying a more commendable spirit of conciliation, walked modestly through what Phillips Brooks had called Richmond's "streets of wickedness."

Unlike Brooks, Lincoln viewed the blackened walls, the fallen chimneys and the heaps of smoldering ruins of the burned and fallen Richmond, "with malice toward none, with charity for all," a policy he had urged in his second inaugural address made exactly one month before he reached Richmond.

Telegraph lines to all points were cut around Danville. It was known that Major General George Stoneman was approaching in a cavalry raid from the southwest. No one knew when or where he would next strike. Major General

W. T. Sherman had left a wake of desolation through Georgia, had "utterly ruined Columbia, South Carolina," he said, and had entered North Carolina with his large army determined to destroy General Joseph E. Johnston's Confederate forces. General Grant was moving from Petersburg in rapid pursuit of General Lee's tired columns.

Confederate Secretary of War Breckinridge had proceeded from Richmond on April 3 to Lee's headquarters. As he approached the rear of the Army of Northern Virginia near Amelia Springs, he observed long lines of army trains still burning—the result of an attack by the Federal cavalry.[19] On April 8 he wired President Davis at Danville: "I left General Lee at Farmville yesterday morning where he was passing the main body across the river for temporary relief. He will still try to move around toward North Carolina," continued the none too optimistic Breckinridge dispatch. "There was very little firing yesterday, and I hear none today. No definite information as to movements of enemy from Junction to Danville. Stoneman's advance reported yesterday to be near Liberty. Lomax reports enemy in considerable force advancing up Shenandoah Valley. No news from Echols, but he is supposed to be close on Stoneman's rear. General Lee has sent orders to Lomax to unite with Echols against Stoneman, and to Colston to make firm defense at Lynchburg." The last part of the message from Breckinridge, "the straggling has been great, and the situation is not favorable," was soon confirmed as the first of Lee's troops, utterly exhausted, began hobbling into Danville.[20]

Suspense in Danville increased in the absence of further news from Breckinridge or Lee. Uneasiness was succeeded by the keenest anxiety, mingled with despair. On Saturday evening, April 8, while President Davis and a group of his advisers were dining at the Sutherlin mansion, Lieutenant John S. Wise, after a hard ride directly from Lee's headquarters, reported that he was convinced Lee would soon be forced to surrender. "In my opinion, Mr. President," he said, "it is only a question of a few days." [21] On the following day, Sunday, April 9, the churches of Danville co-operated with the civil officials in maintaining a spirit of unity among the people by holding a union service which the President and the Cabinet attended.

Confirmation of the crushing report, that the worst had happened, that the seemingly invincible Lee, wedged in between overwhelming forces in both front and rear, had been forced to surrender, was received by President Davis and the Cabinet on Monday afternoon, April 10, when Captain W. P. Graves brought the official word to Danville.

"This news," wrote Mallory, "fell upon the ears of all like a fire bell in the night. . . . They carefully scanned the message as it passed from hand to hand, looked at each other gravely and mutely, and for some moments a silence more eloquent of great disaster than words could have been, prevailed. The importance of prompt action, however, was evident, and in a short time preparations for moving south, before the enemy cavalry could intervene and prevent escape, was in rapid progress." [22] The Cabinet members braced themselves for the ordeal of evacuating Danville, which they knew would be an undertaking almost as trying as that which marked their departure from Richmond.

Danville, though saddened over the loss of Richmond, had only a few days before derived a keen satisfaction over having been made the temporary capital of the Confederacy. Now no one knew how short the time would be before Danville, too, would fall into the Federal hands. Lee's capitulation had changed the whole city in a few hours. It was "crammed with people—soldiers and civilians—pressing southward, some to Johnston's army, some to the Trans-Mississippi, some following President Davis and the flying officials; the most (and they, the surrendered of Lee's army) pushed their way on foot, or perchance with one lame horse to a half-dozen soldiers, ragged, footsore, scarred and weather-beaten, to their far homes in the South, their fighting all ended." [23]

Colonel Harrison, who had rejoined President Davis at Danville after taking Mrs. Davis and her children to Charlotte, directed preparations for removing the officials, archives, and baggage farther south on the evening of April 10. Fortunately the treasure had already been sent on to Charlotte. As it went forward its reputed total had quickly increased by rumors to fabulous sums. So ill was Secretary Trenholm that he was carried to the depot at Danville in an ambulance. Secretary Mallory despairingly wrote: "Nothing seemed to be ready or in order, and the train, with the President, did not leave until nearly eleven o'clock. Much rain had fallen, and the depot could be reached only through mud knee deep. With the utter darkness, the crowding of quartermasters' wagons, the yells of their contending drivers, the curses, loud and deep, of soldiers, organized and disorganized, determined to get upon the train in defiance of the guard, the mutual shouts of inquiry and response as to missing individuals or baggage, the want of baggage arrangements, and the insufficient and dangerous provision made for getting horses into their cars, the crushing of the crowd, and the determination to get transportation at any hazard, together with the absence of any recognized authority, all seasoned by *sub rosa* rumors that the enemy had already cut the Greensboro road, created a confusion such as it was never before the fortune of old Danville to witness." [24]

Finally—but not until President Davis had taken time to write to the Mayor and Council of Danville a letter of appreciation of the courtesies they had extended—the official train of the Confederate Government left Virginia for North Carolina, where the anxious Confederates hoped to find a safer location for the re-establishment of their capital.

While the Confederate leaders were retreating toward Greensboro, the Northern press, assuming the War was over, expressed opinions as to how the Confederate President and Cabinet should be treated. "It is doubtful whether Jeff. Davis will ever be captured. He is, probably, already in direct flight for Mexico, and it may be that he will reach that refuge," said the *New York Times*. "But if he is caught he should be hung. . . . He was the prime mover in the rebellion. . . . He was the head and front of the conspiracy that precipitated the South into Revolution, and he has ever since been the head and front of the confederacy. . . . To endeavor to save him from retributive justice is to outrage every enlightened sentiment, every unperverted instinct. . . . To forgive his followers, will be noble and wise. To forgive Jeff. Davis himself, will be a miserable and most mischievous weakness," was the conviction of the *Times*.[25]

The *New York Tribune* flatly contradicted the *Times* by declaring that Davis not only did not instigate the "Rebellion" but was one of the latest and most reluctant of the notables to renounce definitely the Union. The *Tribune* condemned the movement to punish the Confederate leaders and begged that no vindictive impulse be suffered to imperil the victory. This paper further pointed out that a single Confederate led out to execution would be enshrined in a million hearts "as a conspicuous hero and martyr" and that the feeling would be immeasurably intensified if Jefferson Davis were hanged.[26]

Decisions about the treatment of the Confederate President and Cabinet were premature at this time in view of the fact that they had not yet been captured by the Federals and did not have the slightest intention of allowing themselves to be captured. They were making their way as quickly and as safely as possible from Danville into North Carolina.

Although the Confederacy had lost Virginia, and with

that state General Lee and his army, President Davis was determined to continue the struggle "with fresh defiance" as he had proclaimed in Danville. He hoped the Confederate forces in North Carolina would be sufficiently strong to repel Grant and Sherman. If that could be done, then he and the Cabinet would re-establish the capital of the Confederate Government in Texas or some other part of the South remote from desolated Virginia.

CHAPTER II

CONFEDERATE GOLD

SLOWLY and cautiously the train bearing the officials of the crumbling Confederacy passed from Virginia soil into North Carolina during the early hours of April 11, 1865. The darkness of the night intensified the anxiety of the noted passengers. Stoneman and his six thousand veteran raiders who had left eastern Tennessee the week before were not far away—that much the Confederates knew and that was enough to force upon them the disturbing knowledge that before they had proceeded far along the road to Greensboro their journey might be abruptly ended. Stoneman's object was to wreck bridges, culverts, depots, tear up railroad tracks, sweep away other aids to transportation and communication, and to destroy all supplies which his men, who were living off the country, could not consume. If accomplished, this would isolate Johnston's army in North Carolina and deliver it into the hands of Sherman. Stoneman's men did their work so thoroughly that as the Confederates were entering Greensboro the bridge they had crossed just outside the city was being burned by the raiders![1]

The distinction and prestige enjoyed by the Confederate President and Cabinet in Danville virtually disappeared when they alighted in Greensboro. North Carolinians, learning of General Lee's surrender and hearing ugly rumors of Sherman's "bummers" who were just at this time in their midst, were dazed and bewildered by the losses the South had already suffered. Shadows of greater misfortunes crossed their weary vision upon the arrival of the Davis administration, which they not only had not supported with enthusiasm but had often bitterly opposed. Inhabitants of the city stood in dread of threatened reprisals if comfort were given the "Rebel Chiefs," as the Federals called the Confederate statesmen. Consequently, neither were homes opened nor hospitality of any kind offered.[2]

North Carolina was not without reasons for her rift with the Richmond officials. The disaffection which had always existed in Greensboro had increased early in 1864 when a Union meeting, headed by some of its important people, was held and complaints lodged against "the state of things in Richmond" and about prison conditions in Salisbury. These Greensboro people regarded it "an outrage on our rights to be governed by foreigners from Maryland." The then Confederate Secretary of War, James A. Seddon, received a report which declared that some of the citizens of Greensboro had been insulted and even cursed by Brigadier General J. H. Winder, one of whose unpleasant duties it was to

"The bridge they had crossed just outside the city was being burned"

return stragglers, deserters, and absentees. Winder was labeled a "depraved, corrupt and drunken man, who has received bribes" and who maintained as spies "low rowdies from Baltimore." Even those who were steadfastly loyal to the Davis administration were moved to acknowledge the force and justice of these complaints.[3] Yet President Davis maintained that Winder was "too well bred and well born to be influenced by low and sordid motives." [4]

This Union meeting in Greensboro was one of several held in North Carolina, Alabama, Florida, and other Southern states in 1863 and 1864 by those who believed that the cause of Southern independence had become hopeless and that peace should be sought by the individual states if the Confederate Government failed to bring this result about. Some members of the planter class held this view after they had broken with Davis, but the majority of the more intelligent members of these groups were of Scotch-Irish ancestry or were Quakers who did not share economic interests with slaveholders. The ignorant who held no particular convictions were largely influenced by Northern propaganda. W. W. Holden, a political opportunist, was largely responsible for the movement in North Carolina. As editor of the Raleigh *Standard* he exerted considerable influence. Governor Zebulon B. Vance, aided by Thomas Bragg, one-time Attorney General of the Confederacy, was, however, successful in keeping that state in the Confederacy.[5] But by April 11, 1865, when President Davis and his Cabinet arrived in Greensboro, the morale of the population was entirely shattered. Lee's farewell message to his army was being tearfully accepted as the end of the War. People were more concerned with present needs for food and clothes than for a retreating government with a doubtful future.

Secretary of the Navy Mallory was so shocked by the lack of hospitality that he reproached Greensboro with the statement that "this pitiable phase of human nature was a marked exception to the conduct of the [other] people upon this eventful journey." [6]

"Wait, sir, until we get into my native state, South Carolina!" was the boast of Colonel Lubbock. [7]

"The possessor of a large house in . . . [Greensboro], and perhaps the richest and most conspicuous of the residents [John Motley Morehead] came indeed effusively to the train, but carried off only Mr. Trenholm," stated Colonel Harrison. "This hospitality," he added, "was explained by the information that the host was the alarmed owner of many of the bonds, and of much of the currency, of the Confederate States, and that he hoped to cajole the Secretary into exchanging a part of the 'treasury gold' for some of those securities. It appeared that we were reported to have many millions of gold with us. Mr. Trenholm was ill during most or all of the time at the house of his warm-hearted host, and the symptoms were said to be greatly aggravated, if not caused, by importunities with regard to that gold." [8]

Through the resourcefulness of Colonel John Taylor Wood, one of the President's aides, a temporary home was arranged for President Davis in Greensboro. Colonel Wood had inherited an adventurous spirit and a colorful tradition from his grandfather, General Zachary Taylor, twelfth President of the United States. Since Davis's first wife was a sister of Wood's mother, the Colonel was a nephew of the

President of the Confederacy and was naturally anxious to provide comforts for his kinsman. He had preceded the presidential party to Greensboro by a few days to make provisions for his wife and children while he was accompanying the President and Cabinet. In his family's modest

The "Cabinet Car"

quarters he and Mrs. Wood furnished a small, second-story room with a bed, a few chairs and a desk, for President Davis, over the determined protestations of their landlord.[9] This house was located on the site of the present (1938) National Theater.

The Cabinet, undaunted, made a temporary office for the conduct of business and sleeping places for themselves in a dilapidated, leaky boxcar. They called it the "Cabinet Car." From their Navy Store they drew bread and bacon and depended on "foraging" for eggs, coffee, and flour. Tin cups, tin spoons, and pocket knives were substituted for the more conventional silver and china when the Cabinet dined none too formally in Greensboro. The morale of the official family was strengthened by Lubbock's large stock of Texas anecdotes, Mallory's Seminole Indian war stories, and Benjamin's inexhaustible wit and good humor as one member overcame hunger "with a piece of half-broiled 'middling' in one hand and a hoe-cake in the other"; a second member divided "his attention between a bucket of stewed dried apples and a haversack of hard-boiled eggs"; a third one sternly ran "his bowie knife through a ham as if it were the chief business of life"; and a fourth member swallowed "his coffee scalding hot that he might not keep the venerable Adjutant-General waiting too long for the coveted tin cup." [10]

In Greensboro the Cabinet was relieved of one great worry—the $500,000 treasure. Captain Parker and his guard of sixty young midshipmen, who had transported it from Danville to Greensboro on April 6, when conditions in the lower part of Virginia held very little promise for the Confederacy, stopped only one day in Greensboro. He left there two boxes of gold sovereigns, approximately $35,000, for the President and Cabinet, and $39,000 for Johnston's army. He then took the balance of the treasure on to Charlotte, deposited it in the mint, and placed a heavy guard over it.

Having carried out his instructions, he endeavored to report by telegraph to Secretary of the Navy Mallory and Secretary of the Treasury Trenholm that his responsibilities had been discharged. Unable to get a message through to them, he investigated conditions between Charlotte and Greensboro and discovered, to his amazement, that Stoneman had raided Salisbury, fifty-three miles south of Greensboro, shortly after the treasure train had passed through that city. He learned also that the Federals had cut off all means of communication between the treasure train and the Cabinet.[11]

Stoneman's men had been so eager to get into Salisbury, seat of the famous prison they so violently hated, that they had swept aside the small force of Confederate defenders, wrecked the railroad tracks connecting Salisbury with the outside world, destroyed the depot, prison buildings and prison inclosure, spoiled vast quantities of corn, cotton, salt, rice, wheat, medical supplies, and arms, burned all the rations they could not use, and had taken more than one thousand prisoners.[12]

Captain Parker, alarmed over the crushing blow dealt Salisbury, sensed the danger of the proximity of Stoneman's raiders to the Confederate treasure, for which he was responsible. He knew of the various rumors which had enlarged the treasure to the impossible sum of $13,000,000, and that Stoneman would soon hear them. Parker further reasoned that Stoneman would then concentrate all his seasoned forces on its capture and that the Federals could without difficulty overpower the comparatively small Confederate guard. Consequently he immediately had the treas-ure removed from the mint at Charlotte and packed in a train with a large supply of sugar, coffee, bacon, and flour from the naval storehouse near-by. Fearing also that Stone-man might discover Mrs. Davis at Charlotte and make her a prisoner, he persuaded her and her family to join the wives and children of the treasury clerks who had boarded his outgoing train. Just as President Davis and the Cabinet were entering Greensboro, Captain Parker and his treasure train enlarged by a company of uniformed men, principally from the Portsmouth Navy Yard, were leaving Charlotte. These men, who had volunteered to help the midshipmen, increased the total guard to approximately one hundred and fifty men, thirty of whom were negro servants.

When the treasure train reached Chester, South Carolina, April 13, it was necessary to transfer the gold and silver to wagons, since there was no railroad to the next destination. While the loading was taking place, Mrs. Davis dined with Brigadier General and Mrs. James Chesnut at their tempo-rary home. When the wagons carrying the treasure were ready to start, Mrs. Davis and the other women boarded an ambulance and the men walked, but when they came to a five-mile stretch of mud and the ambulance could not pro-ceed with its heavy load, Mrs. Davis, carrying her baby in her arms, walked that distance through the darkness and in mud over her shoe tops.[13] Progress was slow but they covered a sufficient distance, about six miles, to avoid an attack in the event of a night raid on Chester. They camped at the red brick Woodward Baptist Church, arranged pallets on the benches for the women and children, and Captain Parker, head of the expedition, slept in the pulpit. The communion table was offered as a bed to Mrs. Davis but this she declined. A severe storm during the night made the entire group deeply grateful for shelter.

Assuming that Stoneman was close on their heels, Captain Parker and the Confederate sailors pushed on as rapidly as possible. They had breakfast at Mrs. Isaiah Mobley's on the Ashford Ferry Road and spent the night of April 14 at the plantation of Lieutenant Edward C. Means, in whose home Mrs. Davis and her children were made comfortable. The next day they crossed the Broad River on a pontoon bridge and thereafter took the precaution to station rear guards at each bridge they crossed. At Newberry, where they arrived Sunday, April 16, the treasure was transferred to a train and carried to Abbeville, where Mrs. Davis decided to remain with friends. The Newberry newspaper did not believe that General Lee had surrendered and announced that the rumor "must be an unmitigated falsehood of the enemy."

Captain Parker was determined to get as far from the Federals as possible. He tentatively planned to take the treasure to Macon, but, after having carried it by wagon from Abbeville across the Savannah River to Washington, Georgia, he changed his mind upon learning of the Federal occupation of much of that state. Following a brief rest in Washington, in the course of which coffee and sugar were exchanged for eggs, butter, poultry, and milk, he resolved after consulting leading citizens, to take the treasure to Augusta, Georgia.[14] It was well for the treasure that Parker did not take it to Macon because two days after it had safely reached Augusta, Major General Gustavus W. Smith, a former Confederate Secretary of War, was captured at Macon by Major General J. H. Wilson and his men.[15]

Back in North Carolina President Davis and the Cabinet had been considering with Generals Johnston and Beauregard "our present condition and future operations," as Davis phrased it. Though he was "fully sensible of the gravity of our position," said Davis, "I did not think we should despair. We still had effective armies in the field, and a vast extent of rich and productive territory both east and west of the Mississippi, whose citizens had evinced no disposition to surrender. Ample supplies had been collected in the railroad depots, and much still remained to be placed at our disposal when needed by the army in North Carolina." The Confederate President, however, sought information about the army in North Carolina and what, in the judgment of Generals Johnston and Beauregard, who were in command of that army, "it was feasible and advisable to do as a military problem."

Johnston and Beauregard met President Davis and the Cabinet at Colonel Wood's quarters in Greensboro on April 12, the day after their arrival from Danville. The meeting was continued on the following day when General Breckinridge joined them, after he had made the long trip by horseback from General Lee's headquarters.[16] It was hardly to be expected that Davis and Johnston could even at this critical time harmonize a lifetime of acrimonious differences. Johnston and Beauregard expressed their unqualified judgment that it was not in the power of the army in North Carolina to resist Sherman's advance. Johnston's conviction was that it would be the "greatest of human crimes for us to attempt to continue the war; for, having neither money nor credit, nor arms but those in the hands of our soldiers, nor ammunition but that in the cartridge-boxes, nor shops for repairing arms or fixing ammunition, the effect of our keeping the field would be, not to harm the enemy, but to complete the devastation of our country and ruin of its people." Johnston compared the military strength of the Confederate and Federal armies and pointed out that the former was outnumbered by the latter at least seventeen to one. His recommendation was that President Davis "exercise at once the only function of government still in his possession, and open negotiations for peace." [17]

In sharp opposition to Johnston's proposals, President Davis appeared convinced that it was futile for the civil authorities of the Confederacy to attempt negotiations. They had already been refused all terms other than unconditional surrender. Furthermore, he said he had reason to believe that the spirit of the army of North Carolina was unbroken and that the soldiers had earnestly protested against surrender. Davis pointed out also that even if the army were finally forced to give up, better terms could be secured by keeping organized forces in the field. Secretary Benjamin was the only member of the Cabinet who agreed with Davis. In view of the overwhelming majority against him, the Confederate President yielded, he said, to the judgment of his constitutional advisers and approved Johnston's proposal that he, Johnston, negotiate with Sherman for terms of peace.[18]

General Grant, in Washington, D. C., was expecting to hear hourly from Sherman that Johnston had surrendered. Such was his report to President Lincoln at his last Cabinet meeting on April 14, which Grant attended. Assuming that the War was virtually over, Lincoln and his advisers discussed policies for bringing the South back into the Union. In addition to Lincoln and Grant there were present William Seward, Secretary of State, Lincoln's rival for the Republican presidential nomination in 1860; Edwin M. Stanton, Secretary of War; Gideon Welles, Secretary of the Navy; Hugh McCulloch, Secretary of the Treasury; William Dennison, Postmaster General; James Harlan, Secretary of the Interior, and James Speed, Attorney General, the last two being from Kentucky, for whose loyalty to the Union they were chiefly responsible.

Making it clear that his policy would be one of conciliation toward the South, Lincoln emphasized his conviction, so Welles reported, that if harmony and union were to be restored, resentment would have to be extinguished. Lincoln hoped there would be no persecution of the South. He believed the Confederate leaders would flee to foreign countries "when they became satisfied their cause was hopeless. He [Lincoln] often expressed a wish," further reported Welles, "that they might be facilitated in their escape, and no strenuous efforts made to prevent their egress. This was more strongly enjoined upon me, perhaps, than upon any other member of the Cabinet, by reason of the blockade, which was rigidly enforced. In consequence of the fall of Wilmington, ocean communication with the rebels had almost entirely ceased, and escape by water was extremely difficult." [19]

The surrender of the Confederate Army in North Carolina was imminent. The loss of this, the only large organized force remaining in the field east of the Mississippi River, would precipitate the collapse of the governmental structure of the Confederacy. If Johnston's parley with Sherman failed, as Davis believed was more than likely, the high functionaries of the South would be left without adequate protection and therefore subject to capture. Openly exposed to these increasing dangers, President Davis and the Cabinet left Greensboro, North Carolina, on April 15 with an escort of Tennessee cavalry under the command of Brigadier General George G. Dibrell.[20] With them also was a company of Kentucky cavalry under Captain Given Campbell to act as scouts, guides, and couriers.

The railroad extending south of Greensboro had been wrecked by Stoneman's raiders; hence there was little choice in the means of transportation. Secretaries Breckinridge and Mallory and Postmaster General Reagan rode on horseback with President Davis, while Secretary Benjamin, Attorney General Davis, Secretary of the Treasury Trenholm and some of the older army officers, including General Cooper, were accommodated in ambulances, carriages, and wagons.

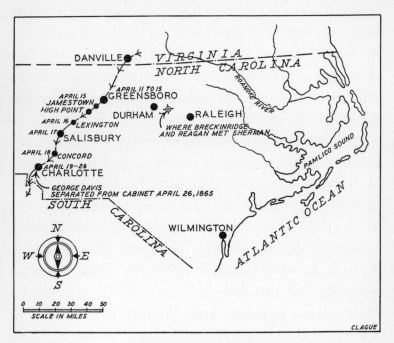

*The route followed by the Confederate Cabinet
from Danville to Charlotte*

The exodus was extremely slow and was accompanied by endless confusion. Hoodlums had begun stealing horses and raiding the quartermaster and commissary supplies. It was with the utmost difficulty that Chief Clerk Clark was able to make up a full train of wagons and ambulances for the transportation of the official papers, the $35,000 in specie that had been left in Greensboro by Captain Parker for the President and Cabinet, and the necessary provisions for the Government officials and their baggage, so general had become the pillaging, even shooting.

"Heavy rains had recently fallen, the earth was saturated with water, the soil was sticky red clay, the mud was awful," said Colonel Harrison. His responsibility for keeping the expedition in motion was an almost superhuman undertaking. Not far out of Greensboro he overtook the old ambulance, drawn by broken-down horses, that was carrying Benjamin, General Cooper, George Davis, and Jules St. Martin, Benjamin's brother-in-law who had been Chief Clerk in the Department of Justice. This vehicle was proceeding with such difficulty that it was forced to turn into the fields from time to time. Whenever the wheels would get stuck in the mud, George Davis and St. Martin would pry them out with fence rails. Through all these hardships Benjamin would cheer his companions by reciting Tennyson's "Ode on the Death of the Duke of Wellington"! [21]

It took not more than ten miles of this kind of travel to exhaust members of the expedition so as to force them to camp for the remainder of the night. This stop was near Jamestown. Some of the party, according to Colonel Harrison, were entertained at a house "at the top of the hill," where they were given the first good meal since leaving Virginia.[22] The next morning the retreating Government passed through High Point, seventeen miles below Greensboro, and remained the night of April 15, in camp four miles east of Lexington and nineteen miles south of High Point. Not unlike the inhabitants of Greensboro, the people in this section of North Carolina, fearful of the retribution that might follow from the Federals, remained indifferent to the comfort of the Confederate leaders.[23]

Zebulon B. Vance, Confederate Governor of North Carolina, reached Greensboro from Raleigh too late to join the retreating expedition. For the time being his round, unwhiskered face had lost its good-humored smile. Worry had restrained his usual rosy, sociable manner and had dishevelled his long, black hair which was ordinarily combed back from his forehead without any dividing line. His arrangements for an interview with Sherman had miscarried and he was eager to advise with Davis about the future. When he finally overtook Davis, the Confederate President invited him to a conference with the Cabinet. Davis appeared full of hope, Vance said, and "told me of the possibility, as he thought, of retreating beyond the Mississippi with large sections of the soldiers still faithful to the Confederate cause, and resuming operations with General Kirby Smith's forces as a nucleus in those distant regions."

Vance went on to say that Davis intimated rather than expressed a "desire that I should accompany him, with such of the North Carolina troops as I might be able to influence to that end. He was very earnest and displayed a remarkable knowledge of the opinions and resources of the people of the Confederacy, as well as a most dauntless spirit." In his report of this interview Vance said there was a sad silence around the council board following this statement by Davis, after which several members of the Cabinet spoke in support of the President's plans. The last Cabinet member to speak, Secretary of War Breckinridge, expressed his opinion that Governor Vance was not being dealt with candidly. His belief was that the Confederate Government's hopes of accomplishing the results outlined by Davis were so remote and uncertain that he would advise the governor to remain in North Carolina and to do the best he could for his people.

"Well, perhaps, General, you are right," remarked Davis. And when Vance explained that Breckinridge's views coincided with his own sense of duty, Davis arose and bade Vance farewell with the following words: "God bless you, sir, and the noble old state of North Carolina." [24]

While President Davis and the Cabinet were proceeding southwestward from Greensboro, General Johnston was interviewing General Sherman. Johnston was so much encouraged by his first conference that he telegraphed General Breckinridge to join him immediately. He believed the eloquence that had made that Kentuckian famous would so strengthen the Confederate appeal for peace that Sherman would agree to terms more liberal than those which General Grant had given Lee, although many in the North, including Ralph Waldo Emerson, regarded Grant's terms as too generous. Beauregard, with a weather eye for criticism from the executive department, urged Johnston to insist on the presence of a member of the Davis Cabinet to protect

Johnston, he said, from the "invidious and ungenerous remarks which would certainly be made, otherwise, by the surroundings of the President, relative to any terms he [Johnston] might agree upon with General Sherman." [25]

The Confederate Secretary of War, General Breckinridge,

Sherman's wake of desolation

left the presidential party at Johnston's request, accompanied by Postmaster General Reagan, who had proposed the bases for negotiations with Sherman. Early the next morning Governor Vance joined them a few miles east of Hillsboro, but neither Reagan nor Vance went with Breckinridge and Johnston to Sherman's headquarters. Sherman would not consent to include in the proposed terms of peace provisions for the Confederate President and the Cabinet. Johnston was of the opinion that Sherman realized the capture of the civil officials would prove embarrassing and that he, Sherman, wanted them to escape.[26] Sherman later revealed that he had in mind his confidential talk with President Lincoln, that Lincoln was not at liberty to commit himself but that Lincoln intimated that Davis "ought to clear out." [27] While Breckinridge and Johnston were with Sherman the Confederates were given the startling news of Lincoln's assassination, but it was deemed of the highest importance, said Vance, that this information be kept secret until the negotiations were terminated.[28] As the famous generals sat discussing terms of surrender, little could General Sherman have suspected that in less than three weeks General Breckinridge would be escaping down the Indian River in Florida past old Fort Pierce where this modern Attila, as the *London Times* called Sherman,[29] had begun his military career.

President Davis and the other members of the Cabinet had, in the meantime, crossed the Yadkin River by the railroad bridge and about sunset on April 17, Easter Sunday, entered Salisbury, seventeen miles below Lexington, with some hesitation because of Stoneman's recent raid on the city. The President and several of his colleagues were hospitably lodged by the Rev. Thomas G. Haughton at the rectory of historic St. Luke's Episcopal Church. It was reported that the head of the Confederacy was cheerful at tea and talked with a small group of friends who surrounded him here until rather late in the evening.[30] Taking no

chances on the safety of the presidential party, Colonel
Harrison and a guard slept on the rectory porch. From
Salisbury the Cabinet group went on to Concord where, on
the evening of April 18, ten of them, including President
Davis, were given accommodations at the home of Judge
Victor C. Barringer on Union Street.[31] The next morning
they started toward Charlotte, which Lord Cornwallis had
called a "hornet's nest" in Revolutionary days.

Refugees from exposed areas had, throughout the War,
crowded into Charlotte for protection and maintenance.
By the latter part of April, 1865, the city was completely
overrun by paroled soldiers, deserters, and stragglers. Just
before President Davis and the Cabinet reached Charlotte
they were met by Major General John Echols, who had
arranged accommodations for Secretary Trenholm at the
home of William F. Phifer, for Attorney General George
Davis at the residence of William Myers, and for Secretary
Benjamin, St. Martin, and Harrison himself at the house
of Mr. Weil, which Harrison had previously rented for Mrs.
Davis. Notwithstanding his towering presence—he stood
six feet four inches and weighed over two hundred and fifty
pounds—General Echols had been unable, he explained to
Harrison, to secure proper quarters for President Davis because Stoneman's cavalry had threatened to burn the house
of anyone who acted as host to the Confederate President.

"There seemed to be nothing to do," reported the bewildered Colonel Harrison, "but to go to the *one* domicile
offered. It was on the main street of the town and was

45

occupied by Mr. Bates, a man said to be of northern birth, a bachelor of convivial habits, the local agent of the Southern Express Company, apparently living alone with his negro servants, and keeping a sort of 'open house' where a broad, well-equipped sideboard was the most conspicuous feature of the situation—not at all a seemly place for Mr. Davis" and three of his staff officers, Colonels Wood, Johnston, and Lubbock, thought Colonel Harrison. Charlotte was not ready to become the Confederate capital as Attorney General George Davis hoped it would be.

As Davis entered the Bates house at the corner of Tryon and Fourth Streets he was hailed by a column of cavalry and asked to make a speech. Coming out on the steps, he thanked the soldiers for their greeting, highly complimented their gallantry and efficiency, and expressed his own determination not to give up hope for the Confederacy. At this time he received a telegram from General Breckinridge announcing the tragic assassination of Abraham Lincoln. The immediate general comment was that Lincoln's removal was a calamity to the South.[32] With serious misgivings the Cabinet reflected on the attitude of Andrew Johnson as Vice President and upon his record of marked hostility toward the Confederate leaders against whom he had made bitter attacks. The fact that Andrew Johnson had opposed Abraham Lincoln in 1860 and had supported Breckinridge for the presidency was now no comfort to Breckinridge and his colleagues in the Confederate Cabinet. Radicals in the North interpreted Lincoln's death as a divine rebuke to those who favored a lenient course toward the Confederacy. An unrestrained desire for vengeance on the South soon followed their deep grief. While President Davis and his Cabinet were awaiting word from Johnston as to what terms he could secure from Sherman, Easter sermons were being delivered in the North, more on the God of Vengeance than on the God of Peace; few were the exceptions. Severest punishment was demanded in unmeasured terms for the "traitors," as the Southerners were designated. The fruits of victory must be preserved, they contended, if the Union were to be preserved, "one and indissoluble."

Many Southerners were quick to repudiate the outrage upon the laws of chivalry, honor, and decency which the murder of Lincoln symbolized. A leading clergyman, the Rev. George M. Everhart, Rector of St. Peter's Church, Charlotte, preached vigorously April 23, 1865, the first Sunday after Easter, on the folly and wickedness of Lincoln's assassination.[33] According to a contemporary report: "President Davis and a part of his Cabinet, General Cooper and the military notables, with members of Congress and prominent citizens, made up a congregation the like of which Charlotte had never seen before, and, will, doubtless, never see again." [34]

The shooting of the President of the United States was, according to the rector, "a blot on American civilization, which in this nineteenth century of the Christian era is doubly deep in infamy. It is the tapping of a fountain of blood, which, unchecked, will burst forth and flow onward through the South as well as the North, and bear on its gory bosom a reign of terrour, like unto which that in the days of Robespierre would fade into insignificance."

The minister also warned that anarchy was already threatening the whole American continent "with its outbreaks of passion and madness, crime and outrage . . . this event, unjustifiable at any time, but occurring just now, renders it obligatory upon every Christian to set his face against it—to express his abhorrence of a deed fraught with consequences to society everywhere, and more especially to Southern society. . . ." [35]

As President Davis walked away from St. Peter's Church with Colonels Johnston and Harrison he said, with a smile: "I think the preacher directed his remarks at me; and he really seems to fancy I had something to do with the assassination." [36] Shortly after this occasion Colonel Harrison left Charlotte for Abbeville to look after Mrs. Davis and to make general plans for the retreat of the Confederate officials farther south.

Ten days after the North had celebrated Grant's victory and the South had generally accepted the situation, there was still definite doubt in the mind of the Confederate President as to whether the Confederacy was or was not at an end. Davis's disinclination to accept defeat was due probably to a complete faith in the righteousness of his cause, to the persistence of his own strong will, and also to advice given him by overoptimistic followers. Lieutenant General Wade Hampton, after reading the terms Johnston proposed to Sherman, wrote Davis vehemently protesting against their acceptance. While the military situation of the Confederacy was gloomy, he admitted, it was by no means desperate. He assured Davis that there were not less than forty thousand (probably many more) Confederates in arms east of the Mississippi, and a large force in the Trans-Mississippi Department. Hampton prophesied, without giving any reasons for it, that a war would soon break out between the United States on one side and both England and France on the other, in which event, he wrote, Southern men would be forced to fight by the side of their former slaves and "under Yankee officers." As another argument against the surrender of the Confederate Army in North Carolina, Hampton advanced the theory that the South would have to pay the debt incurred by the North for the War. A re-entry into the Union under any terms, Hampton believed, would force the South to suffer "base and vulgar tyranny," and "the horrors of war coupled with all the degradation that can be inflicted on a conquered people." No sacrifice, he wrote Davis, would be too great to escape "this train of horrors" and he urged fighting to the extreme limit. Hampton boasted that if he had under his command twenty thousand mounted men in North Carolina he could force Sherman to retreat in twenty days.[37]

That Davis still nourished the forlorn hope of reviving the Confederacy became evident at the next Cabinet meeting. As soon as General Breckinridge and Postmaster General Reagan reached Charlotte from the Sherman-Johnston parley, President Davis assembled the Cabinet for a meeting in the directors' room of Dewey's branch of the Bank of North Carolina on South Tryon Street, later the home of the *Charlotte Observer,* to consider the military convention Johnston had made with Sherman.[38] The propositions in this convention stated that if the Confederate States would cease to wage war for the purpose of establishing a separate government, the United States Government would receive them back into the Union with their state governments unimpaired and with all the constitutional rights recognized. Furthermore, the United States Government would guarantee protection for persons and property in the South. Discussion of this Johnston-Sherman agreement gave this meeting of the Cabinet a place of first importance in the history of the Confederate Government inasmuch as the decision involved meant life or death to that government.

Writing to Mrs. Davis about the momentous decision soon to be made, President Davis explained that he had asked each member of the Cabinet to give him, in writing, his opinion, first, upon the acceptance of the terms of the agreement; and, second, upon the mode of procedure, if accepted. Referring to the various eventualities, he wrote to her: "For myself, . . . it may be that, a devoted band of cavalry will cling to me, and that I can force my way across the Mississippi, and if nothing can be done there which it will be proper to do, then I can go to Mexico and have the world from whence to choose a location." [39]

Recommendations of the Cabinet on these two questions, including that of Secretary Trenholm, which had to be secured from his sickroom, were in substantial agreement with that of Postmaster General Reagan.[40] He stated the facts so logically that there could be but one conclusion. Argued he: "General Lee, the General-in-Chief of our Armies, has been compelled to surrender our principal Army, heretofore employed in the defence of our Capital, with the loss of a very large part of our ordnance, arms, munitions of war, and military stores of all kinds, with what remained of our naval establishment. The officers of the Civil Government have been compelled to abandon the Capital, carrying with them the archives and thus to close, for the time being, at least, the regular operations of the several departments, with no place now open to us at which we can re-establish and put those departments in operation, with any prospect of permanency or security for the transaction of the public business and the carrying on of the Government.

"The Army under the command of General Johnston has been reduced . . . and this force is, from demoralization and despondency, melting away rapidly. . . . General Johnston is of opinion that the enemy's forces, now in the field exceed ours in number by probably ten to one. . . . The Army west of the Mississippi . . . is inadequate for the defence of the country west of it. The country is worn down by a brilliant and heroic, but exhausting and bloody, struggle of four years. Our ports are closed as to exclude the hope of procuring arms and supplies from abroad. . . . The supplies of Quartermaster and Commissary Stores . . . are limited . . . and our railroads are so broken and destroyed as to prevent, to a great extent the transportation and accommodation of those remaining. Our currency has lost its purchasing power . . . and the people are hostile to impressments. . . .

"There is danger . . . that a portion, and, probably, all of the States will make separate terms with the enemy as they are overrun. . . . With these facts before us, and under the belief that we cannot now reasonably hope for the achievement of our independence, which should be dearer than life, if it were possibly attainable and under the belief that a continuance of the struggle, with its sacrifices of life and property and its accumulation of sufferings, without a reasonable prospect of success, would be both unwise and criminal." Judge Reagan urged with these arguments a speedy endorsement of the Johnston-Sherman agreement.[41] This agreement was approved April 24 by the President and Cabinet at this, the most important Cabinet meeting since the fall of Richmond. The terms of Sherman were more generous than those given Lee by Grant, a fact which later caused Sherman much unjust criticism in the North.

When the Sherman-Johnston agreement was reported to President Andrew Johnson it was disapproved, as President Davis had prophesied it would be. Johnston was, however, offered the same terms which were accorded Lee. Rather than continue hostilities he surrendered his forces on April

26 contrary to the order sent him by the Confederate President "to retire with his cavalry." Davis believed if Johnston had struck out toward Alabama he could have enlarged his army sufficiently to "vanquish any troops which the enemy had between us and the Mississippi River," and when safely in Texas, Johnston's forces could be joined to those of the Trans-Mississippi Department.[42]

Although the surrender of Johnston's army completed the capitulation of all remaining Confederate forces east of the Mississippi River, with the exception of those in Alabama and Mississippi under the command of Major General Richard Taylor, President Davis remained firm in his determination to maintain a resistance to the Federals. He called the Cabinet together April 26 at the Phifer home on North Tryon Street,[43] where Trenholm was ill, and mapped out plans for the continued retreat of the Confederate Government through South Carolina, Georgia, Alabama, and Mississippi across to Texas. Attorney General Davis resigned at this time to remain in Charlotte long enough to look after his motherless children and, if possible, his property in Wilmington. After discharging these responsibilities he expected to escape from the Federals as best he could.[44] President Davis and the other five members of the Cabinet, followed by a long wagon train of baggage, supplies, the archives, and the $35,000 in specie, guarded by a large cavalry escort, moved out of Charlotte April 26, 1865, with the hope of re-establishing the Confederacy west of the Mississippi River.

War hysteria in the North impelled the *Boston Transcript* to describe Davis as a "haughty, insolent and malignant traitor" who "appears now before the world in the character of a swindling bankrupt and fugitive thief, running away both from justice and his creditors, with the assets of the Confederacy he has sunk in boundless debts, accompanying him in wagons." [45] This powerful index to current opinion in New England, madly intent on completely vilifying the Confederate President, went on to say:

"Jeff. Davis made a speech at the beginning of the war in which he sneeringly asserted that such was the love for the dollar in the North, that it could not be even scourged into a conflict for the defence of the Union. . . . The last known of the rebel ex-(execrated) President was that he was somewhere in the mountains of North Carolina, evidently determined, if possible to get to Texas. He sneaked out of the rebel capital, having first appropriated to his own private use all the real money left in Richmond. Talk about love of the 'Almighty Dollar'! The meanest 'Yankee' out of the penitentiary would have carried off only the amount belonging to him." [46]

CHAPTER III

PURSUIT

E DWIN M. STANTON, impulsive and vindictive Secretary of War of the United States, had just severely rebuked Sherman by publishing the repudiation of Sherman's proposed terms to Johnston when word reached Washington that the Confederate President and Cabinet had left Charlotte. Stanton immediately telegraphed the Federal commanders in that region orders to "take measures to intercept the rebel chiefs and their plunder." He informed them that the Confederate treasure, or "plunder" as he chose to call it, was estimated to be between $6,000,000 and $13,000,000.

Stoneman's cavalry, having raided parts of Virginia, North Carolina, and South Carolina, was at that time returning to Tennessee. The Federal soldiers had supposed the War was over and had set their hearts on soon getting home. Stanton's orders changed their plans completely and irritatingly. Stunned and enraged by news of the assassination of President Lincoln, which had just reached them, their first impulse was for revenge on the South. Stoneman was instructed to send them across the mountains into South Carolina. He placed Brigadier General W. J. Palmer in command of the pursuit, arranged a concentration of two

Pursuit

brigades at Asheville, sent them to the headwaters of the Saluda River to scout down the river through South Carolina toward Augusta, Georgia, and commanded them to follow Davis and the Cabinet "to the ends of the earth" if necessary. He also concentrated 2,000 infantry at Asheville, ordered them to "clear that region of all rebels," and to hold the pass through the Blue Ridge Mountains.[1]

56

This new assignment of finding Jefferson Davis and the Cabinet somewhere in the vast territory reaching out from the western part of North Carolina to the Atlantic Ocean and to the Gulf of Mexico seemed well-nigh impossible of achievement; first, because the Confederates were passing through country thoroughly known to their escort; and, second, because they were aided by adherents who could be depended on not to divulge the secret route. Forced marches with only a few hours out for rest and sleep were necessary throughout the day and well into the night. It was, for the Federal cavalry, the hardest riding of the War. Fresh hoof-prints were in evidence in many roads but there was no means of ascertaining which road had been used by the retreating Confederates.

From Charlotte, the Confederate Government expedition moved southwestward through a part of South Carolina considerably apart from the smoldering path of the War. Plantations and small farms which they passed had not been visited by the ravages of war and remained typical of the prosperity enjoyed in ante-bellum days. Paradoxically the retreat here almost resembled a triumphal tour, as people lined the streets of small towns to greet the Confederate leaders when they passed. Many of the ladies shed tears of sympathy.

No sooner had the expedition crossed over into South Carolina than Colonel Lubbock's boast of his native state's hospitality was fully realized. As they neared a handsome mansion "a bevy of ladies approached the gate," related Colonel Lubbock, strewed beautiful flowers before Mr. Davis's feet, and "insisted on the President and his party dismounting. . . . They would not listen to us going further that day, and we spent the night." This was, according to Lubbock, the home of Colonel A. B. Springs,[2] near Fort Mill, about seventeen miles from Charlotte. Another part of the expedition was lodged at the home of Colonel William E. White, near-by.

Secretary of the Treasury Trenholm found himself too ill to continue the journey with the Cabinet and resigned at Fort Mill on April 27.[3] Postmaster General Reagan was appointed to succeed him. Before leaving the home of Colonel Springs on April 29, President Davis assembled on the lawn the Cabinet members and high officers of the military escort, to consider carefully the best route for the further retreat of the Confederate Government.[4] They now knew that the Federals were pressing in on this part of the country. Since the railroad bridge over the Catawba River had been burned, the Confederates crossed on a ferry at Nation Ford. "What a sight to see Jeff Davis and Breckinridge and the Cabinet standing on the pontoon. Dickinson and I thought of the Bruce and his retreat in the mountains surrounded by a few of his faithfull followers," exclaimed Tench F. Tilghman, a Marylander in charge of part of the baggage train of five wagons. Then he sadly added: "The cause has gone up. God only knows what will be the end of all this."[5]

At Yorkville (now York) the escorting cavalry scouted the

58

surrounding country thoroughly in order to be prepared for an unexpected attack from the Federals. The high officials, having stopped overnight with Dr. James Rufus Bratton, resumed their journey on the morning of April 30. They proceeded to Unionville (now Union), where dinner was provided at the home of Brigadier General William H. Wallace, who had not yet returned home from the front. Leaving for the southern part of the county, they spent the night of April 30 at the home of Mrs. J. R. R. Giles. Their next stop was for midday dinner at the historic "Cross Key" house, the home of Mrs. Warren Davis, near the Union County line about thirteen miles west of Unionville. Crossing the narrow, muddy Saluda River, they went to the home of the mother of General Martin Witherspoon Gary at Cokesbury, where they spent the night of May 1.[6]

Tilghman said they passed "some very pretty houses with elegant gardens" on the way to Cokesbury. Two of his comrades "breakfasted at a fine house" and "had an elegant breakfast. They also enjoyed a dish of strawberries, 1st of the season of which I got none," he complained, but, compensating for that oversight "young ladies were out in the porches to bow and wave their handkerchiefs. Bouquets were given us and we marched gaily on." Learning from their scouts that the Federals might be not more than ten miles distant, the Confederates rode out of Cokesbury early the next morning, expecting at any moment an assault. Stoneman's men, as they had been ordered, had been a "surprise and a terror" wherever they had appeared.

Finding that the Confederates had two days' start of
him, and that there were several rivers to cross on the way
to Georgia, at which small parties could successfully hold
the fords and ferries and destroy the bridges while the main
body was pushing on, General Palmer determined not to
pursue Davis and the Cabinet on a direct line, he said, but
to "strike by way of Spartanburg, and Golden Grove for the
head of the Savannah River, near Anderson, which would
enable me," he explained, "to effect a junction with the
other two brigades of the divisions which had marched from
Asheville, N. C., toward Anderson, and also to cross the
headwaters of the Savannah River at Hatton's Ford." He
learned from prisoners who had fallen in his hands from
the Davis escort that the Confederates were concentrating
at Abbeville. His supposition was that they would go on
to Athens, Georgia, where he hoped to overtake them.[7]

The Confederate President and his Cabinet were approach-
ing Georgia through that part of South Carolina in which
John C. Calhoun was born, reared, and practiced law. When
Mrs. Davis arrived at Abbeville, chief city of this region,
with the Confederate treasure guarded by midshipmen, she
had received the most heartfelt welcome since leaving
Richmond. She had remained at Abbeville at the home of
Mrs. Armistead Burt, niece of Calhoun, until President
Davis had sent Colonel Harrison from Charlotte to take her
and her sister and the Davis children farther south. Upon
his arrival Colonel Harrison remarked that the large and
comfortable homes of Abbeville were so lavishly embowered

with honeysuckle, yellow jasmine, wistaria, and a great variety of other flowers that a true picture of the "Sunny South" was presented. But Colonel Harrison was by no means sure that Abbeville would remain undisturbed much longer and therefore took his charges on to Washington, Georgia.[8]

In the meantime, Captain Parker, whose command of midshipmen and volunteer naval guards had carried the Confederate treasure to Augusta, Georgia, after leaving Mrs. Davis in Abbeville, had become very much concerned over his responsibility. For three weeks he had been held accountable for nearly all the money the Confederacy possessed. He had transported it from Richmond to Danville, from there to Greensboro, from Greensboro to Charlotte, then over to Chester, Newberry, and Abbeville in South Carolina, and finally to Washington and Augusta in Georgia. The ranking officials of the Army and Navy at Augusta would not share with Captain Parker responsibility for the safekeeping of the treasure. They were convinced, they said, that the War was over. Further complicating Parker's problem was an order from Secretary of the Navy Mallory to disband his corps of midshipmen. Obeying it involved an abandonment of the treasure. He ignored it.

Parker determined, instead, to locate President Davis and turn over to him the gold and silver with which he had been entrusted. He reorganized his guard, took the treasure back to Washington on a train and then in wagons across the Savannah River to Abbeville, South Carolina. He realized it was likely to be captured by Stoneman's men, but he was apparently less worried by that than by the threats of paroled Confederate soldiers, who, with the conviction that the spoils belonged more to them than to anyone else, demanded a division. Otherwise, they contended, the Federals would capture it and if so the Confederates would never get it back.

Two days after the President and his Cabinet had left Charlotte, Captain Parker returned the Confederate treasure to Abbeville and stored it in a warehouse in the public square. Groups of the large number of recently paroled soldiers there threatened to break into the warehouse and take what they regarded as their share of the gold. Confident that the midshipmen were sufficiently strong to resist such attacks, Parker relaxed from his strenuous duties on the evening of May 1 and attended a May party. He was awakened early the next morning by the guard with the terrifying cry, "the Yankees are coming." The entire guard was at once pressed into service to pack the treasure again— for the last time—and load it on the train for Newberry. By daylight the transfer had been effected and the engine was fully steamed, ready to go. Just at that time across the countryside could be seen armed horsemen approaching Abbeville—they were soon recognized as the advance guard of President Davis and the Cabinet.

With the well-deserved feeling that he had performed with distinction a difficult task, under the most harrowing conditions, Captain Parker turned the treasure which he had

guarded with such extraordinary fidelity, over to Acting
Secretary of the Treasury Reagan on May 2, and made his
final report to President Davis just one month after he and
the guard had taken the Confederate gold and silver out of
Richmond.[9] The midshipmen, whom he then disbanded,
were, he said "the best sentinels in the world . . . prompt in
action, and brave in danger, their conduct always merited
my approbation and excited my admiration. During the
march across South Carolina, footsore and ragged as they
had become by that time, no murmur escaped them and
they never faltered." [10]

At Abbeville President Davis, the Cabinet, and the high
army officers were hospitably entertained at the Burt, Perrin,
and other mansions. Danger of their capture had increased,
however, with the addition to their train of a half million
dollar treasure. When a report reached Abbeville that a
detachment of Federal cavalry had raided Anderson, only
thirty miles away, and that in all probability Abbeville
would be their next objective, President Davis assembled on
May 2 what he called "a council of war" at the home of
Major Burt.[11]

"It was a historic scene," was the comment of one who
was present at this meeting. "Mr. Davis presided, with
General Bragg, who had become by the surrender of Lee,
Johnston, Beauregard and Cooper, the senior general of the
Confederacy, on his right hand, and General Breckinridge,
Secretary of War and Major General, on the other side.
Next came Brigadier General S. W. Ferguson, a gallant

and enterprising South Carolinian, a West Pointer, a pet of Beauregard's and a favorite of Davis; next came Gen. George G. Dibrell, a plain, practical, sensible, middle-aged Tennessee clerk and merchant, who was beloved by his men

*The Burt mansion, Abbeville, where President Davis
found shelter*

and had justly won his spurs by long, hard, skillful, devoted service; next, on a little sofa, sat two young men—Brig. Gen. Basil W. Duke and Col. William C. P. Breckinridge—well known among the troops from Kentucky in the Confederate Army; and then, near General Bragg, sat General J. C.

Vaughn of East Tennessee, a brave soldier and an earnest man." [12]

President Davis, in a spirited and eloquent appeal, re-affirmed his faith in the righteousness of the Southern position and urged a continued prosecution of the War. When his hearers did not agree, he appeared not to understand how evident to them was the hopelessness of his vision; how definitely they all felt that the War was over and that a maintenance of the Confederate Government and its military organization was as undesirable as it was impossible. He seemed to realize finally, when those about him did not respond, that there was seemingly no further hope for the Confederacy. When he left the meeting his bearing lacked some of its usual erectness—apparently a painful and reluctant recognition that his leadership was at an end. [13]

At the Charlotte meetings of the Cabinet, President Davis had been able to maintain the formalities of the civil government, but the passing of a week had marked the collapse of all semblance of actual governmental procedure. An indication of this new condition was evident when another member of the Cabinet resigned. It was Secretary of the Navy Mallory, who, much depressed, explained that his family responsibilities would prevent his accompanying President Davis to the Trans-Mississippi Department or to a foreign country. He offered, however, to guide Davis as far as the southern part of Florida, where, because of his intimate knowledge of its coast, he believed he could assist the President to escape by boat to Texas.[14] When another official proposed to Davis that with an escort limited to four naval officers he attempt to escape to the East Coast of Florida and from there to Cuba or to the Bahamas, he appeared to resent the idea that his retreat might be looked upon as a flight.[15] Breckinridge and Reagan felt very strongly that Davis should now provide for his personal safety. They advised him to disguise himself as a soldier, go to the coast of Florida, take a ship to Cuba and in an English vessel cross the Gulf of Mexico to the mouth of the Rio Grande. There, in the Trans-Mississippi Department, they would meet him, they assured him, with as many troops as they could lead overland. But President Davis replied that he would not leave Confederate soil while a Confederate regiment was on it.[16] While this discussion was taking place, the Federals, by occupying important points in Alabama, were making a western retreat impossible and were holding Thomas H. Watts, Confederate Governor of that state and former member of the Cabinet, a prisoner.[17]

Conditions were now at such a critical point that those composing the escort of the Confederate Government had lost some of the awe in which they had previously held President Davis and the Cabinet, though they were still willing to help them escape. The trip from Charlotte, North Carolina, across South Carolina had been taken so slowly and the amount of baggage carried in wagons and ambulances had seemed so utterly unnecessary that some of the officers and soldiers had become impatient. A rather extreme opinion was expressed by General Duke who said that none of the Cabinet, with the exception of Breckinridge, "knew what was going on, what was going to be done, or what ought to be done." [18]   Although South Carolinians extended Davis unstinted hospitality and assistance in his retreat through their state, there were many who had ceased to support his leadership. The decided conviction of one of South Carolina's Confederate Senators, James L. Orr, was that "we have failed through the egotism, the obstinacy and the imbecility of Jeff Davis." [19]   The judgment of those surrounding Davis was probably best summed up by General Breckinridge when he said to one of the soldiers who at Abbeville asked him what course to pursue: "My young friend, I advise you to return to your home in Richmond by the nearest available route." [20]

However much the President and remaining members of the Cabinet might wish to follow that advice, they were not entitled to paroles and were not, therefore, free to follow the course being taken by the soldiers. George Davis, former Attorney General, had left the Cabinet in North Carolina and had gone to Camden, South Carolina, the home of his brother, the blind Episcopal bishop of that state,[21] and was endeavoring to leave the country by a secret route. Trenholm, former Secretary of the Treasury, had remained in South Carolina, too ill to go farther than his home "De Greffin" near Columbia,[22] where he was subject to immediate arrest. Mallory had just resigned from the Navy Department and was preparing to submit to arrest after he had joined his family in Georgia. President Davis and the remaining half of the Cabinet—Benjamin, Breckinridge, and Reagan—continued with their plans to escape to the Trans-Mississippi Department.

The treasure had been packed in wagons and was ready for an early departure from Abbeville.[23] Arrangements were made to pay it to the escorting officers and soldiers after they reached Georgia. Many official papers of the government were destroyed in Abbeville by the President's aides, Johnston, Lubbock, and Wood, assisted by Chief Clerk Clark. The more valuable ones were left by Colonel Johnston in the secret care of Mrs. Henry J. Leovy, his hostess. Those soldiers who did not want to be disbanded were expected to follow Davis and the Cabinet across the Mississippi River.[24]

In the North, insistence that the South be punished was stressed with vigor in the pulpit, on the platform, and in the press. It was known that the military power of the Confederacy was crushed but some Northerners suspected that the South possessed an arrogant spirit and that it would remain defiant and untamed. "We trust that the government will spare no efforts to catch Jeff. Davis, and all his lieutenants in treason, not already in its hands," declared the *New York Times*. "Most of them are undoubtedly in flight for Texas, thence into Mexico. Traversing a belt of country all through which there are very many still attached to them and anxious to facilitate their escape, they have many chances in their favor.

"Yet it is a ride of a thousand miles to the Mississippi; and this ride must be taken on horseback, as all the great lines of railroad are either destroyed or in our possession. The Mississippi itself, if rightly guarded, cannot easily be crossed without observation. With prompt activity on the part of the government, it is not unlikely that capture can yet be made."

Advocating a large reward for the capture of President Davis and his associates, the *Times* added: "These rewards ought to be large enough not only to stimulate the exertions of the loyal men of the South, and of that numerous class, who though calling themselves Secessionists, have been haters of the Richmond Administration, but also to tempt the very friends and adherents of the rebel leaders.

"Even should these rewards fail to produce the captures, they would do much to attach disgrace. The very fact that these men fled the country with a price on their heads, would put them more distinctly into the category of criminals. Its moral effect would be far worse for their names than if they left without any serious attempt to prevent it," concluded the Northern editorial.[25]

CHAPTER IV

A CONFEDERACY IN THE WEST?

General
Kirby Smith

PRESIDENT DAVIS evidently had no intention of allowing the Federals to capture him and his Cabinet. On the contrary, he persisted, even after the surrender of Lee's and Johnston's armies, in the belief, shared by but few others, that the Confederacy could be revived. His colleagues in the Cabinet, with the exception of Benjamin, advised him to abandon the idea of continuing a leadership which, while still respected, was without power. With but few exceptions his military chieftains urged not only a cessation of hostilities but an immediate surrender of all forces remaining in the field.

After General Lee's surrender, President Davis said he intended, if there should be "no prospect of a successful resistance east of the Mississippi . . . to cross to the Trans-Mississippi Department," where he believed General Edmund Kirby Smith and Major General J. B. Magruder would continue to "uphold our cause." [1] His confidence in the Confederate leadership west of the Mississippi River was strengthened by the advice of Colonel Lubbock. When news of Appomattox reached Texas, General Kirby Smith aroused the loyalty of his followers with a none too prudent order which told them: "with you rests the hope of our nation [the Confederacy], and upon your action depends the fate of our people. I appeal to you in the name of the cause you have so heroically maintained—in the name of your fireside and families so dear to you— in the name of your bleeding country, whose future is in your hands.

"Show that you are worthy of your position in history. Prove to the world that your hearts have not failed in the hour of disaster, and that at the last moment you will sustain the holy cause which has been so gloriously battled for by your brethren east of the Mississippi.

"You possess the means of long-resisting the invasion. You have hopes of succor from abroad—protract the struggle and you will surely receive the aid of nations who already deeply sympathize with you. . . .

"The great resources of this department, its vast extent, the numbers, the discipline, and the efficiency of the army, will secure to our country terms that a proud people can with honor accept, and may, under the Providence of God, be the means of checking the triumph of our enemy and securing the final success of our cause." [2]

President Davis also believed that the Confederate forces

in the Trans-Mississippi Department could be sufficiently enlarged to continue the war "until," he said, "our enemy, foiled in the purpose of subjugation, should, in accordance with his repeated declaration, have agreed, on the basis of a return to the Union, to acknowledge the Constitutional rights of the States, and by a convention, or a *quasi* treaty, to guarantee security of person and property. To this hope I persistently clung, and, if our independence could not be achieved, so much, at best, I trusted might be gained." [3]

Texas (which was alone as large as France and Belgium), Arkansas, Missouri, Louisiana, Arizona, New Mexico, and the Indian Territory, comprised the extensive Confederate territory west of the Mississippi River known as the Trans-Mississippi Department. The larger part of this vast Confederate country, far removed from the battlefields, thinly populated, without large rivers, undeveloped, almost without railroads, and possessing a long line of frontier, was virtually untouched by Federal troops and was capable of remaining unconquered for many years. Because of its complete absorption in the War, the Confederate Congress had not been able to organize this large part of its territory so far away. Officials of the state governments in this area had maintained a semblance of law and order but their control began to wane rapidly as the War progressed.

When, on July 4, 1863, the Trans-Mississippi Department was abruptly and almost completely separated from the Confederate States east of the Mississippi River by the fall of Vicksburg, a critical situation arose. The Federals held

the Mississippi River and had overrun Missouri and parts
of Arkansas and Louisiana, thereby cutting off the Trans-
Mississippi Department from its principal sources of military
supplies. Overland communication with Richmond was

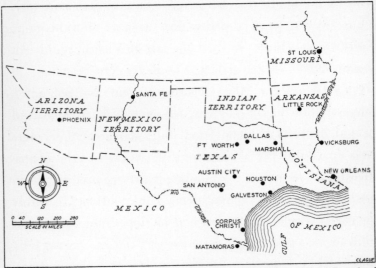

Copied from map dated June 30, 1863, in *Atlas to Accompany the Official Records of
the Union and Confederate Armies, 1861–1865*

*"Kirby-Smithdom," toward which the Confederate Government
was retreating*

rendered infrequent and precarious. Contact between the
Trans-Mississippi Department and Richmond was, however,
sometimes possible by sea. Its success depended on the
ability of the blockade-runners to evade the Federal blockading squadron in the Gulf of Mexico, whose watchfulness
was directed primarily toward the coast of Texas.

Anarchy in the Trans-Mississippi Department, under such conditions, was prevented only by the assumption of unusual military and civil powers by the Commanding General, Kirby Smith, one of the seven full generals in the Confederate Army. These powers, delegated by President Davis and the Confederate Congress, were a virtual assumption of the functions of the President as well as those of the Cabinet. Three weeks after the fall of Vicksburg, General Kirby Smith announced to all officers, civil officials, and agents on duty in the Department that, because of the inaccessibility of the Confederate capital, their instructions would henceforth come from him. So great, in general, was the confidence of the people in his ability and integrity that he succeeded in maintaining a strong military government and an orderly department. The civil functions, which he exercised with reluctance and caution, presented his most difficult problems.[4]

This thirty-nine-year-old dictator, son of Judge Joseph L. Smith of Litchfield, Connecticut,[5] whom President Monroe had sent to Florida in 1822 to preside over the Superior Court, had been trained at West Point where for a time he taught mathematics. His first real military service was in the Mexican War. Later he was engaged in Indian warfare on the Texas frontier. Resigning from the United States Army in 1861, when he held the rank of major, he entered the Confederate Army as a lieutenant colonel and was wounded at Bull Run. The next year he inflicted a severe defeat on the Federal forces at Richmond, Kentucky.

"My power in the Trans-Mississippi Department was almost absolute," Kirby Smith explained. "I bought cotton through my Cotton Bureau at three and four cents a pound, and sold it at fifty cents in gold. It passed in constant streams by several crossings on the Rio Grande, as well as through Galveston to the agents abroad." [6] This remarkable result was not, however, achieved with the stroke of a dictator's pen. General Kirby Smith organized bureaus and, at the suggestion of President Davis and the request of the governors of states in the Department, established a complete military and civil administrative system patterned after the Confederate Government.[7] In the administration of this gigantic system the Commanding General was forced to solve many perplexing problems, such as the conflict of regulations with state and local laws, the opposition of a minority to his dictatorship, and the suppression of private speculation.

The production of meat and grain on a mammoth scale helped to make this western "empire" self-supporting. Looms, factories, and foundries were located at important points in which such necessities for the army as clothing, blankets, tents, and other textiles were made.[8] Many supplies, however, such as munitions, had to be purchased from Mexico, the West Indies, and Europe. Without money, Kirby Smith used the only important marketable commodity—cotton. In order to do so, it was necessary to create a virtual monopoly for his cotton bureaus.[9] Through the alertness and resourcefulness of agents who were sent to the crossings on the Rio Grande, trade was continued and extended in the northern states of Mexico, where foreign buyers assembled and offered gold for cotton. A safe passage for the exchange of Confederate commodities with Europe was maintained through the co-operation of French and Mexican authorities.[10] The success of this plan involved the delicate diplomatic necessity of cultivating the friendship of Mexico and of insuring the sympathetic co-operation of frontier officials.

In order to enlarge the commercial relations of the Trans-Mississippi Department, the number of blockade-runners operated by General Kirby Smith was increased by dismantling and refitting the Federal warships captured on the Texas coast. Despite the Federal patrol on this coast, the Texas blockade-runners carried on a thriving trade with Matamoras, Havana, Nassau, and European ports. They brought in arms, powder, lead, caps, saltpeter, hardware, bagging, rope, drugs, dry goods, shoes, and salt, for which pay was made in cotton.[11]

"Of all the States of the Southern Confederacy," announced the *New York Times* of June 1, 1865, "the State of Texas has suffered the least—immeasurably the least—by the war. . . . Its comparative security has attracted to it tens of thousands of settlers from other parts of the South—from Louisiana, Alabama, Missouri, and also from the Cis-Mississippi States. Its population, by the last census, was 600,000; but there is reason to believe that it now counts over 1,000,000, about three-fourths of whom are white.

Thriving "Kirby-Smithdom"

Though its ports have been blockaded, neither its agricultural nor its general resources have materially suffered. Its crops of cereals have been good, and its cotton crop larger than ever. For a great part of its cotton crop it has found an outlet by way of Matamoras; and the large price in coin commanded by this article has made money abundant and general supplies plentiful." When the Confederacy east of the Mississippi River collapsed during the month of April, 1865, and as its governing officials were moving southward, President Davis knew that the Trans-Mississippi Department was not only self-supporting but prosperous. Moreover, it was, in general, secure from the threat of Federal invasion.

Not to be swayed from his determination to continue the struggle for Southern independence, Davis reflected on the possibility of gathering up the loose ends of the broken government and disorganized military forces in the East, transporting them across the Mississippi River, and creating there a new Confederacy, defended and supported by cotton. His determination was intensified by the danger of capture, which increased daily as he remained in the East. As he retreated through North Carolina he made Texas his objective.

In the judgment of some of President Davis's advisers, an overland retreat to the West was impossible due to Federal occupation of much of Georgia, Alabama, and Mississippi, through which states he intended to make his way. Several of these officials, convinced that they would be forced to choose another route, planned an escape by water for the President and Cabinet. Colonel Charles E. Thorburn, naval purchasing agent and blockade-runner, who had joined the Cabinet at Greensboro on April 12, was entrusted with this mission. Colonel Wood, aide to the President, arranged with Colonel Thorburn to ride south considerably in advance of the presidential expedition, make ready a small but seaworthy vessel he had hidden in the Indian River on Florida's East Coast, and rejoin the Confederate high officials in the northern part of Florida. From there he was to conduct them to the waiting ship.[12] Once around the peninsula of Florida, the Gulf of Mexico afforded a straightaway of about nine hundred miles to "Kirby-Smithdom,"[13] as the Trans-Mississippi Department was sometimes called. Galveston or Matamoras, the Mexican port which had been such an important center of communication for the Confederates, offered a safe entry into Texas.

In the meantime Northern leaders were demanding that the Confederate officials be caught before they could escape to foreign lands. "The gallows," shrieked an editorial in a leading New York paper, with grim delight over the prospect of satiating its desire for vengeance, "and not expatriation should be their fate."[14] The murder of Lincoln had not only lessened the tendency toward conciliation between the North and the South, a policy Lincoln had fostered, but it had stirred the Northern impulse to avenge his death, a loss which some Northerners, in the high emotion of their grief, attributed to the South. This desire for revenge, which was expressed through the press, the pulpit, and other mediums, became unreasoning, even fierce, as tension rose in this critical period.

General Kirby Smith realized that, if the Confederacy east of the Mississippi collapsed, even "Kirby-Smithdom" might eventually be forced to surrender. He proceeded, therefore, to make overtures to the Mexicans. One of his agents was commissioned to present several considerations designed to arrest the attention of his Imperial Highness, Maximilian, gain his sympathy, and secure his aid. By quoting statements made in the North, even in Congress, General Kirby Smith developed a strong plea by which he hoped to convince Maximilian that, if the Confederate States were conquered, the next step on the part of the Federals would be to attack Mexico in order to annex an even larger territory than that which the United States had boldly and without right taken from Mexico less than two decades before. The General's conclusion was a convincing appeal to the Emperor to realize that the "future interests of the Confederate States and of the Empire of Mexico" were identical in their defensive policy against the United States, which, Kirby Smith endeavored to prove, was already "nursing and maturing" further schemes of ambition and of territorial aggrandizement.

Although he disclaimed any authority to represent the Confederacy officially through diplomatic channels, the Trans-Mississippi dictator made it clear that the Con-

federates would be "willing to enter a liberal agreement
based upon the principle of mutual protection from their
common enemy." He assured his Imperial Highness that
"many trained soldiers inured to the hardships of the field,
and inspired with a bitter hatred of the Federals" were
available for such service as the Mexican Emperor might
require.[15]

In preparation for the worst that might befall the Trans-
Mississippi Department, General Kirby Smith informed
Maximilian of his intention to seek refuge personally at
the Imperial Court. He intimated that if he himself went
to Mexico his influence could be a factor in inducing
Southerners to colonize below the Rio Grande.[16] While
these negotiations were going on, the General was devoting
his best efforts to keeping the Trans-Mississippi in readiness
for the arrival of the President and his Cabinet. Plans were
being matured for the organization of an army of fifteen
thousand at Marshall, Texas, to join the Richmond officials
upon their arrival from the East. These Texans expected
that President Davis would lead the combined expedition
into Mexico and place it at the disposal of the Emperor
Maximilian if "Kirby-Smithdom" could not be held against
the Federals.[17]

Such was the situation, inspired by an able, active, and
venturesome leader, General Edmund Kirby Smith, in the
Confederate territory west of the Mississippi River toward
which President Davis and the Cabinet, as they left South
Carolina, were marching.

CHAPTER V

OF FREEDOM AND IMPRISONMENT

A FTER Appomattox, South-
erners were so confused and
apprehensive, and the ordinary methods of communi-
cation were so generally
disrupted, that only those
who chanced to be along the
secret route followed by the
Confederate President and
Cabinet knew the where-
abouts of those officials.
"Great curiosity is naturally felt North and South,"
stated the *Richmond Evening Whig* of April 25, 1865, "to
learn what has become of Jefferson Davis, the head and
front of the greatest rebellion the world has yet seen. . . .
His one object now is to escape to the Trans-Mississippi
and he cannot regard himself out of extreme danger until
he has run the gauntlet of the United States Armies now
operating in Alabama. . . . [His escort of] two thousand
horsemen form today a gloomy cavalcade as they toil along
the southern sandy roads under a southern sun. . . . Davis,
Breckinridge, Trenholm, Benjamin, St. John and Reagan

all ride in the centre of that forlorn band. . . . They bear with them no affection of the people of Richmond, though they have left us a lasting memento in the charred and blackened ruins of the fairest portion of our beautiful city."

This critical attitude was no doubt inspired by the censorship of the Federal military power which had controlled Richmond since the Confederate Government was moved from its capital three weeks before. More representative of the general attitude of the Southern people was the statement of the Edgefield, South Carolina, *Advertiser:* "We would like to inform our readers where these gentlemen [President Davis and the Cabinet] are and what they are doing, but we cannot. Their whereabouts and doings are shrouded in mystery unfathomable to mortal ken. We would not insinuate for a moment that President Davis is not in the right place and doing the right thing; we believe he is. We honor and trust him still, and hold the opinion that he will yet prove himself to be what we thought him when we placed him in the presidential chair." The Augusta, Georgia, *Constitutionalist* announced the receipt of information "on creditable authority" that the President and Cabinet had returned to Richmond to open negotiations.[1] President Davis and the Cabinet were, however, heading in the opposite direction from Richmond, toward the Trans-Mississippi Department, the last week of April, 1865.

At the same time an aide of General Sherman was hurrying to Key West, Florida. Arriving there on May 1, this officer informed the Federal garrison that the Confederate President and his Cabinet had succeeded so far in their plans to leave the country and asked for co-operation in a final effort to capture them. On May 2, the day on which President Andrew Johnson, tricked into believing that the Bureau of Military Justice possessed evidence proving that the assassination of Lincoln was "incited, concerted and procured by and between Jefferson Davis" and other Southern leaders, announced a reward of $100,000 for the capture of President Davis,[2] Rear Admiral Cornelius K. Stribling dispatched a vessel from Key West up the West Coast of Florida to instruct officers in all the ports to catch Davis and his colleagues before they could escape. He also ordered the fishing boats and all other craft out of Key West to return to that place and all cruising vessels to guard, with utmost vigilance, the entire coast. As a further precaution, two expeditions were sent to cruise inside the reef and among the keys to Cape Florida. A third, under Commander George H. Cooper, was ordered on May 3 to take possession of Key Biscayne near the present (1938) city of Miami and to guard the passages from Bear Cut to the north end of Key Biscayne as well as to the Gulf Stream.[3]

Up in South Carolina where the Confederate officials had stopped temporarily, it was cold and rainy. As Stoneman's men were thought to be fast approaching Abbeville, time was becoming more precious than ever. At midnight of May 2, when it was darkest, President Davis, Secretary of State Benjamin, Postmaster General Reagan, who was also Acting Secretary of the Treasury, and former Secretary of the Navy Mallory, accompanied by the President's Staff and a small escort, hurriedly left Abbeville. Captain Clark, Chief Clerk of the Executive Office and Quartermaster Watson Van Benthuysen, assisted by a small number of

highly trusted officers and men, immediately followed the President with his baggage, papers, and two boxes of specie. By riding briskly they reached the Savannah River at daylight on May 3, crossed on a pontoon bridge near Fort Charlotte Plantation below Vienna,[4] and arrived at Washington, Georgia, that evening. Benjamin so sensed the danger of capture that he separated from the escaping party before it reached Washington, with the understanding that he would rejoin President Davis in Texas.[5] Throughout the long and perilous journey from Richmond, Benjamin had been the "life of the party." His inexhaustible stock of anecdotes, recited with unusual dramatic power, punctuated by puffs from his fragrant Havana cigars, had cheered his colleagues and relieved the tension of their undertaking.

The remainder of the expedition followed with the treasure of the Government and that of the Richmond banks, under the command of Secretary of War Breckinridge. Great fatigue and the gradual disorganization of the straggling troops had prevented him from sending men from the encampment about six miles west of Washington for enlargement of the Davis escort[6] to protect the President in the event of an attack by Federals. Reporting from the encampment to President Davis, Breckinridge wrote: "Nothing can be done with the bulk of this command. It has been with difficulty that anything has been kept in shape. I am having the silver paid to the troops, and will in any event save the gold and have it brought forward in the morning when I hope Judge Reagan will take it. Many of the men have thrown away their arms. Most of them have resolved to remain here under Vaughn and Dibrell, and will make terms. A few hundred men will move on and may be depended on for the object we spoke of yesterday. . . . Threats have just reached me to seize the whole amount [of the treasure] but I hope the guard at hand will be sufficient." Breckinridge then ordered the distribution of the silver to the troops, according to statements certified by the brigade commanders.[7]

General Breckinridge arranged for the "few hundred men" who could be depended on to remain together for a few days and for each group to march in a different direction. He expected to confuse the pursuing Federals in this manner and to divert them from the Confederate President. As Secretary of War he gave an honorable discharge from the army to the other troops and urged them to surrender promptly to Federal authorities.[8]

Washington, a city founded in colonial days and the center of a district of wealthy Georgia planters, had been entirely removed from the seat of war, and its inhabitants had been spared much deprivation and suffering. It was the home of Robert Toombs, first Confederate Secretary of State, who, bitterly disappointed that he had not been made President, was jealous of Davis. While Reagan was his guest at this time, he was much impressed by the fact that Toombs no longer had a quarrel with Davis and that he was willing to call together some of his most trusted followers in that part of Georgia, enlarge the Davis escort, and see the Confederate President safely across the Chattahoochee River at the risk of his own life. This, Judge Reagan assured him, was not necessary.[9] Mallory, accompanied by Brigadier General L. T. Wigfall of Texas, took a train from Washington to Atlanta, eighty-five miles to the west, and went on from there to join his family at Lagrange and await the action of the Federal Government.[10]

At Washington, Georgia, President Davis and his colleagues were accommodated in the bank building on the north side of the public square by Dr. J. J. Robertson, cashier of the local branch of the Bank of the State of

Georgia. In this building, now the site of the county court-house, he held a meeting on the morning of May 4. Those attending were Judge Reagan, holder of two Cabinet port-folios, Colonels Johnston, Lubbock, Wood, Thorburn and other members of his staff and escort. At this meeting President Davis spoke with surprising calmness and hope-fulness of uniting the scattered forces of the Confederacy and of re-establishing the Government west of the Missis-sippi River.[11] He performed at this time his last official act as President by appointing Captain M. H. Clark Acting Treasurer.

The camp of the much-reduced Davis escort at Silver Springs, about one mile from Washington, was astir early Thursday morning, May 4, with preparations for departure. The President's guard was disbanded, the train was reduced to one wagon and two ambulances, and the extra horses were distributed among the men. The President's baggage, the remaining papers of the President and Cabinet, and the two boxes of specie amounting originally to $35,000 when they had been placed in the President's train at Greensboro, were carefully packed in the ambulances. The President's letter and message books, which Clark had removed, were sewed in blankets and hidden in Washington until such time as he could return and take them out of Georgia under more favorable conditions. The stores, except the few the escort needed to carry, were given out in the town.

Late in the morning, when all was in readiness, the Presi-dent and his most trusted companions rode away, his erect

Brackets indicate settlements that did not exist in 1865

The route followed by President Davis and his escort
from Charlotte to Irwinville

military bearing and his always calm and dignified manner commanding the full respect and admiration of everyone. When a stop for rest and food was made early in the afternoon, Tilghman, who remained faithfully on duty with the baggage train, was so saddened by the situation that he found it difficult to describe his feelings as he sat near President Davis and his staff, listened to their conversation, and saw the "head and representative of a great and mighty people fleeing for his life to quit the country. . . . He [Davis] seems yet hopeful but I fear our noble cause is gone." Davis's gray eyes, the outstanding feature of his face, appeared to have lost some of their lustrous power.

Shortly after President Davis's departure from Washington, General Duke brought the treasure train to within one mile of town where, under a large elm tree, Captain Clark assumed his duties as Acting Treasurer of the Confederacy. A summary of disbursements, based on his reports and supplementary records, is as follows:

Amount of gold and silver coin
and silver bullion in the Confederate
Treasury when the treasure train left
Danville, April 6, 1865, about $327,000.00

Paid to soldiers in Greensboro,
about $ 39,000.00

Removed from the treasure train
at Greensboro and taken with the

Brought forward	39,000.00	327,000.00

President and Cabinet; separated from Davis near Sandersville, Georgia, May 6, and sent on to Florida (for disposition of these funds, see pages 115-116), about   35,000.00

    Paid to Major E. C. White near Savannah River to pay escorting officers and troops about $26 each, about   108,000.00

    Paid to Major R. J. Moses for soldiers' provisions in Washington and Augusta, about   40,000.00

    Paid to John C. Breckinridge, for transmission to the Trans-Mississippi Department   1,000.00

    Paid to James A. Semple, a bonded officer of the Navy, who, with an assistant, agreed to take it, concealed under the false bottom of a carriage, to Charleston or Savannah and then ship it to a Confederate agent in Bermuda, Nassau, or Liverpool, or some other foreign port for the account of the Confederate Government, about   86,000.00

Brought forward	309,000.00	327,000.00
Paid to Colonels Johnston, Lubbock, Thorburn, and Wood, $1,510 each (taken by Federals except amounts carried by Wood and Lubbock)	6,040.00	
Paid Captain Given Campbell for scouts	300.00	
Paid Acting Secretary of the Treasury Reagan (taken by Federals)	3,500.00	
Paid to midshipmen and other naval guards of the treasure train	1,500.00	
Paid to Lieutenant Bradford for the marines	300.00	
Paid for miscellaneous expenses	6,360.00	
Total expenditures,[12] about	$327,000.00	$327,000.00

The funds of the banks of Richmond, amounting to approximately $200,000, were deposited in a vault in Washington.[13]

As soon as they had concluded the business of the Treasury Department, Judge Reagan and Captain Clark left Washington and overtook President Davis and his escort in camp not far from Warrenton "in a miserable out of the way place, the President wishing to be as secluded as possible," wrote Tilghman.

When Davis left Washington, Georgia, his object was to go far enough to the south to pass below the points reported to be occupied by Federal troops. "I expected to cut my way through to a place of safety with the two detachments of cavalry along with me, but they have become so much demoralized . . . that I can no longer rely on them in case we should encounter the enemy," explained the Confederate President.

"I have therefore determined," he continued, "to disband them and try to make my escape, as a small body of men elude the vigilance of the enemy easier than a larger number. They will make every effort in their power to capture me and it behooves us to face these dangers as men. We will go to Mississippi, and there rely on Forrest, if he is in a state of organization, and it is to be hoped that he is; if not, we will cross the Mississippi River and join Kirby Smith, where we can carry on the war for ever." [14]

Proceeding on the false theory that the escaping Confederates would pass through Athens, Georgia, General Palmer achieved one of the hardest cavalry marches of his career and captured that university city on May 5. Not knowing, of course, that Davis had covered a day's march south of Washington, he sent out his men to search every swamp and other hiding place in that region. [15] While

Palmer was engaged in this futile attempt, Davis was hurrying southward. Near Sandersville, on May 6, he, Reagan, Johnston, Lubbock, Wood, Thorburn, and a few scouts led by Captain Given Campbell rode ahead of the baggage train with the understanding that they would rejoin Captain Clark and his guards near Tallahassee or Madison, Florida, where Captain Clark and his guard agreed to take it. Before the two groups separated Clark paid to Johnston, Lubbock, Thorburn, and Wood $1,500 in gold each. Their receipts indicated that these officials had accepted the "property of the Confederate States, for transmission abroad." They would need it, Captain Clark said, "for supplies en route and to buy boats in Florida." He also gave each one $10 in silver "for small uses." Judge Reagan was prevailed upon by Clark to place in his saddle bags $3,500 in gold coin.[16] There remained in the baggage train an amount in excess of $25,000.

Davis and his small group, riding ahead, crossed the Oconee River. Near Dublin they overtook Mrs. Davis and the children whom Burton N. Harrison had conducted out of Abbeville on April 29 and who had left Washington just before the President arrived there. Mrs. Davis, not wishing her husband's escape to be endangered by an addition to his group, continued with Harrison, who hoped to find a way out of Florida to some foreign port. Learning that several thousand Federal cavalrymen had camped at Hawkinsville, Davis crossed the Ocmulgee River twenty-five miles below that town. Hearing rumors of an expected assault by stragglers on his wife's train, he seriously delayed his own progress in order to afford her adequate protection. On the night of May 9 he overtook Mrs. Davis near a small creek in the level pinewoods about one mile from Irwinville.[17] This was about sixty-five miles north of their anticipated haven across the Florida border and about seventy-five miles southeast of Macon.

When it became known that General Johnston had surrendered to General Sherman, Major General Wilson spread his large cavalry force out like a fan from Macon, in the confident expectation that some of his men would intercept the Confederate "fugitives," as he called them. From Atlanta one division was watching all roads north of the mouth of the river, and detachments were proceeding to Newnan, to Carrollton, and to Talladega, Alabama, as well as to the northeastern part of Georgia, at Athens, which Palmer had just captured, and to Washington. A second division was directed to picket the Ocmulgee River from the mouth of the Oconee River, by way of Dublin, with instructions to follow the Confederate leaders to the Mississippi if necessary. A third division was picketing the Ocmulgee and Altamaha Rivers as far as the mouth of the Ohoopee. Another force was stationed along the Flint River and the crossings of the old Muscogee & Macon Railroad to Albany. A small detachment was sent to Columbus.

Brigadier General Edward M. McCook, on his way to Tallahassee to receive the surrender of the State of Florida, sent out scouting parties to the north and eastward from

Tallahassee and Thomasville. Almost a continuous line of troops stretched from the Etowah River in the northwestern part of Georgia down to the northern part of Florida.[18]

Colonel Thorburn, who had devoted almost one month to maturing plans for the escape of the Confederate leaders, had decided that the only safe route led through Florida and around to Texas by water. He separated from President Davis very early on the morning of May 10 to carry out his daring plan. His varied experiences in the War had prepared him to meet this, the most acute emergency of his life. He had many times experienced the thrill of running the blockade and as an officer on the *St. Nicholas* he had helped capture the *Monticello,* the *Mary Pierce,* and the *Margaret,* all in Chesapeake Bay dangerously near the Federal capital. Later, when as a secret agent of the Confederate State Department he was returning from Europe with highly confidential state papers, he threw them overboard when the *Cornubia,* on which he was traveling, was captured.[19] Past dangers must have appeared insignificant to him as he sped through the darkness of the morning of May 10, 1865. Unexpectedly he ran into the pursuing Federals near Irwinville and was fired upon. Turning in his saddle for a moment, he shot the foremost of his pursuers and saw his victim tumble from his horse. This enabled him and his negro servant to outdistance the Federals, who had reason to believe they were about to capture Davis. Protected by the darkness Thorburn was able by hard riding to reach the Florida border. He continued south with utmost caution for fear the Federals had already penetrated that state. Near Lake City he met Captain Louis M. Coxetter in an old railroad passenger coach and arranged with him to make ready the vessel which Coxetter had kept waiting in the Indian River on the East Coast to take Davis and the Cabinet to the Bahamas, Cuba, or Texas.[20]

It was characteristic of Thorburn's efficiency that he had secured for this bold undertaking an experienced and daring blockade-runner. Coxetter had been on the *Trent* when Mason and Slidell were arrested, and in order to deceive the Federals after that experience he had often used the name of Mitchell, his middle name. He had been captain of such successful blockade-runners as the *Fanny and Jenny,* the *Herald,* and the *Jeff. Davis,* on which large shipments of cotton had been taken to the Bahamas and cargoes of ammunition brought back to Charleston and other ports. One of the prizes he had taken was the *Alvarado* with $70,000 worth of wool, goat skins, old copper and iron, and medicines from Africa. He had also captured the *John Welch,* the *Enchantress,* the *S. J. Waring,* the *Santa Clara,* the *John Carver,* the *Mary E. Thompson,* and the *Mary Goodell.*[21] No wonder the Federal Rear Admiral S. F. du Pont, regarded Coxetter as the most skilled seaman on the Atlantic Coast.[22]

But even Captain Coxetter's competence could not guarantee a safe passage through the Federal net that was then being drawn about Florida. When it was learned that President Davis was nearing the Florida border and would probably attempt to escape through the islands along the East Coast or down the West Coast south of Tampa, the Federals began to draw their lines more tightly. Lieutenant J. J. Hollis with a detachment of soldiers was ordered to

Federal vessels carefully guarded the coast

proceed to Cape Sable, the tip end of the peninsula, "to intercept any parties who might be making their escape." [23] A watch could be maintained almost indefinitely on this, the southernmost point of land on the West Coast of the peninsula, inasmuch as there was an abundance of game on the savannahs and in the pinewoods and hammocks near-by.

While Federal troops were guarding Georgia and Florida to prevent the escape of President Davis, he was slowly approaching the Florida border. Not even Southerners, except the small group that followed him, knew of his whereabouts at this time. "We are still ignorant of President Davis' movements," wrote a Floridian, "but it is rumored that he is making his way, with a large body of cavalry into the Trans-Mississippi Department, and that he proposes to make another stand there; and if defeated, he will retreat into Mexico, and tender his services to Maximilian. This distracts our young men very much, and many are leaving to join him before the parole is administered. President Davis is excusable for such plans for himself, but I hope that he will not mislead our impetuous youth. The South has been overcome in honorable combat; no heart-burnings or grumbling will wipe out the fact; we had better submit gracefully to the defeat, and return to the allegiance to which we were born, although it is bewildering to learn that Lincoln walks unmolested the streets of Richmond, making 'Union' and 'Peace' speeches, and that our arch-enemy, Beecher, proclaims from Sumter's walls his abolition teachings." [24]

This alarmed concern over the Confederate President's ability to influence a large number of Confederate soldiers to follow him to Texas was not based on any justification. General Richard Taylor had surrendered on May 8 all the Confederate land and naval forces in Alabama and Mississippi, which removed the possibility of enlarging the Davis escort and blocked the passage to the Mississippi with Federal occupation of the territory. When Davis camped near Irwinville, Georgia, on the following night, May 9, there were with him less than a dozen men: his secretary, Harrison, his three aides, Johnston, Lubbock and Wood,

Thorburn, two scouts, and several negro servants. Of the three members of the Cabinet who had resigned, George Davis and Trenholm were still in South Carolina and Mallory was in Georgia. Two others, Benjamin and Breckinridge, had also left the President and were on their way to the coast of Florida. One member of the Cabinet only, Reagan, remained with Davis. The escort of more than two thousand cavalry who had guarded the President and Cabinet through North and South Carolina, having crossed over the Savannah River into Georgia, were waiting to be paroled.

Two days before the Confederate President camped near Irwinville, Lieutenant Colonel B. D. Pritchard and a regiment of Federal soldiers left Macon with orders to "capture or kill Jefferson Davis, the rebel ex-President." [25] Early on the afternoon of May 9, they succeeded in striking the trail of the Confederates, rushed on toward Irwinville that night and in the gray dawn of May 10, 1865, one month after Lee's surrender, reached the Davis camp.[26] His capture was described by the Confederate President as follows:

"My horse and arms were near the road on which I expected to leave, and down which the [Federal] cavalry approached; it was therefore impracticable to reach them. I was compelled to start in the opposite direction. As it was quite dark in the tent, I picked up what was supposed to be my 'raglan,' a water-proof, light overcoat, without sleeves; it was subsequently found to be my wife's, so very like my own as to be mistaken for it; as I started, my wife

thoughtfully threw over my head and shoulders a shawl.
"I had gone perhaps fifteen or twenty yards when a
trooper galloped up and ordered me to halt and surrender
to which I gave a defiant answer, and dropping the shawl
and raglan from my shoulders, advanced toward him; he
leveled his carbine at me, but I expected, if he fired, he
would miss me, and my intention was in that event to put
my hand under his foot, tumble him off on the other side,
spring into the saddle, and attempt to escape. My wife,
who had been watching, ran forward and threw her arms
around me. Success depended on instantaneous action, and,
recognizing that the opportunity had been lost, I turned
back, and, the morning being damp and chilly, passed on
to a fire beyond the tent." [27] Davis and the entire group
of Confederates were placed under arrest. Acting Treasurer
Clark and his group who were guarding the President's
heavy baggage, private papers, and the balance of the treasure, having separated from Davis and his escort a few days
before, escaped the notice of the Federal scouts and proceeded
on to Florida.

Disappointed that the other Cabinet members were not
captured with Davis, the *New York Herald* assured the
Northern public that such disposition of the Federal cavalry
had been made as would prevent the ultimate escape of
Benjamin, Breckinridge, and the other "Cabinet officers and
fellow criminals." [28]

As Mrs. Davis, ex-President Davis, and his fellow prisoners
were being taken on their own horses across Georgia from

Irwinville to Macon, the next highest ranking Confederate official, Vice President Alexander H. Stephens, was arrested at his home, "Liberty Hall," at Crawfordsville, Georgia. The common fate of the President and Vice President of the Confederacy did not lessen the strong feeling produced by their past differences in policies. Stephens described his meeting with Davis, which took place under the vigilant eyes of guards as they were being carried down the Savannah River, shortly after they had become fellow prisoners on the steamer at Augusta, as follows: "Mr. Davis came out on deck soon after I got up. It was our first meeting since our parting the night after my return from the Hampton Roads Conference [with Lincoln] to Richmond. Much as I disagreed with him [Davis] and much as I deplored the ruin which, I think, his acts helped to bring upon the whole country, as well as on himself, I could but deeply sympathize with him in his present condition. His salutation was not unfriendly, but it was far from cordial. We passed but few words; these were commonplace." [29]

Within a few days the Confederate President was in chains behind the prison bars of Fortress Monroe, in defence of which *Harper's Weekly* said, "No appeal to history, no argument drawn from the fact of war can obscure the plain fact that Davis' life is forfeit to the law." Davis and the other Southern political leaders were regarded by the majority of Northerners as the living embodiment of treason on whom was concentrated the blame for four years of strife. Vengeance was demanded. Their "treason was the highest crime known to the constitution. . . . The Government of the United States owed it to itself to spare no effort to arrest the acknowledged chief of the conspiracy. It has secured him, and no sound reason can be urged why the law should not take its course," declared this "Journal of Civilization," which *Harper's* claimed to be.

"Jefferson Davis must be tried for treason. If convicted he must be sentenced. If sentenced he must be executed. . . . Can any lesson be so permanently impressive as the final proof by the solemn sanction of the supreme authority that treason against the United States is not a political difference of opinion, but a crime whose enormity will not remit the legal penalty?" [30] concluded *Harper's*.

Expressions of inveterate hatred toward the defeated Confederate leaders and demands for their lives, by one section of the Northern press, were criticized by the *London Saturday Review*. Mindful of the fact that Jefferson Davis was one of the most efficient, if not the most efficient, Secretaries of War the United States had had up to 1861; that he was dominant in the two previous administrations, those of Franklin Pierce and James Buchanan; that Breckinridge had occupied next to the most exalted position in the United States immediately preceding the War; and that Benjamin, Mallory, and Reagan had served with distinction in the United States House of Representatives and Senate, this foreign periodical reminded "American politicians" that they ought to "remember the discredit which they inflict on their country by reckless imputations on antagonists who formerly held high places in the councils of the Union." [31]

The exultant satisfaction of the Federals over the capture of the President, the Vice President, and the Postmaster General of the Confederacy was somewhat lessened when it was learned that Colonel Wood, aide to Davis and captured with him, had succeeded in bribing his guard with two twenty-dollar gold pieces and had escaped. He knew that his personal relation to President Davis and his destruction of Federal ships would be avenged by the severest punishment if he remained in captivity. He reached the Florida border five days later, forded the Withlacoochee River, and one mile north of Madison consulted J. H. McGinnis, a Confederate veteran who was well-acquainted throughout the state and able to give valuable information. As Colonel Wood rode twelve miles southward into Madison late that night he saw two Federal parole officers but fortunately for him they did not recognize him.[32]

Breckinridge was within forty miles of Irwinville, Georgia, when he learned of the capture of President Davis; he immediately informed the forty-five men who were escorting him southward of his resolution to risk an attempt at escape. "I will not," he is reported to have said, "have one of these young men to encounter one hazard more for my sake." Taking an affectionate farewell of them, he, as cool and as gallant as ever, started into exile,[33] in the full realization that he, the extreme Southern Democratic candidate against Lincoln in 1860, perhaps the most popular symbol of the Southern system, was one of the Confederate leaders most

hated by the North. Many regarded him, as did Lord Charnwood, as "a gentleman not otherwise known than as the
standard bearer ... of the undisguised and unmitigated claims
of the slave owners." [34] He had occupied the office of Confederate Secretary of War just long enough to have the bitter
criticism of the North focused upon himself as a member
of the Confederate high command. He knew he was in
danger of execution, if captured. One of Breckinridge's
sons, Clifton, and a son of James B. Clay, were arrested
about eleven miles below Macon on the Ocmulgee River
the night of May 10. A letter was taken from the boys in
which the Confederate Secretary of War stated: "Should
my friends ever know my part in the occurrences of the
last three months [the brief period during which he had
been a member of the Confederate Cabinet], I venture to
think it will give me an increased claim on their confidence
and regard." [35]

Sensitive to the danger about him General Breckinridge
exercised the utmost vigilance in directing his course through
the most isolated part of southeastern Georgia. His camping
sites were carefully selected and his trail was completely
washed over by the incessant rains that followed him several
days after the capture of his chief. Finally he crossed over
the Georgia border into Florida and on the night of May 15
was entertained by Judge Benjamin F. Wardlaw near Madison. The next day Breckinridge went on into Madison, fifty
miles east of Tallahassee, to see Daniel G. Livingston, to
whom he carried a letter from a South Carolina kinsman,

D. F. Livingston, and there met Colonel Wood. Noting that the General's horse had given out, Livingston provided him with a fleet-footed mare and gave him a letter to Lewis M. Moseley on the Suwannee River. Thus fortified the Confederate Secretary of War prepared to enter the "underground" passage through Florida.[36]

CHAPTER VI

"YANKEES BEAT HELL, ANYHOW"

TO be a conquered people is a novel experience, and we have daily both amusing and mortifying incidents in our unadaptedness to the change," commented a Tallahassean as General McCook arrived in the Confederate capital of Florida on May 10, the day President Davis was captured not far beyond the Georgia border. This writer went on to say that although the "emancipation of slaves had been discussed as a probable result of the war, yet we in Middle Florida were so removed from the advance of occupation of the south by the army that we had not realized that this was an accomplished fact." [1]

Ports and towns near the coast had been captured early in the War by the Federals, and, with few exceptions, had remained under Federal control. Refugees from such settlements had, therefore, sought temporary homes in the uninvaded areas of the inland. The settlements extending from Tallahassee east to the Suwannee River, particularly Madison, were the center of these refugee colonists. It was to this comparatively secluded part of Florida that the three members of the Confederate Cabinet—Benjamin, Breckinridge, and George Davis—who were seeking an "underground" passage to a foreign country, were proceeding.

When on May 6 President Davis, his aides, and Judge
Reagan had separated from the small baggage train of one
wagon and two ambulances near Sandersville, Georgia, it
was with the understanding that they would rejoin it near

Suwannee River

Tallahassee or Madison. If, by interference of the Federals, Davis were prevented from uniting his small escort
with the baggage train, the understanding was that Captain
Clark, who was in charge of the train, would take the
money (more than $25,000), official papers, and baggage to
Cuba or to Mexico.

Captain Clark had with him a group of the most trusted

young men of the Confederacy, members of prominent families, some of whom were related by marriage or friendship to the Confederate President. They were Captain Watson Van Benthuysen, who had acted as Quartermaster of the baggage train since the President and Cabinet left Charlotte, and his brothers, Captain Alfred C. Van Benthuysen and Captain Jefferson Davis Van Benthuysen. Born in Brooklyn, New York, they had been taken to New Orleans in the 1850's by their father. Their aunt had married Joseph Davis, brother of the Confederate President. Also in the group were five "Eastern Shoremen" of Maryland—Captain Fred Emory, William Sidney Winder, John White Scott, William Elveno Dickinson, and Tench Francis Tilghman—two scouts from Captain Given Campbell's company, and five negro servants, including Watson, the President's cook.[2]

At first the train consisted of one four-mule wagon and two ambulances, but one of the ambulances was soon abandoned.[3] The train was carefully guarded during the night by the men, who served in relays of two.

Captain Clark and his guards were making good progress toward Florida on May 7, the day after Davis had separated from them, when they sighted three sentinels, who they believed were the advance guard of a column of Federals. The Confederates immediately turned off into the woods and camped in a secluded place until they had reason to conclude that there was no further danger of capture. One of their scouts became alarmed at this time and deserted. The deeper they penetrated into southern Georgia the scarcer and poorer became the houses, but milk, chickens, and other provisions were still obtainable.

When, only a few miles distant, President Davis was being captured on May 10, his papers and baggage were being safely transported by the faithful Clark and his loyal associates across two streams, the first of which, according to Tilghman, was "Gum swamp where we had to unload our wagon and ambulance. The things we put in an old scow which we found at the crossing and bailed out. The other was a most beautiful stream of the clearest water. This stream is called Sugar Branch. Soon after crossing this we camped on the road to Jacksonville where we got plenty of milk, etc., and some very nice venison. . . ."

The Davis baggage train crossed over the Ocmulgee River on May 11 but its guards, hearing that a Federal steamer was expected at any time, waited until night to take the wagon and ambulance over. They heard no more of the Federals that night and felt, Tilghman said, "tolerably safe." As they continued their journey they became bored by the monotony of the pine barrens which they had seen for days. When they passed a cemetery, one member of the party claimed it to be the first sign of civilization that he had seen in a hundred miles and a "sure index of passing the residence of a doctor."

As a diversion Captain Clark proposed to write a book of his experiences since leaving Richmond on April 2 and discussed for many hours the chapter headings he would use. Winder was very ill for several days and had to be carried in the ambulance. Tilghman feared he would be "left on the road yet." As they neared Florida the fleeing Confederates saw "splendid magnolia trees in the swamps and in a few days they will be in bloom," wrote Tilghman. "We ate ripe blackberries on the way, the earliest I ever saw and will soon find plenty I hope. What will be our destiny is uncertain but we are all hopeful. Most likely we shall go to Cuba and thence God only knows. I am getting very anxious for news from the dear ones at home. To think I have not seen my babies since July [almost one year] and not one word since last August. God bless and keep them safe." Tilghman recovered his spirits the following day and wrote, "I think it almost certain that we shall go to Cuba and if so anticipate a good time."

The baggage train was taken across the Allapaha River and on May 15 entered Florida, when, wrote Tilghman, "the country suddenly changed and became fine." Just before camping that night a gentleman from a plantation they had passed brought them "some elegant fish, bread and clabber," on which they "feasted sumptuously." From this newly made friend Tilghman and his colleagues learned "the Yanks have occupied the State of Florida and are paroling all the State troops. After ten days all not paroled are to be outlawed and we shall be among the number beyond a doubt as it is not our intention to apply for one."

Still unaware that Jefferson Davis had been captured and was being taken to prison, these loyal followers continued to transport and guard the Confederate President's heavy baggage, private papers, and the two boxes of gold sovereigns of the Confederate treasury with which they had been entrusted. They camped the night of May 16 at a Mr. Beason's farm. The next day they crossed the Withlacoochee River, a tributary of the Suwannee, and also the Pensacola & Georgia Railroad tracks. Here they learned that Joseph Cabell Breckinridge, son of the General and one of the midshipmen who had guarded the Confederate treasure on its long trip, was in Madison. They feared the General had been captured, but as a matter of fact he was at that time only a few miles distant on his way to Gainesville. Benjamin had crossed the Suwannee River a few days before and had also entered one of the "underground" passages of Florida.

An unexpected danger faced the Davis baggage train on May 17. Tilghman wrote that he and the other officers guarding the valuables were made "very uneasy today by the appearance of a deserter who had joined the Yanks and is now home. He left suddenly tonight and we fear an attack from him and his band." Also the negro servants were "getting uneasy" and were likely to desert them. Both dangers disappeared, however, in the course of an arduous drive of twenty miles, after which they camped near a Mr. Irvin's house and bought from him forage for the horses, food for themselves—"a fine pig and plenty of chickens"— and "some nice blackberry wine which we needed." Their host "bled us freely it is true," wrote Tilghman, "but we stood it for the stomach's sake."

Late on the afternoon of May 18 they crossed the Suwannee River at Moseley's Ferry, where two members of the Confederate Cabinet, Benjamin and Breckinridge, two days apart, had preceded them. Here they heard that Davis had been captured but refused to believe it.

While the Davis baggage train was on May 19 being guarded northwest of Gainesville at the plantation of Captain Martin, Colonel John Taylor Wood was spending that night at "Cotton Wood," the plantation of David L. Yulee, at the present town of Archer. Wood explained to Yulee that the Confederate President had sent his heavy baggage on to Florida four days before his capture. Three days later Clark and the guard of officers went south on Alligator Road west of Gainesville to avoid possible detection by the Federals who had occupied that town. They stopped at noon at the "White House," home of Edward Haile about twelve miles northwest of Gainesville, and were "hospitably treated and refreshed by a very nice drink of brandy," said Tilghman. That evening they arrived at the Yulee plantation with the baggage, papers, and money. Yulee, who had been the first United States Senator from Florida after its admission to the Union, was absent at that time but Mrs. Yulee received them hospitably.[4] It was here on May 22 that they learned positively from Mrs. Yulee that their chief had been captured twelve days before. "Of course the last hope is gone of the Confederacy," wrote Tilghman, "and our only course, as we are in the Department surrendered by General Johnston is to go somewhere, deliver ourselves up and be paroled.

This I had hoped to have been spared but there is no alternative."

That night, after they had partially recovered from the disillusionment wrought by the shocking news of Davis's capture, Captain Clark announced to the Van Benthuysen brothers and several of the Marylanders who were in his tent, that the capture of President Davis placed upon him, as Chief Clerk of the President's office, personal responsibility for the safekeeping of the Davis papers and baggage, and, as Acting Treasurer of the Confederate Government with "verbal orders from the Secty of the Treasury [Reagan]," the care of the balance of some $25,000 remaining in the Confederate Treasury. He proposed to hide the papers and baggage in Florida until he could return for them. Clark explained that under some discretionary powers granted him by Judge Reagan he would pay to members of the guarding party a fair salvage from the specie in recognition of the risk and trouble borne by them. He further announced that he would place the remaining funds in England to await orders from President Davis and Secretary Reagan. If, however, he were prevented from communicating with Davis and Reagan, he explained that he would use the funds for the defence of the Confederate President and Cabinet when they were tried by the United States Government.

This announcement produced a heated discussion between Clark and Watson Van Benthuysen. The latter declared that the specie had been turned over to him as a quartermaster fund, that he had exclusive control of it, that the Confederate Government had ceased to exist, and that all quartermasters and financial agents would appropriate such funds as remained in their care. Van Benthuysen told Clark that he had consulted his two brothers and the five Marylanders and with their approval he would lay aside one quarter of the entire fund for the benefit of Mrs. Davis and her children, which he, himself, a distant kinsman, would take charge of, and that he would divide the balance equally among those who had guarded the funds, papers, and baggage. Inasmuch as Van Benthuysen was sustained by all those present, Clark was compelled to waive his claim but he required a written statement from Van Benthuysen, endorsed by those present, as an official proof that he had endeavored to perform what he believed to be his duty as Acting Treasurer of the Confederacy.[5]

The day on which this decision was reached, May 23, Captain Van Benthuysen took possession of the last of the Confederate funds and proceeded to divide them. The approximately $35,000 which had been transferred at Greensboro five weeks before from Captain Parker's treasure train to that of the President and Cabinet had been reduced, by the heavy expenses of the flight through parts of North and South Carolina, Georgia, and Florida and by payments for salaries, to an amount in excess of $25,000.

This balance, according to a reported statement of Watson Van Benthuysen and supplementary papers, was distributed as follows:

Captain Watson Van Benthuysen, 400 gold
sovereigns at $4.85 . . . .$1,940.00
Captain Alfred C. Van Benthuysen, 400 gold sover-
eigns at $4.85 . . . . 1,940.00
Captain Jefferson Davis Van Benthuysen, 400 gold
sovereigns at $4.85 . . . . 1,940.00
Captain Fred Emory, 400 gold sovereigns at $4.85 . . 1,940.00
W. E. Dickinson, 400 gold sovereigns at $4.85 . . . . . . 1,940.00
W. S. Winder, 400 gold sovereigns at $4.85 . . . . 1,940.00
T. F. Tilghman, 400 gold sovereigns at $4.85 . . . . . . 1,940.00
John W. Scott, 400 gold sovereigns at $4.85 . . . . 1,940.00
Captain M. H. Clark, 400 gold sovereigns at $4.85 . . 1,940.00
To each of the above, $55 for traveling expenses 495.00
One month's pay to Captain Clark 125.00
To Howard and Staffin, (Davis's cook and guard)
each $250 . . . . 500.00
To five negro servants $20 each 100.00
Miscellaneous 250.00

Total [6] $18,930.00

It was the understanding of Clark, Dickinson, Scott,
Tilghman, and Winder that Watson Van Benthuysen retained the balance of 1,400 gold sovereigns at $4.85 ($6,790)
for Mrs. Davis and her children.[7]

Clark and Watson Van Benthuysen did agree, however,
that they could find no safer place than the Yulee plantation
for hiding the President's baggage and the papers. In the

absence of her husband, Mrs. Yulee obligingly assumed responsibility for the papers and baggage. To her fifteen-year-old son, C. Wickliffe Yulee, was entrusted the task of secreting them. He "delightedly performed it," he said, with the assistance of a faithful companion, Lieutenant John S. Purviance, by burying them, in one trunk and two chests, "at midnight in a cow stable, where a few hours later, no trace of the work could be seen." [8]

At the conclusion of this business, wrote Tilghman, "we mounted our horses and each, with all his worldly goods in a very small bundle behind him, rode off."

Captain Clark remained in the neighborhood of the Yulee plantation a week after his associates had left to make sure the Davis train had not been followed by the Federals. Then he went to Atlanta where he placed Watson, Davis's cook, in the charge of Lieutenant Joseph Cabell Breckinridge. Clark found Washington, Georgia, heavily garrisoned by the Federals and concluded it would not be wise to attempt to remove until later the executive letter and message books he had hidden there a month before.

Proceeding to Abbeville, he carefully examined, over a five-day period, the Confederate papers left there in the care of Mrs. Henry J. Leovy. And according to a rule given him by Colonel John Taylor Wood, he destroyed all applications for exemptions, detail appointments, and promotions, but retained all letters and telegrams from generals, governors, members of the Cabinet, and prominent senators and members of Congress, all papers relating to the organization of the army and such other records as would likely be of value in recording the life of the Confederacy. The selected papers Clark packed in a trunk and advised Mrs. Leovy to hide them in the country. From other confidential friends in Abbeville he secured the papers of General Bragg and the records of the Attorney General and arranged for their secret

care. Although he declined to take the oath of allegiance to the United States, Captain Clark was not molested as he proceeded to Baltimore.[9]

When Yulee returned to "Cotton Wood" plantation and learned of the disposition of the Davis baggage and papers, he was consulted by the Van Benthuysens about what they personally ought to do. "Upon learning from them that they had made their way to Florida with the purpose and expectation of reaching Texas from the coast, I at once said to them," Yulee wrote, "that in my judgment their duty was to report themselves at once to the proper officers in Florida, take their parole, return home to their families, and resume the duties of civil life. That I considered the idea of any further protraction of the military struggle an absurdity and that the forces under General [Edmund Kirby] Smith could have no hope of maintaining themselves against the large Union armies liberated by the surrender of the Confederate forces east of the Mississippi." These distant relatives of Davis concluded to take Yulee's advice and arranged to leave at the Yulee plantation for later transfer to their homes in New Orleans, their blooded Kentucky mares.[10]

Unexpectedly arrested in Gainesville, Yulee decided to send his wife and children to the home of her father, "Duke" C. A. Wickliffe, former Governor of Kentucky and Postmaster General in Tyler's Cabinet. Having accepted the Davis baggage and papers for safekeeping, he arranged for a Mr. Meader to transfer them from "Cotton Wood" plantation to Waldo and place them in the care of M. A. Williams, the agent there of the Jacksonville & Cedar Keys Railroad which Yulee owned.[11]

Soon the Federals learned, from one of the negroes who had driven the Confederate wagon, that the Davis baggage had reached Florida. United States Secretary of War Stanton immediately wired orders to capture the property. Brigadier General Isaac Vogdes, in command of Federal troops at Jacksonville, sent Captain O. E. Bryant and eight negro soldiers to Gainesville for that purpose. There they secured additional information and proceeded at once to the Yulee plantation, where they learned from Mrs. Yulee that the trunk and two chests had been sent to Waldo. Before leaving "Cotton Wood" the Federals took possession of the Confederate President's French rifle musket (described by Captain Bryant as "a most murderous weapon"), the ambulance, and three saddle horses that had been left with the Yulees. Bryant and his negro soldiers then went to the plantation of Edward Haile where they took the wagon, the mules, and three more saddle horses which had been a part of the baggage cavalcade. Upon arriving at Waldo, Captain Bryant was surprised to find the trunk and chest "unguarded by even a lock" in a storeroom adjoining the home of the railroad agent.[12]

Captain Bryant had the negro soldiers carry the Davis trunk and two chests to Jacksonville, where Vogdes and several other Federal officers examined the contents and found them to be: three woolen coats, one linen duster, three pairs trousers, three woolen waistcoats, one woolen tippet, one small dressing case, two towels, one pistol (nine shooter), one case of ammunition, one silk undershirt, one silk necktie, one pistol holster, two dressing robes, eight linen shirts, eighteen pairs socks, five undershirts, six pairs of drawers, one double-barreled revolver, quantity of smoking and plug tobacco, brush, comb, razor strop, one pair of gaiters, one pair of slippers, two toothbrushes, one pistol case, one pair of holsters with pistols enclosed, two full packages of metallic cartridges, two pairs of lace shoes, two pairs of boots, one pair gauntlets, one roll courtplaster, one woolen shirt, one small bundle containing eyeglasses and a plain ring, private correspondence, blank envelopes, note paper, $20,000 in Confederate paper money, six boxes of cigars, one portfolio, and portraits of Mr. and Mrs. Davis and of General Lee.[13]

One set of valuable official records was found. These were letters from five members of the Confederate Cabinet—Benjamin, Breckinridge, George Davis, Mallory, and Reagan—written at Charlotte and presenting to President Davis recommendations that the original agreement covering Johnston's surrender to Sherman be accepted by the Confederate Government. There was also found among these papers a key to the cipher used by the Confederates in official communications.[14] This property of Davis was sent to Washington where it remained until 1874 when some of it was returned to its owner.[15]

After the Eastern Shoremen of Maryland had mounted their horses and, as Tilghman reported, "each, with all his worldly goods in a very small bundle behind him rode off" from the Yulee plantation, they proceeded to seek paroles. Tench Tilghman and Sidney Winder stopped overnight at "Kanapaha," the plantation of Thomas Evans Haile, eight miles southwest of Gainesville, near Arredondo. Tilghman gratefully remarked, "we were received and treated very kindly by Mr. Haile indeed, and a clean bed and entire undress after so many nights on the ground was elegant."

Two other Marylanders, "El" Dickinson and John Scott, were accommodated a quarter of a mile away at the home of Haile's brother-in-law, James Chesnut.

Starting the next day for the Federal headquarters at Jacksonville, the four Confederate officers made a stop at Gainesville, remained overnight at the plantation of Elias Earle, at the present site of Earleton, and enjoyed a swim in nine-mile-long Sante Fé Lake northeast of Gainesville. This route carried them through country that was "horribly poor and sandy," and through the once prosperous but then almost deserted village of Middleburg. Near Black Creek they were the guests of George Ozias Branning. At Starke they were forced to pay exorbitant prices for corn for their horses. Finally they arrived at Jacksonville, May 26.

"Today we have been subjected to a trial such as I had hoped never to have been called on to endure," wrote Tilghman. "We were halted by negro pickets and taken to a tent where our names were registered by a negro sergeant. We were then stripped of our revolvers and escorted into town. The remarks of the negro soldiers were unendurable. I feel disgraced and degraded."

Fortunately the $2,000 in gold sovereigns each one carried in the bottom of his pantaloons, which were stuffed in his boots, was not disturbed. They registered at the Taylor House and sold their horses for $50 each. They then met a "character" named McCall "who in less than an hour got $5 from John [Scott] to buy whiskey which up to bed time John has not seen," wrote Tilghman. Captain Alfred Van

Benthuysen of New Orleans and Captain Fred Emory of Maryland, who had left the Yulee plantation by another road, were paroled at Baldwin and from there walked twenty miles into Jacksonville.

The Marylanders were not allowed in Jacksonville to take

Confederates paroled

the oath of allegiance to the United States but were given a pass to Hilton Head, at the mouth of the Broad River on the South Carolina coast about forty miles east of Savannah. After waiting for a steamer until June 7, they secured passage for $5.50 each and embarked. One stop was made at Fernandina, which Tilghman called "an old antedeluvian town built on the sand." Hilton Head, Federal head-quarters for the district, was reached on the night of June 8. At last on June 10 they took the oath and were, Tilghman wrote, "informed that we were free to go anywhere we chose in the United States." Late that afternoon they boarded the S. S. *Haze* and started home with many problems as to the present as well as to the future, still unsolved. One such puzzling question had arisen about the amazing growth of Hilton Head. "When the war broke out there was not a single house except the plantation house and quarters," wrote Tilghman. "Now a considerable town has sprung up with an immense business capital. Billiard rooms, restaurants and even a theatre are among the attractions of the place. Yankees beat hell, anyhow!"

CHAPTER VII

"UNDERGROUND" PASSAGES

THE capture of Judge Reagan, Postmaster General of the Confederacy, with President Davis on May 10, 1865, increased the confidence of the Federal pursuers in their ability to capture the other five members of the Cabinet—Benjamin, Breckinridge, George Davis, Mallory, and Trenholm. Rumors were rife as to how they were escaping.

Federal commanders stationed in various parts of Florida were warned as early as the middle of April that the highest Confederate officials would probably attempt to escape from the Florida coast. One rumor indicated that three or four thousand troops were gathering in the vicinity of Tallahassee to aid the Government leaders to escape from its port, St. Marks, twenty miles south. Federals at Pensacola heard that the Confederate ram, *Stonewall,* was approaching that coast and would take the Cabinet on board. The mouths of the Suwannee, Wacassassee, Crystal, and Withlacoochee Rivers, and the harbors of Pensacola, St. Marks, Cedar Keys, Bay-

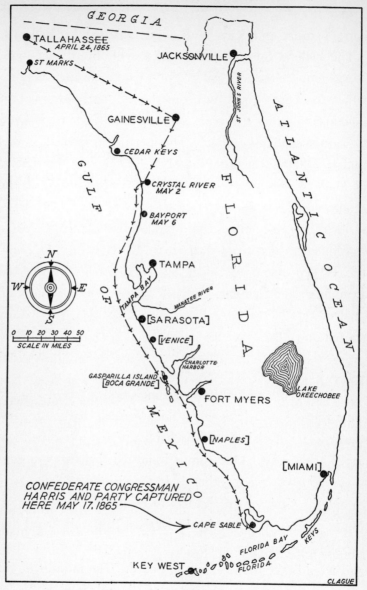

Brackets indicate settlements that did not exist in 1865

The route followed by Confederate Congressman Thomas A. Harris

port, Tampa, and Key West were guarded by Federals.
The Federal commander at Jacksonville heard that some
"suspicious characters" had recently passed through Gainesville with a small boat and some boxes that might contain
gold and that they had offered $1,000 in gold to be conveyed
to Tampa or Sarasota Bay. This party was headed, it was
understood, by a Captain Johnson of Key West, a close friend
of Mallory. He was one of the few men, according to the
report, who knew the secret passes through the Florida keys,
inside of which fugitives could remain unmolested for years.

While he was at Cedar Keys Brigadier General John New-
ton learned that these "suspicious characters" were thirteen
in number and that three of them were thought to be high
civil officers of the Confederacy and that they had already
started down the coast. He immediately gave chase, searched
every vessel and closely scrutinized the shore from Cedar
Keys to Key West, and then picketed the reef from Key
West east to Indian Key. From that point the naval officers
conducted the search to Cape Florida on the East Coast.[1]

Lieutenant Hollis and his Federal guard had been waiting
for two long weeks to intercept the escaping Confederates
at Cape Sable, where a luxuriant growth of mangroves
fringed the Bay of Florida and densely grown semitropical
trees and shrubbery formed hammocks and were made
almost impenetrable by clustering cactus.

At two thirty, on the morning of May 17, Hollis arrested
seven "persons of importance," including Brigadier General
Thomas A. Harris, a Confederate Congressman from Mis-

souri. This group of refugees, which the captors suspected included Breckinridge, Mallory, and other members of the Cabinet, had left Tallahassee on April 24. They were reported to have made their way partly by railroad and partly with the aid of three teams, one of six horses and two of four horses. From Tallahassee they traveled to Gainesville and then sixty miles southwestward to Crystal River, near the old town of Pierceville where five years before James R. Randall, author of "Maryland, My Maryland," had taught school. On May 2, the Missouri official and his friends launched the small boat they had brought down from Gainesville, passed Bayport on May 6, and proceeded down the coast, sailing at night and hiding by day. After two weeks of such travel, just as they were about to leave Florida for Cuba, Lieutenant Hollis and his men apprehended them at Cape Sable.[2] But no member of the Cabinet was found in the captured party. Benjamin, Breckinridge, and George Davis had found secret passages into Florida, each of the three choosing a different route. So far Mallory in Georgia and Trenholm in South Carolina had not been arrested.

Moving with the utmost secrecy, lest he arouse the suspicion of the Federal patrol, General Breckinridge, upon his arrival in Madison, Florida, May 15, consulted Brigadier General Joseph J. Finegan and other leaders about the route along which he would be least likely to be overtaken or intercepted by the enemy. General Finegan, whom President Davis and the Confederate Congress had thanked a year before for his "skill and gallantry displayed in achieving the signal victory" of Olustee when the invading Federal forces were turned back from Florida,[3] had been for three years in charge of the larger part of the Confederate forces in that state. He was, because of this experience, well qualified to provide an "underground" passage for General Breckinridge.

Bidding his son, Cabell, farewell, General Breckinridge, accompanied by his aide, Colonel James Wilson of Kentucky, and his negro servant, Thomas Ferguson, who had served him throughout the War, hurriedly left Madison on horseback May 16, 1865.[4] He went east toward St. Augustine along the old Bellamy road, built by slave labor. At the time of its construction it had connected the two centers of population, St. Augustine and Pensacola, and passed through the newly established capital, Tallahassee. When General Breckinridge traveled over this road, the country through which he rode included not many of the less than eighty thousand people of the state. At the Suwannee River, about twenty-five miles east of Madison, he and his followers spent the night at the home of Lewis M. Moseley. There he learned that Secretary Benjamin had preceded him by two days on his way south. Breckinridge was joined at this place by Colonel John Taylor Wood, who had remained a few hours in Madison to trade horses, and who had finally exchanged with General Finegan by giving the Floridian fifty dollars "to boot."

Colonel Edward Mashburn, Moseley's son-in-law, had been an officer in General Breckinridge's command. Mrs. Mashburn did not know of her husband's whereabouts and was naturally solicitous over his safety. According to Breckinridge, "Col. Wilson relieved her by the statement that her husband would reach home in a few days. I am sorry to say," added the General, "that Col. Wilson had no information on which to found this assurance." Colonel Wilson was fortunately correct in his statement. Colonel Mashburn had been paroled at Greensboro two weeks before and at this time was on his way to Florida.

Mr. Moseley's ferry carried Breckinridge and his escort across the deep and placid waters of the Suwannee River early on the morning of May 16. Massive live oaks formed an almost interlocking archway over this dreamy stream whose banks of limestone had been curiously sculptured by the water. The vivid coloring of cardinals flashing by the travelers contrasted sharply with the gray thickets along the road. Continuing on the seldom traveled St. Augustine road, the Breckinridge party passed through a wilderness of pines—"pine barrens" as Audubon called them—tall pines, miles of them, beneath which grew rank grass, here and there mixed with low bushes and saw palmettos. For nearly twenty miles there was no sign of water as they jogged through the flat, sandy woods, avoiding scores of gopher holes lest their horses stumble. The summer heat of Florida made their progress slow, as did the mosquitoes and other insects which the General described as "countless and intolerable." No sound greeted them other than the swishing of the pines in the light breeze, the hum of the insects, the grunt of "razor-back" hogs, the occasional "bob-white" of a distant quail, and the song of the meadowlark. Much-needed water was found at Double Sinks but it was pronounced "bad."

Without knowing it, Breckinridge and his escort crossed the Santa Fé River at the Natural Bridge, a "bridge" that broadens to a width of three miles as the river passes through an underground channel. The night of May 17 was spent at Collins, a lonely stagecoach station about thirty-two miles east of the Suwannee River near the present city of Live Oak, where they were charged for their lodging. The middle of the next day brought them to Newnansville, former county seat of Alachua County. There they dined with Colonel "Wash" W. Scott, a former Confederate officer. After traveling some thirty-five miles in a southeasterly direction they reached Gainesville that night.

Disappointed at finding the home of former Confederate Congressman James B. Dawkins at Gainesville filled with guests, they suffered the indignity and discomfort of being forced, because of lack of accommodations, to sleep on the floor at a tavern which Colonel Wood feelingly labeled a "filthy hole." They were further disturbed when they learned that a Federal officer and soldiers who had been in Gainesville the previous day were expected to return at any hour. Much of this anxiety was doubtlessly dispelled the next morning, May 19, when Judge Dawkins entertained them at breakfast and helped them organize the next step in their journey.

Although forced by the urgent necessity of getting through Florida as rapidly as possible, it was imperative that General Breckinridge map out his course southward with the utmost care; otherwise the ever-vigilant Federal guards could hardly be circumvented. All ports on the twelve hundred miles of Florida's seacoast were now under the control of the Federals and much of the intervening coast line was being patrolled.

"It would not do to attempt to leave the country from the West Coast of Florida," decided the General. The East Coast was the only part of the state that could not be completely guarded, though several Federal blockade camps remained there. He decided that the East Coast presented the better opportunity for escape.

The next problem was to get a boat. The boat which Colonel Thorburn, after such careful planning with Captain Coxetter, had held in readiness in the Indian River for the presidential party, had been destroyed when the capture of Jefferson Davis was learned, but Captain J. J. Dickison, who had achieved a reputation as the "Francis Marion of Florida," came to the rescue of the Confederate Secretary of War. He hurried over to see General Breckinridge at Gainesville from the little town of Waldo, ten miles away, where his command was about to be paroled, and immediately joined the secret conference. This he described as follows: "It was his [Breckinridge's] earnest desire to reach the Trans-Mississippi department and join Generals Kirby Smith and Magruder before they surrendered, and thought the safest route to this objective point would be by way of Cuba, and wished to know if I could arrange to send him at once. The only means of transportation that I could offer was a lifeboat I had captured with the gunboat *Columbine"* on the St. Johns River.[5]

While General Breckinridge was completing arrangements with Captain Dickison to use the *Columbine's* lifeboat southward up the St. Johns River, Colonel Wood attempted to locate Secretary Benjamin and Colonel Thorburn. Armed with one of Captain Dickison's revolvers, he rode about sixteen miles along the railroad from Gainesville to Archer. At "Cotton Wood" plantation Wood was welcomed by Mrs. David L. Yulee. A few hours after Wood's arrival, Yulee returned from Jacksonville where he had gone to discuss the new status of the Southern States with Chief Justice Salmon P. Chase. It amused Chase to observe "how ignorant he [Yulee] was that during the last four years anything had happened! Slavery was dead—that much was hastily admitted—but what other change the causeless Rebellion could have, or ought to have wrought, he didn't see," Whitelaw Reid reported.

"That there was any modification of the old order of things—that Southern men were not to be heeded whenever they stamped their feet—that every Rebel had not the same rights under the Constitution with every loyal man—were things which, in his seclusion in the interior [of Florida] had never occurred to him," thought Reid.

"He [Yulee] had been appointed a Commissioner to see

whether the Administration would not permit the Governor and Legislature to resume control of the State, and dispense with further military interference!

"While we were at Hilton Head," continued Reid, "General Gillmore had issued an order overturning the effort of the fugitive South Carolina Governor to continue *his* control of his State; and Senator Yulee had just heard of it. He was greatly disturbed, and begged Mr. Chase to tell him whether it could be possible that the Administration would sustain Gen. Gillmore, and thus, by refusing to recognize the only constitutional authorities of the State, plunge them all into anarchy again!

"But worse horrors remained for the sanguine Senator to encounter. He had not recovered from the shock of learning that, instead of being again clothed with the authority of the State, he and his fellow conspirators stood a better chance of being dealt with for treason, when the negro question came up.

"He [Yulee] was desirous that the State officials should control the freedmen. It was suggested [by Chase] that the freedmen, being in some sections in the majority, and in all having the advantage of loyalty, might better control the State officials," was the further report of Reid.[6]

This disillusioning interview with Chief Justice Chase led Yulee to advise Wood to seek terms with the Federals. Colonel Wood reflected on the certain punishment that awaited him. His adventurous spirit had carried him on many a more dangerous mission than his present flight and he was confident of his ability to escape. He disregarded Yulee's counsel and rejoined General Breckinridge on May 20 at "Millwood," the extensive plantation of Colonel Samuel Hamilton Owens, near Orange Lake in Marion County about twenty-four miles south of Gainesville. The large plantings of short staple cotton by the Owens family made this picturesque part of Florida the center of many activities, including a cotton gin and a sawmill.

General Breckinridge, Colonel Wilson, and the ex-slave, Tom, had arrived at "Millwood" the evening before Wood's arrival after a five-hour horseback ride south from Gainesville. They had left Gainesville as quickly as possible after arranging with Captain Dickison for three paroled Floridians, twenty-one-year-old, sandy-haired Sergeant Joseph J. (Jerry) O'Toole, Corporal Richard R. Russell, and Irish-born Private P. Murphy, to bring into service the *Columbine's* lifeboat. Neither Breckinridge nor Wood had been able to determine the whereabouts of Secretary Benjamin who they had hoped might rejoin them for the final dash of their escape.

Colonel Wood regarded this part of Florida as better than any he had seen since leaving Madison. Colonel Owens "lived in a good deal of style," he said, probably not unlike that maintained by the other two hundred and fifty Floridians, each of whom before the War presided over "feudal" domains of more than five hundred acres, manned by fifty or more slaves.[7] Colonel Owens, whom Breckinridge called

135

"an excellent gentleman," also entertained the escaping party the next night, May 20. This was the day the former Secretary of the Navy, Stephen R. Mallory, was arrested at the Benjamin H. Hill mansion in Lagrange, Georgia. Despite almost insurmountable obstacles, Mallory had succeeded in organizing and directing a navy that had achieved a remarkable record. Because of this achievement, he was a marked man. The North regarded him not as the head of a Navy Department but as chief of a system of privateering on a par with piracy. Federal officers arrested him without the least consideration for his comfort. Surprising him at midnight, they hustled him off, half-clothed, charged with "treason and with organizing and setting on foot piratical expeditions." [8]

Breckinridge was comparatively secure from arrest in the central part of Florida. The nearest town, Ocala, was fifteen miles distant and the possibility that Federal troops would penetrate this area in the near future was remote. Friends here, said Colonel Wood, were "very kind and desirous to assist us as far as possible." They therefore continued their flight in a more leisurely manner. On May 21 they went only a short distance and were dinner guests at "Rutland," the plantation of Captain William A. Owens, who had done much at the outbreak of the War to organize and equip the Confederates of Marion County. J. B. Owens, a third brother, had been a delegate to the Democratic Convention in Charleston in 1860, was a member of Florida's Secession Convention, and had also represented Florida in the Provisional Confederate Congress. "Rutland," which had been designed by a Charleston architect and luxuriously decorated with materials from that city, was the most comfortable retreat which General Breckinridge had enjoyed since leaving South Carolina. Colonel Wood observed that the Owens brothers "were wealthy, until this present issue of affairs." He referred, undoubtedly, to the fact that the assessed value of real and personal property in Florida, exclusive of slaves, had shrunk from about $47,000,000 in 1860 to about $25,000,000 five years later, a decrease of nearly 50 per cent and that the freeing of slaves in Florida had destroyed approximately $22,000,000 in values.[9]

While General Breckinridge partook of the overnight hospitality of "Rutland," Colonel Wood proceeded to Silver Springs, six miles northeast of Ocala, with Lieutenant William H. McCardell, whom Captain Dickison had provided as a guide. At the Springs they were guests in the "log cottage hotel" of the Lieutenant's father-in-law, Hiram T. Mann, a former member of the Confederate Legislature of Florida. Ten years before this Judge Mann had entertained here Lady Amelia Murray, an intimate friend of Lady Byron and maid of honor to Queen Victoria. While enjoying the beauty of Silver Springs she wrote one of her notable letters.[10] Colonel Wood was fascinated by the sparkling transparency of the subterranean river that forms the Springs as it rushes from the earth through a vast cavern in a volume estimated at 300,000,000 gallons per day. He declared it to be the "most beautiful submarine view I have ever seen."

Thaddeus Oliver, to whom is attributed the poem, "All Quiet along the Potomac," while stationed in a Confederate camp near Silver Springs, was likewise impressed. Said he: "The River comes out from the Spring in a clear, transparent stream or volume of water large enough for a medium sized steamer to go up without the slightest difficulty . . . the water seems to come out through long breaks or fissures in the solid rock. Through these cracks or fissures pearly radiance streams, as brilliant and much more dazzling than firelight. . . . The bottom of the Spring, except where these fissures are seen, is thickly carpeted with a perfectly green grass that grows beneath the water and seems to be nourished alone by the rays of the sun that penetrate through the water." Oliver added, "These people [in the vicinity of Ocala] are much better than around Gainesville and cannot tolerate a Yankee or deserter. I do not doubt that there are more deserters and tories about Gainesville than in this section but at Gainesville the people say nothing about it and will not expose them. Here they hunt them with dogs." [11]

After Colonel Wood left Silver Springs he passed the old Seminole War landmark, Fort King, and took the stagecoach road south past the site of the present town of Belleview. He rejoined General Breckinridge, Colonel Wilson, and Tom Ferguson near the present site of Summerfield at "Wauchula," the plantation of Colonel A. G. Summer, former Confederate Quartermaster General of Florida. In the absence of Colonel Summer, Milton O'Dell and B. F. Smith

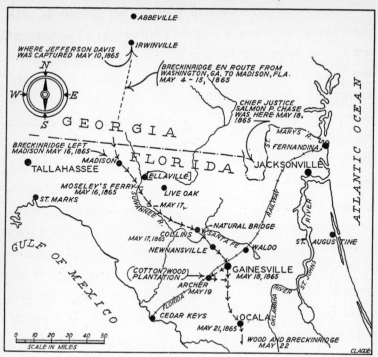

Brackets indicate settlements that did not exist in 1865

The route followed by John C. Breckinridge to Ocala

looked after General Breckinridge and his escort on May 22 and 23.

At "Wauchula," while they awaited the arrival of the lifeboat of the *Columbine,* which Captain Dickison had promised to have delivered to them at Fort Butler on the St. Johns River, the visitors went on a hunting trip in the Marion County woods. The General's comments on this experience relate not to the one deer he killed but to the "ticks or very small bugs," (red bugs), which he said "buried themselves under the skin, and tormented me for days, causing me to scratch until large raw places were made." Although General Breckinridge had been recognized by a number of people in his travels, Colonel Wood believed his secret would be well kept. While the Confederates were hunting on May 23 in Central Florida, the Chief Justice of the United States was becoming acclimated at Key West by imbibing "champerou," a concoction which, according to local report, was the "greatest of all the institutions" of the island city. To a base of curacao were added absinthe, maraschino, and other liqueurs as well as sugar and eggs. This combination produced a compound that according to Whitelaw Reid would puzzle any analytical chemist.[12]

After leaving Colonel Summer's plantation, General Breckinridge turned "up the country a little, and moving eastward" journeyed ten miles to Lake Weir, "a fine sheet of water, some five or six miles across," according to Colonel Wood, who enjoyed a swim in it. Slightly north on the west side of this lake, Mr. James A. Wiggins was host on May 24 to the party at his home, now a part of the Carney Orange Grove.

Skirting the south side of Lake Weir and moving eastward, the Confederates went twelve miles the next day, May 25, just as their friend, ex-Senator Yulee, charged with treason while holding a seat in the United States Senate and with plotting to capture the forts and arsenals of the United States in Florida just before the War began, was being arrested in Gainesville.[13] Breckinridge's next stop was at the plantation of Major Thomas Stark near a point on the road between the present towns of Weirsdale and Umatilla where the bridge crosses the Oklawaha River, the largest tributary of the St. Johns. They crossed this narrow and crooked body of water, colored by vegetation, in what Colonel Wood called a "pungy," while the horses encountered difficulty swimming across the swift current. Here General Breckinridge obtained supplies for two weeks, including sweet potato "coffee" and grits. He made sure of his directions, secured confidential information about the people he might encounter, and launched into the semitropical wilderness, where the trunks of countless palmettos bristled with the regularity of bayonets.

As the Confederates severed their ties with the civilization of the Old South, all traces of their movements of the previous ten days were carefully guarded by the loyal friends who had made possible their "underground" passage from lower Georgia through the settled portions of north and central Florida. Fate had served them well. If good fortune favored them a few days more, they would reach the Atlantic and there they would have at least a slight chance to get out of the country. The Trans-Mississippi Department could no longer be their objective, however, because General Kirby Smith was on May 26, as Breckinridge was approaching the St. Johns River, surrendering his army, the last of the Confederate forces to lay down their arms. Two other goals remained open, Cuba and the Bahamas.

Lieutenant McCardell guided Breckinridge and his men

laboriously through more than thirty miles of heavy sand, scrub, and dwarf pine and oak growth from the Oklawaha River to Fort Butler, opposite the settlement of Volusia, near the mouth of Lake George on the St. Johns. Dull blue "scrub" jays, cooing mourning doves, and numerous rabbits darting ahead kept the Confederates company along the lonely way. Their arrival at this point on the St. Johns River about midday of May 26 marked the end of their long journey by horseback which had begun at Greensboro, North Carolina, on April 15. Awaiting them were the three recently added Florida recruits to the expedition, O'Toole, Russell, and Murphy. These former Confederate soldiers had raised the lifeboat of the *Columbine* from its hiding place and during the preceding eight days had brought it up the river. They were experienced hunters, fishermen, and beachcombers and destined to be of valuable service to Breckinridge in the still long trip ahead.

This new means of transportation was a four-oared open cutter about seventeen feet in length "with a place in front to 'step' a very small mast, so as to use a sail when there was wind, by holding the end of the rope in the hand," explained Breckinridge. By four o'clock in the afternoon, the provisions, camping equipment, firearms, and ammunition were loaded and all preparations were completed for the next step in the escape of the Confederate Secretary of War, while the Grand Jury of the Supreme Court of the District of Columbia was authorizing the issuance of a bench warrant for his arrest.[14]

Breckinridge's original party of four, including Wilson, Wood, and Tom Ferguson, besides himself, had now with the addition of the three Floridians increased to seven. This load weighed the boat so far down in the water that there was not much freeboard left. Before saying goodby to the

Starting up the St. Johns River

escaping party, McCardell sold his shotgun to Colonel Wood and was rewarded with the Colonel's horse for his services as guide.

Depending on the oars when the wind dropped, the Southern statesman and his escort proceeded up the coffee-colored waters of the St. Johns and at nightfall anchored in the middle of the stream, the banks of which were covered with cypresses, palmetto palms, water oaks, and maples.

Before the morning sun could bring the near-by trees out of the lurking shadows and dry out the moisture of the night, a thunderstorm broke. Not only were the men drenched to the skin, but their provisions and some of their ammunition were soaked, and much of their salt had dissolved. Their only safeguard against undue exposure was a "shot" of rum and water. They were able to make some thirty-five miles that day.

General Breckinridge regarded the St. Johns as the most crooked and bewildering stream he had ever seen. "Its general course is almost due north," explained he, "but frequently the boat's head pointed to every point of the compass and we were often puzzled and led astray by false channels that ended in nothing.

"It abounds in cranes, pelicans and other water fowl and great numbers of crocodiles, who sunned themselves on the bank, and slid into the river with a sullen plunge on our approach. Sometimes they would swim across our bow with their black scaly backs just visible, like a gunboat low in the water.

"I shot one with my pistol, and after we got him ashore it required three more balls through the place where his brains should have been, to finish him. He was about 13 feet long, and had under his throat, a little bag, containing a strong musk, which we cut out, Col. Wilson intending to present it in a smelling bottle to some female friend but it was mislaid afterwards.

"We caught some fish in this river, and found some sour

oranges in a deserted orchard, with which, and some dark and dirty brown sugar, we made a very miserable [orangeade]."

As the Confederates pulled the oars laboriously, they overtook Captain George C. Brantley freighting a load of goods, probably the first since the close of the War, from Jacksonville up the river to Mellonville, now Sanford. They also passed the two deserted houses of Hawkinsville on the west bank. That day they were able to make only twenty-three miles before darkness overtook them. At night, in order to avoid the mosquitoes, they again anchored in midstream but only for four or five hours. On the banks of the river was a dense growth of bays and cypresses held tight by clambering vines, all darkened mysteriously by masses of hanging Spanish moss. Colonel Wood added to the food supply by catching bass from time to time, which bit well, he discovered, in the quiet waters of the St. Johns.

Sunday morning, May 28, found the party breakfasting at Eaton's, which, like most places on the river, was deserted. Evidences of a warmer climate in the form of tropical fruits—figs, guavas, bananas, and citrus—greeted them in the old gardens. A fair wind pushed the small craft eight miles across Lake Monroe, which is not a lake but a widening of the river resembling a lake, with Enterprise on the left and Mellonville on the right. This latter settlement was then the terminus of an old military road of the Seminole Indian War days.

As Secretary of War Breckinridge was sailing along in this

isolated part of Florida, in comparative safety, a Cabinet colleague, former Postmaster General Reagan, first member of the Cabinet to be captured, was writing in his solitary confinement at Fort Warren, Boston harbor, a convincing appeal to President Andrew Johnson. As one descendant of poor East Tennesseans to another, he urged the President to change his vindictive policy toward the South. It is not improbable that this document exerted an influence on President Lincoln's successor and was partly responsible for the change in his attitude and policy.[15]

Upon arriving at Holden's Landing, just above Lake Monroe, Colonel Wood and Sergeant O'Toole went inland five miles to Saulsville (Osteen since 1883) and engaged George Sauls to meet them the next day at Cook's Ferry to haul their boat overland from the St. Johns River to the Atlantic Ocean. It was "the only wagon to be found in that desolate country," Breckinridge said. Oxen were numerous, he added, inasmuch as "large herds of cattle were grazed in that country and sold to the northward."

On the following day the Breckinridge party encountered serious difficulties with the sluggish current, which divided itself most unexpectedly. As they approached the headwaters of the St. Johns River they discovered that it was dangerously populated with alligators drifting slowly with just their wicked eyes protruding out of the water. The channel was becoming so narrow and crooked that the General seldom knew which way to go. This part of the river ran through broad, grassy tropical savannahs where on every hand could be seen blue and white herons, snowy egrets, water turkeys, and ducks. Another twenty-mile pull in heat that became excessive when the breeze died out brought the worn travelers on May 29 to Cook's Ferry, just north of where the Okeechobee Branch of the Florida East Coast Railroad now crosses the St. Johns. Near the mouth of Lake Harney, which Sidney Lanier later described as "an expanse of the Upper St. Johns," George Sauls and his ox team were waiting. Private Murphy, who, the General said, had been "very kind and useful," left for his home after he had received $100 for the lifeboat of the *Columbine,* which he claimed was his.

The boat was loaded on the oxcart that night so that an early start could be made the next morning. For the first time in four nights the weary men slept in beds and under a roof. As the danger of the Federals overtaking them in this isolated country was reduced to a minimum, the fugitives could relax and enjoy a good night's rest without the slightest concern for the rain, which came down more heavily than ever. Probably they were not conscious of the ominous hoot of the owls, the eerie cry of the limpkins, the monotonous croak of frogs, or even the lusty, ground-shaking bellow of the bull alligators. They needed rest for the next strenuous part of the flight—the overland journey across what was then a part of Volusia County to the Atlantic Ocean.

At sunrise on the morning of May 30, the celebrated Kentuckian and his fellow adventurers set out on foot from the

St. Johns River and headed southeast, following the ox team with its priceless cargo of boat, provisions, and ammunition. The boat could not be fastened securely on the frame of the oxcart. This added to their worries, and despairingly the

General remarked: "The road (if it could be called one) was full of ruts which rocked everything badly and several times the front wheels ran away from the hind ones, bringing the end of the boat to the ground with a heavy thump."

It was necessary to stop so often to repair damages that they made only eighteen miles that day, their lonely and dreary progress being broken only occasionally by the sight of a big sand-hill crane, rising out of the pathway to settle down a few yards farther away, or a lone buzzard circling high in the air. At dusk they camped at Six Mile Creek, two and one-half miles west of the present town of Mims. Soon smoke from a cheerful lightwood fire was curling up through the broad fronds of palmettos, and the weary travelers were refreshed by a dinner of bacon, eggs, and sweet potatoes. The corn meal had been spoiled by the rains. After dinner swarms of mosquitoes from the swamps made sleeping impossible. The large horseflies had bitten the oxen so savagely that their heads and necks and other parts of their bodies were becoming saturated with blood. The black ox had attracted the tormentors more than the white one and Sauls feared it would not be able to go on. The men were forced to remain awake almost the entire night, only partially protected from the fury of the insects by the smoke of the campfire. Their only compensating satisfaction lay in the knowledge that they were so completely cut off from civilization that capture was virtually impossible. Even the vegetation along parts of the road was limited to occasional clusters of tall palmettos rising out of fields of saw grass which like the Everglades stretched on endlessly. Occasionally there could be seen a flock of the now rare scarlet ibises, or a white heron, solitary and motionless, as if it were a sentinel guarding the silent path of the lonely Confederates.

Finally on May 31 they approached the Atlantic Ocean about fifty miles south of the present site of Daytona Beach and reached the Indian River at Carlisle's Landing, now Lagrange, about three miles north of the present city of Titusville. There they launched the boat and prepared to trust their fortunes to Neptune.

Before taking leave of George Sauls, the Florida "cracker" who had transported their boat from Lake Harney to the Indian River, an incident occurred which General Breckinridge described as follows: "The oxen had suffered most of all and the black one was literally covered with blood. The driver [George Sauls] said he would probably die (I did not think so) and secured five dollars more out of us on the chance of it.

"This was the only person in Florida who dealt closely with us. He was very ignorant, but keener and more provident in all points of a contract than any Yankee I ever saw.

"I think he knew me, but at parting he raised both hands and eased his conscience by declaring that he 'knowed nothing about us,' that he was a poor man, that it was a plain business matter, as anybody could see, and that he was not responsible for consequences." [16]

CHAPTER VIII

ADVENTURE IN PIRACY

G ENERAL BRECKINRIDGE and his escort, highly elated over their success in traversing much of the populated portion of Florida without running afoul of the Federals, had reason to feel optimistic over their chance for escape when they reached the Atlantic Ocean and were near the possible haven of Nassau. At least two dangers, however, made their passage down the coast of Florida hazardous: first, the turbulent ocean which was hardly safe for a mere lifeboat the size of theirs; and second, several camps of Federal guards stationed along the Indian River, down which they expected to sail.

Despite what the General called "the thumps and wrenches it had received," in its trip overland, the lifeboat proved "tolerably watertight." He had "thought it might do for the River" but regarded it as "a very frail thing" for the ocean. Doubtless he had serious misgivings about getting any considerable distance from Florida in it. He must have been comforted, however, when he realized that one member of his party, Colonel John Taylor Wood, had continued the training he had received at Annapolis to such a degree that he had become one of the most skillful and resourceful navigators in America. General Breckinridge probably did not know it—because Colonel Wood was evidently too modest to seek the recognition and promotion that his ability, courage, and energy amply justified—but no man in the Confederate Navy, with the exception of Rear Admiral Raphael Semmes, had captured more Federal vessels than had Colonel Wood.

Like his famous grandfather, "Old Rough and Ready" Zachary Taylor and his cousin, General Robert E. Lee, Colonel Wood was a fighter. As a lad of sixteen he had served in the war against Mexico, from which his grandfather had emerged the most popular hero. He had so mastered the science of seamanship and gunnery that after graduation from the United States Naval Academy he had acted as assistant professor in those subjects. He was a lieutenant, a commander, and finally a captain in the United States Navy for a decade and had served in the Mediterranean and on the Atlantic and Pacific Oceans before resigning to enter the Confederate Navy. It was partly due to Colonel Wood's daring that large quantities of much-needed food and coal were captured from the Federals at Plymouth, North Carolina. He had been an officer on the

Virginia (*Merrimac*) in her historic battle with the *Monitor* in Hampton Roads, the first between ironclads. One of his remarkable exploits was to take the 220-foot commerce raider, *Tallahassee,* up the Atlantic seaboard from Virginia through the lane of commerce past New York, "down" the coast of Maine, and over to Halifax, Nova Scotia, in the course of which he captured numerous Federal merchantmen.[1]

When the Breckinridge party first started down the coast of Florida, Colonel Wood was not forced to grapple with ocean perils. A line of sand reefs and long, narrow islands, enclosing shallow bodies of water, extends along most of the four hundred miles of that coast. Inside this fringe of land a broad arm of the sea, the Indian River, margins the Atlantic for more than two hundred miles from near Cape Canaveral to Key Biscayne. This so-called "river" is a protected waterway, averaging one mile in width, partly salt and partly fresh, through which fairly large boats may pass with safety. Since this waterway is so near the ocean there is almost daily a good sailing breeze. It was near the head of this Indian River that the Confederates launched their boat and it was down this waterway that they directed their course, using a map of Florida that had been published by the War Department in 1856 when Jefferson Davis was United States Secretary of War.[2]

After hauling their small boat across the sand bars and mudflats of the Indian River in the scorching sun, encountering here and there a stingaree, the Confederate adventurers

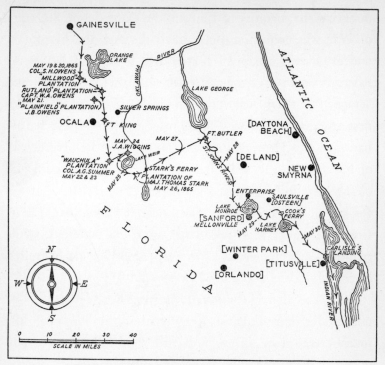

Brackets indicate settlements that did not exist in 1865

*The route followed by Breckinridge and his party
to the Indian River*

started south on May 31. They passed the site of the present
(1938) Indian River City, and, aided occasionally by the
wind, made good progress with the oars. When darkness
overtook them they camped on the west bank. "Indifferent
water," said the General, "was obtained by digging in
the sand."

While the North, in response to President Johnson's
proclamation, was observing June 1 as a day of prayer

honoring the memory of Lincoln, the Confederate Secretary of War was boldly escaping down the Atlantic Coast. At one of several inhabited houses which he and his escort passed, tobacco was exchanged for watermelons with several "crackers" whom Colonel Wood described as the most destitute people he had seen for a long time. They "hardly had rags enough to cover them." Opposite the present city of Eau Gallie, across the Banana River from the south end of the forty-mile long, wedge-shaped Merritt Island, at the Captain John C. Houston place, near the mouth of Elbow Creek, the boat was hauled on shore and caulked, while numerous sandpipers looked on apparently with interested curiosity.

After the damage suffered during the overland transportation from Lake Harney had been repaired, the journey was resumed and soon the site of the present city of Melbourne was passed. When night came on, hoping to avoid the mosquitoes, which attacked them in swarms, they anchored in the quiet of the river. The General indulged in the unpleasant contemplation that a man with his arms tied and face exposed would be killed by these insects in two nights. Disturbed only by the occasional splash of a leaping mullet, they dozed off with the heavy smell of salt marshes deep in their nostrils. Although their lounging positions were uncomfortable, they were lulled to sleep by the murmur of the distant ocean.

By taking advantage of the generally fair wind, at night as well as during the day, they traveled forty-five miles more before again stopping. When the wind died the heat was oppressive, the mosquitoes became increasingly torment-ing, and the sting of sand flies pierced them with the sudden-ness of needle pricks. Colonel Wood, maintaining that the Indian River justly deserved its fame for these pests, explained: "Someone has said that by swinging a bucket around your head twice you could fill it [with mosquitoes]. We can get no rest, except by covering every part of one's person except his nostrils. I tie a towell around my hands and wrists; thin clothes they will pierce. Insects are so bad here that cattle cannot live."

The agonizing irritation of heat and mosquitoes was relieved on the afternoon of June 2 when, as the Confederates passed the site of the present city of Vero Beach, torrents of rain lashed the forlorn mariners so fiercely that they could not see twenty feet beyond their bow. These hardships were slight, however, compared to those experienced by Colonel Wood's grandfather, General Zachary Taylor, when, twenty-eight years before, he and his troops had penetrated the high saw grass of the Everglades, waded through almost impassable stretches of mud, and, finally, on the shores of Lake Okeechobee, approximately forty miles southwest of where the Confederates now found themselves, won a deci-sive victory over the Seminole Indians after a bloody three-hour battle.

All thoughts of their discomfort vanished when the Con-federates realized that within a few miles, at Indian River Inlet, was located a camp of Federal blockaders eager to

intercept escaping Confederates. As they prepared to pass
the camp at night they suspected every mysterious shadow
cast by the palms was that of a Federal. "Approaching
cautiously with muffled oars, we saw a fire on the bank,

Sailing along the Indian River

which we supposed to be the guard fire," wrote General
Breckinridge. "The night was dark, and keeping the middle
of the stream, we glided past without being challenged."

Breakfast that morning, June 3, was presumably consumed with an unusual relish, flavored with the satisfaction
of having effected an escape from very real and imminent
danger. They ate at a large, deserted orange grove belong-

ing to John Philip Herman on Herman's Bay at the present site of Ankona. Oranges were out of season but they were able to take on board a supply of lemons and coconuts. Herman's Grove was slightly south of old Fort Pierce where, a quarter of a century before, General Sherman had been swimming, spearing sharks, catching redfish, and rolling green turtles when he was not fighting Seminole Indians.[3]

If General Breckinridge recalled his last meeting with General Sherman in North Carolina on the previous April 18, he made no reference to it, but with a sly sense of humor noted, "Col. Wilson had a shot at a deer that was quietly looking at us from the bank of the river. From the manner in which it bounded off, stopping occasionally to look back at us, the Colonel thinks it possible he may have missed the animal."

Down the Indian River, now straight and broad, they sailed toward Jupiter Inlet, where they expected to turn into the ocean. When they reached the site of the present city of Stuart they found Gilbert's Bar closed. Colonel Wood observed that the channel at Juniper Narrows, just beyond, was crooked and narrow, just the reverse of what it had been up to that point. Vainly trying to find their way south, they lost a half day among the treacherous shoals, oyster bars, and intricate channels, followed by hundreds of gulls and terns skimming the surface of the water about them. These troubles left them little or no time to enjoy the beauty of the roseate spoonbill to be seen in large numbers there at that time.

The general plan of the Confederates was to go through Hobe Sound, as that part of Indian River just below Juniper Narrows is called, and pass from the Indian River into the Atlantic Ocean at Jupiter Inlet. But Breckinridge, fearing the presence there of another camp of blockaders, considered this proposal too hazardous to attempt. While seeking another opening to the ocean they fortunately located a short haulover, not more than fifty yards wide, and there pulled their boat across to the ocean.

"What a relief it is," exclaimed Colonel Wood, "to get out of the swamps and marshes of Indian River into the blue waters of old Ocean and the freedom from mosquitoes; what enjoyment to us, who have been punctured and bled for the past two weeks." Such had been the sensation experienced by Spanish conquistadores since the founding of St. Augustine in the sixteenth century, as they gazed on the apparently never-ending stretch of white beach bordering the clear blue water.

On the afternoon of June 3 the little boat braved the deep waters, and, sailing south with a fair wind, was unnoticed by a large steamer not more than a mile off shore. Since the brick-towered Jupiter Lighthouse had been put out of operation by the Confederates four years before, there was no beacon to guide the Breckinridge party that night, and so they directed their course by the stars and the roar of the ocean as it beat upon the beach. Jupiter Lighthouse had, however, served the Confederacy in another way. During the War whenever the near-by coast was observed to be clear of Federal cruisers, a previously arranged signal guided into the harbor the small blockade-runners which had come from the Bahamas. The contraband shipments were then transported up the Indian River to the interior settlements.

In the darkness of the night of June 3 another vessel was passed, which Colonel Wilson believed belonged to the Federal blockaders. Its attention was not attracted, however. No campfire was visible and no sound of blockaders was heard as the Confederates passed Jupiter Inlet. All that came within their vision was the glowing, phosphorescent water. Their relief was tremendous when they passed the danger zone and left the twenty-five mile length of mysterious Jupiter Island, fringed with palms and mangroves, where Jonathan Dickenson and a group of English Quakers were shipwrecked in 1696, and where a variety of notables have lived, from Padre Torre of Spanish days down to its present winter colony of notable people from many different places.

Soon after sunrise on Sunday, June 4, a landing was effected about fifteen miles below Jupiter Inlet, not far from the northern limits of the present city of Palm Beach. Sleep and rest were needed after the strenuous tax on their endurance the preceding night. Finding fresh water in Lake Worth, near the old Bleachyard Haulover, the Confederates cooked their breakfast as pelicans dived heavily about them and "fiddlers" darted up the beach. It was far from a modern Palm Beach breakfast that was set before them on this particular Sabbath. Provisions were getting low. There had been no bread for days; the sweet potatoes were nearly gone; and on the ocean beach the only food they could find was the eggs of the huge green turtles. They knew that the female would come to the sandy beach at night, more frequently in moonlight, and crawling up above high-water mark, would dig a hole about one foot in depth with her rear flappers and that in it she would sometimes lay as many as one hundred fifty eggs. Covering them with sand and smoothing the surface, she would crawl back again to the sea, leaving them to be hatched by the sun. By following her tracks they probed the sand with a sharp stick and located the eggs, which are almost the size of a golf ball with skin as white and tougher than parchment which it resembles. For these eggs they hunted industriously. As Colonel Wood described their quest, they were literally "scratching for a living." The eggs were plentiful in June and were much sought after by the bears from the Everglades.

Unwilling to subject themselves longer to the desperate chance of capture by the blockading and patrol camps along the Florida coast, they now decided to sail across to the Bahama Islands about sixty miles east. Realizing the nerve-racking strain and the enormous peril that confronted them on the open sea, the tired and sleepy voyagers rested after the previous night's close vigil and prepared themselves for the still more momentous journey ahead. Late in the afternoon they refreshed themselves with a swim in the clear blue ocean and about five o'clock Colonel Wood read prayers.

They then set out upon the deep waters and risked losing their lives in an effort to reach the British possessions. Their only company was the gorgeously colored flying fish that continually rose before their prow. Their only encouragement came from the friendly glow of the sun as it sank below the many palmettos on the banks of Lake Worth.

United States transport steamer

A strong wind on the morning of June 5 defeated their daring purpose of leaving the coast of Florida. The good fortune they had previously enjoyed now appeared to have deserted them completely; and panic must have seized them as they "saw a large steamer coming down the coast right in our tracks," as the General expressed it.

They rowed swiftly to the shore, hauled the boat up and all except one, who remained with the boat, hid behind the sand dunes as the steamer passed within half a mile. Im-

mensely relieved at not being detected, they returned to the
shore—but their eagerness proved their undoing. They had
been sighted. Immediately the United States transport
steamer bore around and pointed toward the shore. Only
two courses faced them. One was to abandon their boat and
make for the swamps where starvation had brought death
to many a shipwrecked Spaniard. The other possibility was
to bluff the pursuers. They decided to risk the latter.

After the steamer had come within about three hundred
yards of the shore, a boat full of men armed with cutlasses
and pistols was lowered. Leaving Breckinridge, Wilson,
and Tom Ferguson on shore, Wood, O'Toole, and Russell
rowed out and met the Federals about fifty yards from the
beach. By looking stupid, exhibiting the paroles of the
two Floridians, offering to sell turtle eggs and pretending
to be hunting, fishing, and "wrecking" along the coast, they
succeeded in quieting all suspicions of the Federal officer
in charge. When this inexperienced officer inquired if
there were any batteries on shore, Colonel Wood inwardly
registered much scorn, as he noted in his diary, "a battery
on a beach where is not a white man within a hundred
miles!"

The Confederates were immeasurably relieved from the
strain of the danger they had experienced as the Federal
steamer departed. If they had not extricated themselves so
cleverly, imprisonment would have been the minimum
punishment they would have suffered. The party, however,
still faced uncertainty. The continuing head wind forced

them to hug the shore and to abandon, at least temporarily, the hope of reaching Nassau. There still remained the possibility of sailing on down the coast and crossing the Gulf Stream to Cuba, provided they could elude the Federal patrol.

Disguised as "wreckers" they offered to sell turtle eggs to the Federals

About eight o'clock on the morning of June 6 they caught sight of some old tents on shore. Anxiety over the likelihood of its being a camp of blockaders was soon dispelled. Their taut nerves relaxed when the tall, well-formed redmen on land were recognized as Seminole Indians dressed in calico shirts, breech cloths and turbans, their bare legs shining like polished mahogany. Descended from the few hundred who escaped capture in the Seminole Indian War,

1835-1842, a conflict which lasted as long as the Revolution against England and which cost the United States in the neighborhood of $30,000,000, these Indians were engaged in hunting, fishing, and gathering turtle eggs.

Hoping to replenish their fast diminishing food supply, the Confederates landed and approached the Indian camp. All they could obtain was some koonti,[4] which the General pronounced slightly thicker than a pancake when cooked and "ten times as tough." Colonel Wood regarded it as "little better than fried gutta percha." It was, however, gratefully received, as were the few morsels of fish left over from the Indians' breakfast. These the hungry Confederates ate ravenously. With this slight enlargement of provisions they started out briskly and were soon to be rewarded by a stroke of good fortune which compensated largely for recent disappointments and privations.

Colonel Wood's pronounced success as a commerce raider and blockade-runner had caused him to be generally spoken of as a "pirate" in the Northern newspapers. The Confederate Congress had thanked him for his "daring and brilliantly executed plans" that had resulted in the capture of many Federal ships, including the transport schooner, *Elmor,* on the Potomac River; the *Golden Rod,* the *Coquette,* and the *Two Brothers* on Chesapeake Bay; and the gunboats *Satellite, Reliance,* and *Underwriter.*[5] A man of such achievement and experience and endowed with the resolution of a martyr was soon to be needed by Breckinridge as on June 6 he sailed down the coast of Florida.

When they reached the south end of Lake Worth, between the present cities of Lake Worth and Delray, the Confederates were struck with consternation at the sight of a boat coming toward them. With the recent narrow escape from capture by the Federal ship fresh in mind, their first impression was that this newcomer was the Federal guard they had been expecting since reaching the Indian River a week before. But when the supposed enemy changed his course, obviously to avoid the Confederates, Colonel Wood suspected its crew consisted of deserters or escaped convicts from the Dry Tortugas,[6] who were themselves fearful of the consequences of capture.

Observing that the approaching boat was a better sea-craft than their own, though not so fast a sailer, the Confederates determined on an exchange. Their savage-looking whiskers and generally woebegone appearance gave them a bloodthirsty air. The Confederate Secretary of War and his followers became, temporarily, pirates. Colonel Wood's description of the incident is vivid: "The breeze was very light, so we downed our sail, got out our oars and gave chase. The stranger stood out to seaward, and endeavored to escape; but slowly we overhauled her, and finally a shot caused her mainsail to drop. . . .

"They were thoroughly frightened at first, for our appearance was not calculated to impress them favorably. To our questions they returned evasive answers or were silent, and finally asked by what authority we had overhauled them. We told them the War was not over so far as we

*The Confederate Secretary of War and his followers
look like pirates and act the part*

were concerned; that they were our prisoners, and that their boat our prize; that they were both deserters and pirates, the punishment of which was death; but that under the circumstances we would not surrender them to the first cruiser we met, but would take their paroles and exchange boats.

"To this they seriously objected. They were well armed, and although we outnumbered them five to three (not

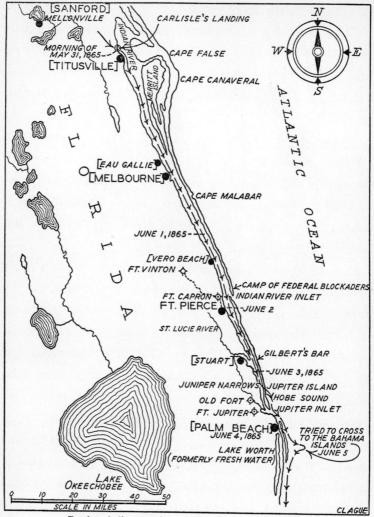

Brackets indicate settlements that did not exist in 1865

The route followed by the Breckinridge party down the Indian River

counting Tom), still, if they could get the first bead on us the chances were about equal.

"They were desperate and not disposed to surrender their boat without a tussle. The General and I stepped into their boat and ordered the spokesman and leader to go forward. He hesitated a moment, and two revolvers looked at him in the face.

"Sullenly he obeyed our orders. The General said, 'Wilson, disarm that man'! The Colonel with pistol in hand, told him to hold up his hands. He did so while the Colonel drew from his belt a navy revolver, and a sheath-knife. The other two made no show of resistance, but handed us their arms."

Colonel Wood threatened the captured crew with every cruel torture his active imagination could invent, but he finally relented so far as to let them off with an exchange of boats! The victims, extremely grateful for this clemency, went through what Mr. Lincoln called the dangerous process of "swapping horses while crossing a stream," and soon headed north in the lifeboat of the *Columbine,* which had been constructed for an entirely different purpose.[7]

General Breckinridge remarked that his aide, Colonel Wilson, was so pleased with the exchange of boats that in a swashbuckling mood he expressed his strong conviction that they could soon trade themselves into the possession of a steamer; and Colonel Wood countered with the wager that with the proper provisions they could now cross the Atlantic Ocean!

The lack of any foodstuffs at this stage of the flight, however, seriously threatened their progress even down the coast of Florida. Their new boat was a stauncher craft and gave them much-needed confidence in their plan to get away from the United States. This confidence was more than welcome, especially to Colonel Wood as he observed along the beach "a great deal of derelict stuff—the remains of vessels and their cargoes"—an unpleasant warning of a possibly similar fate for the Confederates. Three centuries before, the Governor of Cuba had reported to the King of Spain the loss of twenty caravels along this coast and had recommended the establishment of a port for protection. Since that time the ships of many nations had been wrecked upon this stretch of hazardous shore.

The captured sloop was no longer than the lifeboat of the *Columbine,* but it had more beam and was more seaworthy. Half-decked and with a centerboard, Colonel Wood found it "cranky for want of ballast" but it sailed and worked well. As the Confederates proceeded down the coast, Colonel Wood knew that slightly less than two hundred miles to the east was Green Turtle Key in the Bahamas, a natural signal which had guided many a sea dog to Nassau. This Bahama port had been an important point for the arrival and departure of Confederate blockade-runners, where thirst was reported to be quenched with champagne and where, it was said, the reckless old salts who were engaged in this risky business, ate, drank, and made merry with the expectation of dying on the morrow.

"We all took heart so much" over the new boat, stated General Breckinridge, "that we resolved to head for Cuba" and abandon the original plan of sailing across to Nassau. This decision was reached despite the disquieting knowledge that the Federal patrol was stationed at Key Biscayne, along their intended course to Cuba.

CHAPTER IX

ADRIFT IN THE STORM-DRIVEN GULF STREAM

COLONEL WOOD exacted hard and uninterrupted labor from each member of the escaping Confederate crew— General Breckinridge, Colonel Wilson, the two Florida soldiers, O'Toole and Russell, and Tom, the ex-slave—for the better part of the night of June 7, 1865, to pull their recently captured sloop from the ocean over sand bars and reefs against a strong tide and current to the clear blue waters of the bay the Spaniards had named "Biscayne." More than once, throughout that long night, while they battled mosquitoes as bloodthirsty as vampires, and, while rain drenched them again and again, they very likely cursed the decision that had led them to abandon their original plan of sailing across to Nassau. But after they had achieved their goal, the beauty of sun-pierced Bay Biscayne fringed with mangroves and a profusion of other tropical growth, affording a safe waterway forty miles southward, sheltered by numerous keys and coral islands, probably gave them new heart. Grimly, they hoped to pass unnoticed the last station of the Federal patrol which they suspected was in the vicinity. The acuteness of their anxiety was intensified June 8 as they observed an obstacle even more threatening than the Federal patrol.

Colonel Wood, as a well-informed navigator, was no doubt familiar with the lawless type of adventurer this lonely and dangerous lower East Coast of Florida attracted. These desperadoes, variously designated as "seacoasters" or "wreckers," were described as "peoples who watch the misfortunes of navigators, to make a benefit of them . . . and know so well how much ships are exposed . . . that they station themselves a little south of the point, from whence they can with certainty wait for the sight of any ship that is so unfortunate as to be driven ashore: hence, Key Tavernier has become for the last fifty years [prior to 1823] the general rendezvous of the little fleet of small craft. . . ." [1]

As the more violent piratical depredations of earlier days ceased in this part of the world, a "respectable" form of piracy called "wrecking" became a profession. It began during the latter part of the eighteenth century when Florida was an English possession. Skillful and enterprising tars sailed over in small sloops and schooners from the Bahamas to salvage the cargoes of vessels in distress or entirely wrecked in the dangerous navigation of the Florida keys. At first, barbarous practices prevailed. Ships were plundered; crews and passengers were robbed; even murder was committed. Criminal methods by which ships were lured by fake lights placed near hidden shoals

Wrecks along the coast

and dreaded reefs were at times employed by these hardy veterans of the deep. Conspiracy with lighthouse keepers made deception possible in regard to channels. Gradually, however, as the violation of traditions and laws governing "wrecking" decreased, this adventurous undertaking developed into an extensive and well-regulated business for the practice of which licenses were required. So large a percentage of the salvaged goods went to wreckers, lawyers, wharf owners, and auctioneers that for a time Nassau and Key West were almost entirely supported by "wrecking."

Threatening the passage of the escaping Confederates as they sailed down Biscayne Bay was what Colonel Wood called a "nest of tories and deserters from our service" who with wreckers and outlaws, had, during the War, made their headquarters in the old rock ruins of Fort Dallas [2] on the Miami River, now virtually the center of the present (1938) city of Miami. From this outlaw trading post the Confederates knew they must secure provisions before attempting to cross the Gulf Stream to Cuba. The oölitic limestone walls of old Fort Dallas in a setting of luxuriant green foliage, towering coconut trees and brightly plumaged royal poincianas and yellow elders, came into view as Colonel Wood slowly and cautiously piloted the Confederate sloop against the current of the Miami River.

"As we neared the small wharf," related Colonel Wood, "we found waiting some twenty or thirty men, of all colors, from the pale Yankee to the ebony Congo, all armed; a more motley and villainous-looking crew never trod the deck of one of Captain Kidd's ships. We saw at once with whom we had to deal—deserters from the army and navy of both sides, with a mixture of Spaniards and Cubans, outlaws and renegades. A burly villain, towering head and shoulders above his companions, and whose shaggy black head scorned any covering, hailed us in broken English, and asked who we were. Wreckers, I replied; that we had left our vessel outside, and had come in for water and provisions. He asked where we had left our vessel, and her name, evidently suspicious, which was not surprising, for our appearance was certainly against us. Our head-gear was unique; the general wore a straw hat that flapped over his head like the ears of an elephant; Colonel Wilson, an old cavalry cap that had lost its visor; another, a turban made of some number 4 duck canvas; and all were in our shirt-sleeves, the colors of which were as varied as Joseph's coat. I told him we had left her to the northward a few miles, that a gunboat had spoken us a few hours before, and had overhauled our papers, and had found them all right.

"After a noisy powwow we were told to land, that our papers might be examined. I said no, but if a canoe were sent off, I would let one of our men go on shore and buy what we wanted. I was determined not to trust our boat within a hundred yards of the shore. Finally a canoe paddled by two negroes came off, and said no one but the captain would be permitted to land. O'Toole volunteered to go, but the boatmen would not take him, evidently having had their orders. I told them to tell their chief that we had intended to spend a few pieces of gold with them, but since he would not permit it, we would go elsewhere for supplies. We got out our sweeps, and moved slowly down the river, a light breeze helping us. The canoe returned to the shore, and soon some fifteen or twenty men crowded into four or five canoes and dugouts, and started for us. We prepared for action, determined to give them a warm reception. Even Tom looked after his carbine, putting on a fresh cap.

"Though outnumbered three to one, still we were well under cover in our boat, and could rake each canoe as it came up. We determined to take all the chances, and to open fire as soon as they came within range. I told Russell to try a shot at one some distance ahead of the others. He broke two paddles on one side and hit one man, not a bad beginning. This canoe dropped to the rear at once; the occupants of the others opened fire, but their shooting was wild from the motions of their small crafts. The general tried and missed; Tom thought he could do better than his master, and made a good line shot, but short. The general advised husbanding our ammunition until they came within easy range. Waiting a little while, Russell and the colonel fired together, and the bowman in the nearest canoe rolled over, nearly upsetting her. They were now evidently convinced that we were in earnest, and, after giving us an ineffectual volley, paddled together to hold a council of war. Soon a single canoe with three men started for us with a white flag. We hove to, and waited for them to approach. When within hail, I asked what was wanted. A white man, standing in the stern, with two negroes paddling, replied:

" 'What did you fire on us for? We are friends.'

" 'Friends do not give chase to friends.'

" 'We wanted to find out who you are.'

" 'I told you who we are, and if you are friends, sell us some provisions.'

" 'Come on shore, and you can get what you want.'

"Our wants were urgent, and it was necessary, if possible, to make some terms with them; but it would not be safe

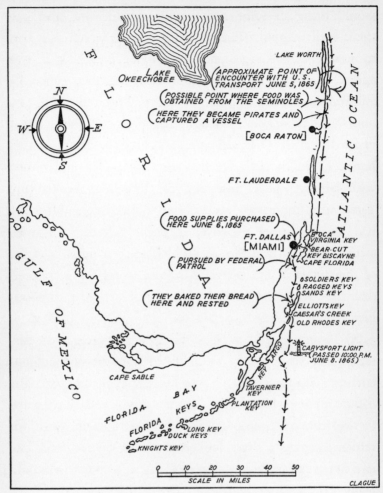

Brackets indicate settlements that did not exist in 1865

The route followed by the Breckinridge party from Lake Worth to the Gulf Stream

to venture near their lair again. We told them that if they would bring us some supplies we would wait, and pay them well in gold. The promise of gold served as a bait to secure some concession. After some parleying it was agreed that O'Toole should go on shore in their canoe, be allowed to purchase some provisions, and return in two hours. The buccaneer thought the time too short, but I insisted that if O'Toole were not brought back in two hours, I would speak the first gunboat I met, and return with her and have their nest of freebooters broken up. Time was important, for we had noticed soon after we had started down the river a black column of smoke ascending from near the fort, undoubtedly a signal to some of their craft in the vicinity to return, for I felt convinced that they had other craft besides canoes at their disposal; hence their anxiety to detain us.

"O'Toole was told to be as dumb as an oyster as to ourselves, but wide awake as to the designs of our dubious friends. The general gave him five eagles for his purchase, tribute-money. He jumped into the canoe, and all returned to the fort. We dropped anchor underfoot to await his return, keeping a sharp lookout for any strange sail. The two hours passed in pleasant surmises as to what he would bring off; another half-hour passed, and no sign of his return; and we began to despair of our anticipated feast, and of O'Toole, a bright young Irishman, whose good qualities had endeared him to us all. The anchor was up, and slowly with a light breeze we drew away from the river, debating what should be our next move. The fort was shut in by a projecting point, and three or four miles had passed when the welcome sight of a canoe astern made us heave to. It was O'Toole with two negroes, a bag of hard bread, two hams, some rusty salt pork, sweet potatoes, fruit, and most important of all, two beakers of water and a keg of New England rum.

"While O'Toole gave us his experience, a ham was cut, and a slice between two of hardtack, washed down with a jorum of rum and water, with a dessert of oranges and bananas, was a feast to us more enjoyable than any ever eaten at Delmonico's or the Cafe Riche. On his arrival on shore our ambassador had been taken to the quarters of Major Valdez, who claimed to be an officer of the Federals, and by him he was thoroughly cross-examined. He had heard of the breaking up of the Confederacy, but not of the capture of Mr. Davis, and was evidently skeptical of our story as to being wreckers, and connected us in some way with the losing party, either as persons of note or a party escaping with treasure. However, O'Toole baffled all his queries, and was proof against both blandishments and threats. He learned what he had expected, that they were looking for the return of a schooner; hence the smoke signal, and the anxiety to detain us as long as possible. It was only when he saw us leaving, after waiting over two hours, that the major permitted him to make a few purchases and rejoin us."[3]

The Confederates left the present site of Miami without

the slightest delay and continued inside the keys down Biscayne Bay, hoping to avoid being observed, but without success. For three or four hours they were chased by a launch, probably a part of the expedition which Admiral Stribling had sent from Key West more than a month before to guard Key Biscayne and the passage to the Gulf Stream. The dependable "pirate" craft, responding to the master seamanship of Colonel Wood, finally outdistanced the pursuers. At least temporarily the safety of the Confederates was no longer imperiled. By afternoon they had reached Elliotts Key, twenty miles below Fort Dallas. As the breeze had become light the ill-fated group landed, relaxed, baked their bread and rested. Feeding on mollusks near them on this island were scores of strikingly handsome flamingoes, uniformly vermilion-scarlet in color. The Confederates could not spare time, however, for observing the beauty of nature; indeed, they barely took time out to eat, so constantly haunted were they by the threat of Federal pursuit.

Down the inland waterway they went, frequently encountering reefs jutting entirely across their course. Running aground repeatedly, they would plunge overboard and haul the boat over while the mosquitoes, according to Colonel Wood, "almost darkened the air" and "their buzzing was like the roaring of the wind." The gathering gloom of the night settled before they could reach the swift-running channel through Caesar's Creek, sheltered on the north by Elliotts and Adams Keys and on the south by

Old Rhodes and other smaller islands. Through the labyrinth of mangrove inlets they worked their way with the greatest difficulty, "pulling, wading and wandering." They endured more punishment from the mosquitoes here than at any other point. By the latter part of the evening they had surmounted the difficulties of Caesar's Creek and were in sight of Carysfort Light.

As Florida's dim outline slowly vanished in the background, John C. Breckinridge, first member of the Confederate Cabinet to leave the country, bade farewell to his native land, his home no longer, and started into exile.

After the plucky mariners had passed out of Lower Biscayne Bay through Caesar's Creek, they stood to the south and west with a fair wind, and prepared to run through the reefs which almost continuously bordered the keys. Suddenly the weather became thick and squally, the sea rose as the heavy rain fell with increasing strength. Lightning flashed in terrifying silver streams as the tempest howled, and the constant cracking of their small craft made them fear it would be dashed to pieces at any moment. New danger appeared to lurk in every crashing wave that broke about them and hurled over them the heavy, biting, salt spray. The sea continued in violent agitation, and soon they were hopelessly lost among the reefs which should have afforded them some protection in such a storm.

"The young men with us were lying in the bottom sick," wrote the General, and Thomas, his negro servant, "was worn out and asleep; Capt. Wood was forward attending to something; I was very tired and just losing myself in a doze and the celebrated Col. Wilson was steering.

"Suddenly I was aroused by a wave going over me and half filling the boat, which leaned over until the gunwale was under the water. At the same moment I observed that Capt. Wood was overboard, and looking round I saw Col. Wilson as stiff as a stanchion holding on like grim death to the rudder and the sail rope. It was his grip on the latter that was about to sink us.

"I knew just enough to shout to him to let go the rope, which he did, and the strain being taken off, the boat finally righted, Captain Wood fortunately caught a rope as he went and had scrambled on board." Had Captain Wood not survived, the Breckinridge expedition would surely have ended here. It was Wood's genius as a seaman that had saved it time and again.

Once they touched on a reef and after several desperate and unsuccessful efforts to sound, they anchored near a beacon, which was probably on the shoal known as the "Elbow." There they remained through the eventful night of June 8, helplessly awaiting the break of dawn.

Laying their course by the North Star, and with the aid of a pocket compass, the size of a dollar, they steered in the early morning toward Cuba into the storm-driven Gulf Stream. Gradually the wind freshened, the sea rose, and the whirl of water was so furious that the boat could not be kept on the course. A steamer passed very near them, but nothing happened. That evening, June 9, according to Breckinridge, "the wind and the sea rose and during the whole night the waves ran very high [two of the yawning waves, said Colonel Wood, were at least twenty feet high]. It seemed to me that she must go under. . . . Capt. Wood looked very grave, but he held the helm

"The chances were against us that night"

himself through the night, cool and collected. He told me afterwards that the chances were against us that night—and that in 19 years' experience of the sea he had never felt in so great peril.

"A worse sea Colonel Wood said he had never seen and he was amazed that the little boat lived through for which he thanked a gracious Savior. It was by keeping the boat nearly head to the great waves that he kept it from filling and turning over like an egg-shell.

"Toward morning the sea went down a great deal and about daylight we came bump upon a United States merchant ship [the brig, *Neptune* of Bangor] and boldly demanded some water which we got. They stared very hard at us, but no explanations were demanded or given," concluded the General. He and his men probably looked more like pirates than officials of the Confederacy. Certainly they presented an appearance not likely to excite enthusiastic admiration. Breckinridge believed it was the dozen biscuits and five gallons of water, unwittingly given them by a kind "Yankee Skipper," together with the fast diminishing supply of rum, that kept them alive, so low were their rations and so parched were their throats after this ordeal of uncertainty and helpless agony.[4]

As the morning of June 10 grew older, they found themselves across the worst part of the Gulf Stream. By afternoon they sighted the Doubleheaded Shot Keys—rocky and barren islets which lie off the coast of Cuba on the northwest edge of Salt Key Bank. The Confederates now knew they were out of the jurisdiction of the United States. Almost miraculously they had escaped the notice of the Federal guard patrolling the waters between Key West and Key Biscayne. Their confident hope of making a safe landing in Cuba increased as the dim outline of the islands bordering the Cuban coast came into bolder relief. Steering southwest they held the expectation of reaching the Spanish-owned land that night.

Having narrowly escaped shipwreck, starvation, and capture in quick succession, they doggedly forced their tiny craft on toward Cuba. Their intensive flight of twenty-six days through Florida had been so completely exhausting and nerve-racking, that Saturday morning, June 10, found them in a seriously weakened condition and suffering from lack of sleep—they had been able to sleep only a few hours out of each of the previous nights. General Breckinridge, regarded as the handsomest man in the South, wrote that on this day he was "very weary" and after sleeping several hours awoke "really sick" and probably not at all handsome, after the loss of much of his remarkable energy and his bold, cavalier manner.[5]

Throughout the day the sun, almost boiling hot, brought down added agony as the men, cramped and feverish, languished in the boat, which rolled with every swell of the ocean. The light hair of Russell and O'Toole was completely bleached; the sun had deeply bronzed them all and excessive exposure to the salt water and heat had swollen and blistered their feet and legs. They forced themselves on, however, hoping to come within sight of land that would assure them of rest and security. The approach of night soon dimmed their hope, although its coolness relieved the almost insufferable heat of the day. As the purple skies of the tropics were obscured by the approach of darkness and as each previously visible object was enveloped in the discouraging blackness of night, the wanderers were mercilessly subjected to an apparently unending period of anxiety and bewilderment. Another night of gloomy reflections closed about them as they continued the voyage with its perils and its increasing tax on their endurance.

As the attention of the six escaping Confederates was strained toward the south to catch the first friendly flash of a lighthouse, the long-awaited gleam was sighted a few hours after dark. It at once proved the proximity of Spanish territory. For the moment the rigorous trials and the glowering dangers they had encountered since they left Richmond more than two months before appeared negligible. At last the Confederate Secretary of War and his compatriots realized that within their reach was safety on a foreign shore.

On the northern coast of Cuba, not more than seventy-five miles east of Havana, is a spacious bay sheltered by a long promontory. At the head of this blue-watered bay in which several vessels were anchored, with picturesque mountains towering in the background, was a brightly tinted Spanish city glowing in sunshine and cooled by soft tropical breezes. This the former Vice President of the United States, John C. Breckinridge, saw on the Sabbath which ended his flight from the United States in 1865. "Steering for it," he said, after a sail of ten or twelve miles up the bay, "we found ourselves at sunrise, on the 11th of June, in the harbor of Cardenas. At my request Capt. Wood again read prayers, and I am sure we all felt profoundly grateful for our deliverance."

As the Confederates heard church bells clang on the Sunday morning which marked their deliverance from the threats of nature and of man, their thoughts must have turned back to their last Sunday in Richmond when General Lee had sent his message to St. Paul's Church and had started the Confederate Cabinet on its flight. It must have seemed inconceivable to them that so much could have happened in the intervening weeks.

Great was the sensation among the thirteen thousand inhabitants of Cardenas over the arrival of the miniature craft that had brought these six Confederates. As soon as the newcomers had identified themselves and cleared their nameless boat, they sought food at the Fonda del Almirante Colon at the corner of the present Real and Jerez Streets, not far from where they had landed. The colony of North Americans in Cardenas, mostly Southerners, were soon aware of the prominence of the travel-worn arrivals and eagerly cared for their needs. Clean clothes and other necessities were generously provided under the leadership of Gumersindo Antonio Pacetti, a refugee from and one time Mayor of St. Augustine, who also gave a dinner in honor of General Breckinridge and his escort. The Confederates were allowed to pay for nothing. A serenade concluded the celebrations.[6] It was an event of historic value and recalled the landing in Cardenas fifteen years before of the first voluntary troops from the United States to land on Cuban soil to help the Cubans gain independence.

In this Spanish colony of her Catholic Majesty, Isabella II, the highest diplomatic post to whose court had been offered

General Breckinridge when Franklin Pierce was President, the Confederates enjoyed their status as ex-officials of another, though fallen, government. The Spanish Governor of the island, General Domingo Dulce y Garay (Marques de Castell-Florit), sent an officer to escort the former Confederate Secretary of War to Havana. Leaving Cardenas at six o'clock on the morning of June 12, 1865, they breakfasted in the fragrant tropical atmosphere of Matanzas.

After traveling through many miles of cane fields, they arrived at the exotic capital of Cuba, where the Southern cause had always been favored, and were given an enthusiastic welcome at the Hotel Cubano. Unusual courtesies were extended General Breckinridge and it was reported that a house was offered him if he would make Havana his home.[7] But Breckinridge made plans to proceed to

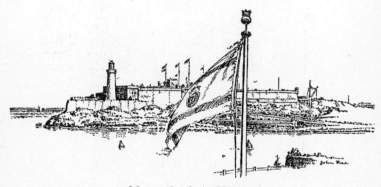

Morro Castle in Havana

England with his fellow Kentuckian, Colonel Charles J. Helm, who had been special agent of the Confederacy in the West Indies. In the meantime movements in Havana were being secretly reported to the Secretary of State at Washington as Breckinridge relaxed from the strain of his incredibly difficult escape from the United States, where a Federal prison had been awaiting him and where hope for his incarceration had not been abandoned.[8]

On June 14, two days after the arrival of Breckinridge in Havana, George A. Trenholm, former Confederate Secre-

The Trenholm mansion in Charleston, now Ashley Hall

tary of the Treasury, was arrested near Columbia, South Carolina. He was temporarily lodged in the city jail in his native Charleston where he had rendered conspicuous public service as civic leader, as bank and railroad director, and as a member of the legislature. His banking houses had exerted great power before and during the War. His property, including his beautiful home, now Ashley Hall, had been confiscated. No longer could he enjoy the rights even of an ordinary citizen. Trenholm was paroled to the corporate limits of Columbia, South Carolina, the latter

191

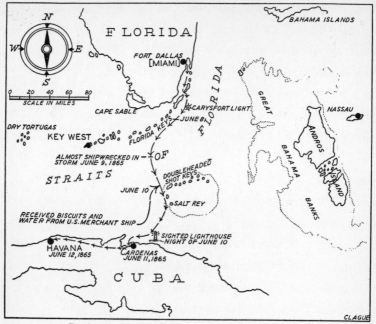

Brackets indicate settlements that did not exist in 1865

The route followed by Breckinridge to safety on Spanish soil

part of June because of his feeble health and in view of the fact "that he has performed many acts of kindness to Union prisoners," according to a Federal report. But when Stanton heard of his release he immediately ordered Trenholm's return to Fort Pulaski.[9]

Three of the six members of the Confederate Cabinet, Mallory, Reagan, and Trenholm were at this time, June, 1865, in prison and sharing punishment with the President and the Vice President of the Confederacy. One member, Breckinridge, had escaped. The resourcefulness of the other two members, Benjamin and George Davis, was being severely tested in keeping out of reach of the pursuing Federals as they attempted to find, as Breckinridge had found, an "underground" passage through Florida to safety on a foreign shore. They preferred expatriation to hanging, the choice of which the *Boston Transcript* gave them. The opinion of this exponent of New England culture was: "The people of the United States should not, in this emergency, be fooled into sacrificing their instincts of justice, because those instincts may be stigmatized by the weak and the wicked as revengeful and vindicative." Its incredible conclusion was: "The whole mass of individual murderers since Cain have not produced in forty centuries so much misery and ruin as these malignant traitors [Jefferson Davis and his associates] have wrought in four terrible years." [10]

CHAPTER X

THE SECRETARY OF STATE PREFERS ENGLAND

 IT became clear to Secretary of State Judah P. Benjamin, after the retreating Government expedition had, for the time being, outdistanced the pursuing Federal cavalry in the lower part of South Carolina and had safely crossed over the Savannah River into Georgia, that he must strike out for himself in order to escape.

There was no longer a military escort of any real effectiveness for the Confederate Cabinet. In a small group, Secretary Benjamin knew he would be recognized instantly. He was short and stout and of decidedly Jewish aspect, facts well-known to the public. As a wise counselor and as one of the South's greatest constitutional lawyers, he had been the most valuable member of the Cabinet. He was undoubtedly the best-known high official next to the President and Vice President and ranked third in the succession. His career before the war had been one of unusual distinction. At the height of a legal career of national significance he had become a leader in promoting and organizing the railroad which later became the Illinois Central. In 1853, he was elected to the United States Senate from Louisiana and served in that capacity until his resignation in 1861.

Probably more to spare the feelings of his chief than in any real expectation of ever reaching Texas, Secretary Benjamin left President Davis on May 3, 1865, between the Savannah River and Washington, Georgia, with the understanding that he would rejoin him in the Trans-Mississippi Department.[1] Actually he was determined to go to the place farthest from the United States, if it took him to the middle of China, according to his colleague, Postmaster General Reagan.[2]

Horseback riding to one of his physique was extremely uncomfortable and his identity could not, without difficulty, be concealed in that mode of travel. Benjamin therefore secured a buggy, and, accompanied by Colonel H. J. Leovy, started toward Florida,[3] after leaving $900 in gold with a friend in Georgia for delivery to his sisters at Lagrange.[4] After he had consumed a week in hiding from the Federal troops he was overtaken May 11, twenty-four miles from Irwinville, Georgia, by Colonel John Taylor Wood from whom he learned of the capture of President Davis. Wood observed that Secretary Benjamin was disguised as a French gentleman, Monsieur Bonfal.[5]

"With goggles on, his beard grown, a hat well over his face, and a large cloak hiding his figure, no one would have recognized him as the late secretary of state of the Confederacy," noted Colonel Wood.[6] When he was asked if the initials "J.P.B." on his trunk would not betray him, he replied that he did not think so because there was a Frenchman traveling in the Southern States who had the same initials and that he, Benjamin, could speak broken English like a Frenchman.[7]

Secretary Benjamin disguised as a French traveler

Unnoticed by the Federal patrol, Secretary Benjamin slipped down into Florida. Four days after seeing Colonel Wood, he crossed the Suwannee River at Moseley's Ferry, two days before General Breckinridge passed that point on his way through Florida.[8]

"I found my most successful disguise to be that of a farmer," explained Benjamin. "I professed to be traveling in Florida in search of land on which to settle, with some friends who desired to move from South Carolina. I got a kind farmer's wife to make me some homespun clothes just like her husband's. I got for my horse the commonest and roughest equipment that I could find. . . ." [9]

By avoiding towns and using the least traveled roads in sparsely populated sections, Benjamin progressed southward, he said, at the rate of about thirty miles a day. He had intended following General Breckinridge's plan of escaping down the Indian River on the East Coast of Florida, but, learning that no vessel was available and that there was considerable risk of detection there, he decided to try the West Coast. Aided by loyal Confederates,[10] he was taken secretly to a thirty-six hundred acre sugar plantation at the present (1938) town of Ellenton near the Manatee River, formerly the property of Major Robert Gamble. Here Captain Archibald McNeill, who had been deputy commissary agent of the Manatee section under Confederate Captain James McKay, extended him the hospitality of the Gamble mansion. This massive

"Farmer" Benjamin

structure, which gave the impression of an immense Greek temple rising out of a luxuriant tropical garden, was built a decade and a half before the War. Its foundations and structure were as sturdy as were those of Stratford Hall, General Lee's home on the Potomac. Major Gamble utilized

The Gamble mansion near the Manatee River

the engineering skill he had acquired at West Point in its construction. The material was shell brick, or tabby, consisting of sand, water, and lime, the last being made from oyster shells which had been burned, crushed, and sifted. The immense beams, the wide plank flooring and other woodwork had been hewn from cypress and oak timbers on the plantation. Its walls were as thick as those of a fortress. Eighteen gigantic pillars colonnaded all but the back of the house, and, extending twenty-five feet in height, supported the roof. The Confederate Secretary of State was warmly welcomed to this imposing ante-bellum mansion.[11]

Captain McNeill, Benjamin's host, and other Confederate leaders in south Florida, were being sought by the Federals at this time. Fearing that a gunboat might enter the Manatee River, a continuous watch was maintained from the upper verandah of the large, gray Gamble mansion. Shortly after Benjamin's arrival, the Federals made a surprise entry into the mansion for an inspection. They may possibly have suspected that Benjamin or George Davis or both were hidden there. Captain McNeill and the highest official of the Confederacy barely had time to dash out through the kitchen into the dense thicket in the rear. While searching the woods adjacent to the mansion, the Federals were at one time within a few feet of the securely hidden Confederates. Fortunately a sneeze or a cough did not betray them at this critical moment. With the approach of darkness the Federals returned to their gunboat and Mr.

Benjamin became more impatient than ever to get out of Florida.[12]

Now known as "Mr. Howard," Secretary Benjamin crossed the Manatee River and was taken into the home of Captain Frederick Tresca near the town of Manatee. While here Mrs. Tresca ingeniously sewed plaits in the back of Benjamin's waistcoat and waistband for the concealment of his gold. Since he was corpulent, his garments afforded space for an adequate supply.[13]

Tresca, a native of France, had gained much knowledge of the coast before the War in piloting his freight sloop, *Margaret Ann,* from Cedar Keys to Key West. He had run the blockade from Florida to Nassau and was thoroughly posted on the inside water route down the West Coast. Possessing the cool courage, daring, and experience required for such an adventure, he agreed to take Secretary Benjamin to the Bahamas.[14]

Studied preparations for the dangerous trip consumed about two weeks. A Methodist minister, the Rev. Ezechiel Glazier who had been a member of Florida's Secession Convention, transported Benjamin overland to a point on Sarasota Bay near the present location of Sarasota. Tresca and H. A. McLeod, a tall, sturdy ex-Confederate sailor met him there in a small yawl, the *Blonde,* which with much difficulty they had secured. Finally on June 23, the Confederate Secretary of State set out for a foreign land.[15]

The lower West Coast of Florida, down which Benjamin sailed, consists of countless bays and harbors. The vast expanses of lowlands bordering this coast are drained by numerous creeks and quiet rivers, the chief of which are the Caloosahatchee, the Peace, and the Myakka. As Benjamin's boat approached Charlotte Harbor, a magnificent, sheltered bay, his captain caught a glimpse of a Federal gunboat just as one of its small boats was being launched preparatory to chasing the Confederates.

"We put in at Gasparilla Pass," reported McLeod, "and as there was no wind, we lowered the mast as soon as we got behind the island, pulled our boat under the mangrove bushes until completely hidden, lay down in it and waited.

"The pursuing boat came on, searching diligently, and once came so near that we could hear them talking; but we kept quiet, so quiet, indeed, that above the voices of our enemies, and the taunting song of the mosquitoes, against whose attack we were quite helpless, rose the hollow sound of our beating hearts."

As soon as the Federal gunboat returned to the Gulf, Benjamin and his two loyal friends made a landing on Gasparilla Island. Suspecting the return of their pursuers, they dared not build a fire for the cooking of their supper until late that night lest the smoke indicate their position. They then made coffee, fried bacon, and cooked the red fish they had caught. Securely hidden, they remained on Gasparilla Island the following night also, to keep clear of possible Federal patrol in the Gulf.[16]

If Benjamin's companions were at all superstitious, the two nights they spent on this lonely and mysterious island must have been an extremely uncomfortable experience. Hardly more than a half century before these Confederates reached it, Gasparilla Island had been the infamous headquarters of the notorious pirate, José Gaspar, a former officer  in the Spanish Navy, who, on account of his numerous and valuable captures and his murderous and rapacious disposition of those he found on board the prizes, had become the terror of the seas surrounding Florida. Now the center of fishing, yatching, and other recreational life, this beautiful island had been the scenes of drunken revelry, murder, and rape.

Benjamin's small craft succeeded in leaving the former lair of the Spanish pirate without being sighted by the Federals. It then passed Pine Island at the mouth of Charlotte Harbor, one of the "islets that extended out into the sea," according to Ponce de Leon who careened one of his ships, the *San Cristóval,* on it in May, 1513, after his discovery of Florida.[17] As the escaping Confederates sailed south, they passed Sanibel Island and carefully hugged the shore as they were exposed to the Gulf waters for a long stretch near the present town of Naples.

When Benjamin arrived at Cape Romano he was able to vary his fare. Prior to that time it had consisted chiefly of fish. Some delicious bananas of which he was fond were now added. It was almost impossible to obtain water and he and his companions were reduced to the extremity of drinking the juice of coconuts.[18] They seldom encountered human life as they made their way south of Cape Romano, past thousands of small, low islands covered with heavy vegetation, and left Cape Sable, the southernmost point on the West Coast where the Harris party had been captured two months before. The Confederates received the kindest treatment from the men they did see, many of whom had lost themselves in this isolated part of the world to escape the rigors of conventional living or to avoid punishment for crime.

At Knights Key, Captain Tresca was able to secure a larger boat with a leg-o'-mutton sail, for the passage into the open sea, since the *Blonde* was only about sixteen feet in length. More confident of reaching their destination in the larger boat, they sailed past Indian Key, halfway between the present cities of Miami and Key West, where for many years wreckers had maintained a prosperous station, and where more than a century ago a tourist hotel had been operated. Indian Key also, a quarter of a century before, had been the scene of a bloody massacre of white settlers by "Spanish" Indians.[19]

Four days more brought them on July 10 to the Bimini Islands. "Squalls and water spouts and tropical storms came near finishing us," wrote McLeod. "The water came down in sheets. I took a tin pan and baled desperately and Mr.

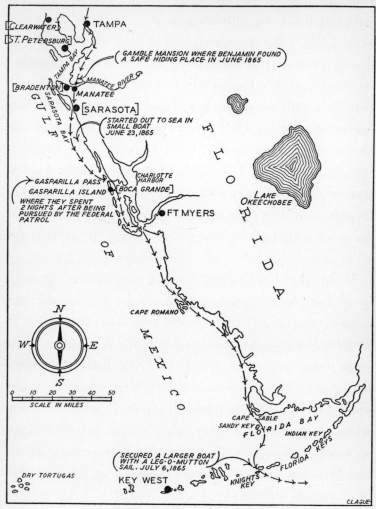

Brackets indicate settlements that did not exist in 1865

The route followed by Benjamin to Knights Key

Benjamin used his hat; and turning to me, said with a smile, 'McLeod, this is not like being Secretary of State'." [20]

Benjamin paid Captain Tresca $1,500 in gold for his passage of more than six hundred miles, which had required seventeen days.[21] "During much of the trip he [Benjamin] enlivened the tedious hours and lessened the strain on our nerves by his cheerful spirit and humorous speeches," was McLeod's final comment.[22]

Light-hearted and relieved that the risk of his capture was now at an end, Secretary Benjamin took passage in a small sloop, loaded with sponges, for Nassau. But his escape was far from achieved. On the following day, Benjamin said, "the sloop foundered at sea, thirty miles from the nearest land, sinking with such rapidity that we had barely time to jump into a small skiff that the sloop had in tow before she went to the bottom.

"In the skiff, leaky, with but a single oar, with no provisions save a pot of rice that had just been cooked for breakfast, and a small keg of water, I found myself at eight o'clock in the morning, with three negroes for my companions in disaster, only five inches of the boat out of water, on the broad ocean, with the certainty that we could not survive five minutes if the sea became the least rough." [23]

By a stroke of incredibly good fortune the sea remained calm all day. Late in the afternoon the four shipwrecked men were rescued by the H. B. M. Lighthouse Yacht, *Georgina*. Though this vessel was on a tour of inspection of Bahama lighthouses, its Captain Stuart obligingly carried

Brackets indicate settlements that did not exist in 1865

*The route followed by Benjamin from Knights Key
in his flight to safety*

Secretary Benjamin back to port. Having thus returned to
Bimini he chartered a sloop and started to Nassau on the
afternoon of July 15. So baffled was this boat by calms,
squalls, and head winds that six days were needed to reach
its destination. Despite this trying experience and his complete exhaustion, Secretary Benjamin wrote that he was
"contented and cheerful under all reverses." [24]

Leaving Nassau on July 22 in the *Britannia,* a small schooner, the former Confederate Secretary of State was favored with good weather on the trip to Havana. He arrived there, sun-scorched and ragged, on July 25 and was received, he said, with "great kindness and attention" by Southern sympathizers and escaped Confederates, among whom was General Kirby Smith who had just arrived from Vera Cruz, Mexico. In order to reach England, Benjamin found it necessary to change to a larger ship at St. Thomas. When this larger vessel was about sixty miles out from land a serious fire was discovered in the forehold. "By dint of great exertion," wrote Benjamin, "and admirable conduct and discipline exhibited by all on board, the flames were kept from bursting through the deck till we got back to the harbor of St. Thomas, where we arrived at about three o'clock in the morning with seven feet of water in the hold poured in by the steam pumps, and the deck burned to within an eighth of an inch of the entire thickness.

Colonel Leovy, who, accompanying Benjamin from Abbeville, South Carolina, had for two weeks assisted him to circumvent the pursuing Federals down through Georgia, left the Confederate Secretary of State near Monticello after they had reached the safer roads in Florida. Leovy then returned to his home in New Orleans.

Benjamin never appeared "so great as during that time of adversity," said Leovy. "Traveling in disguise, sleeping at night in log huts, living on the plainest fare, subjected to all the discomforts of such a journey, with all his plans shattered and without definite hope for the future, his superb confidence and courage raised him above all; and he was the great, confident, cheerful leader that he had been in the days of his highest prosperity." [25]

The change to the uneventful routine of a quiet ocean voyage to England, which was his final reward, must have been more than welcome to the former Confederate Secretary of State. Such a change would also have been eagerly made by Benjamin's Cabinet colleague, the former Confederate Attorney General, George Davis, if he could have substituted uneventful routine for the months of desperate uncertainty and privations which he was undergoing in his attempt to escape from another part of Florida.

CHAPTER XI

"CLEAN BEYOND GOOD MORALS"

GEORGE DAVIS, former Attorney General of the Confederacy, was not accounted for until a week after two of his colleagues in the Cabinet, Reagan and Trenholm, had served terms in prison and had been released. George Davis had been the first member of the Cabinet to resign. This action was taken on the advice of his colleagues who felt it was his duty to arrange a place of safety for his young children who were with him in Charlotte, North Carolina, when on April 26, 1865, the Confederate Cabinet left that city.

George Davis of course knew that he would be arrested if he remained in that section of the country which was being rapidly overrun by the Federals. After making arrangements for his children, he hastily left for Camden, South Carolina, and stopped over at the ivy-covered bishopstead, occupied by his brother, the Rt. Rev. Thomas Frederick

Davis.[1] Leaving there on horseback, he traveled under the assumed name of "Hugh Thompson" and carried nothing except such clothing as he could pack in his saddle bags.[2] For five weeks he succeeded in eluding the Federal troops in South Carolina, Georgia, and the northern part of Florida as he made his way southward.

On June 3 Davis reached the plantation of his cousin, Mrs. Thomas Hill Lane, about twenty miles southwest of Lake City, fifteen miles east of which settlement the Battle of Olustee, the most important engagement of the War in Florida, had occurred more than a year before. So closely was his identity guarded that even Mr. Lane, who had never seen his wife's cousin, did not know at first who he was. After a two-day rest with the Lanes, he moved on to the plantation of James Chesnut, a Confederate veteran, about twelve miles northwest of Gainesville.[3]

During the ten days the former Attorney General was secreted near Gainesville by his loyal friends, the Chesnuts, he possibly learned something of the policy being developed by the Federal Government toward the South. Gainesville was one of the "important points in the central and eastern portions of Florida" which Major General Q. A. Gillmore had ordered occupied "to secure quiet and good order." This order made it clear that his subordinates were expected to "act promptly, justly and with energy" as "lawlessness must be suppressed, industry encouraged, and confidence in the beneficence of the Government established." [4]

Just how the "beneficence of the Government" was to be

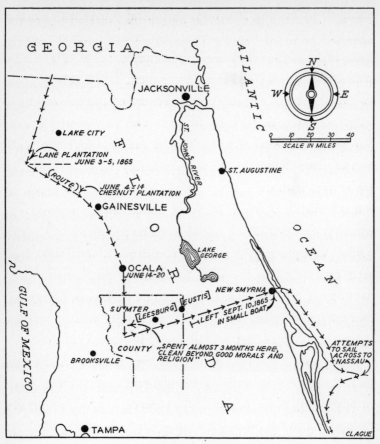

GEORGIA

JACKSONVILLE

ATLANTIC

LAKE CITY

LANE PLANTATION
JUNE 3-5, 1865

(ROUTE)

JUNE 4-14
CHESNUT PLANTATION

GAINESVILLE

ST. JOHN'S RIVER

ST. AUGUSTINE

LAKE
GEORGE

OCALA
JUNE 14-20

OCEAN

SUMTER [LEESBURG] [EUSTIS]

NEW SMYRNA

LEFT SEPT. 10,1865
IN SMALL BOAT

GULF OF MEXICO

COUNTY "SPENT ALMOST 3 MONTHS HERE,
CLEAN BEYOND GOOD MORALS AND
BROOKSVILLE   RELIGION"

ATTEMPTS
TO SAIL
ACROSS TO
NASSAU

TAMPA

CLAGUE

N
W   E
S

SCALE IN MILES
0   10   20   30   40

Brackets indicate settlements that did not exist in 1865

*The route followed by George Davis from near Lake City
to the ocean*

established in the Confederate territory was as yet undetermined. General Lee, Alexander H. Stephens, Judge Reagan, and a "multitude of American citizens who have served the rebellion in a civil or military capacity" were quoted as having described conditions upon which the Union could be restored. A leading Northern periodical proceeded to make light of the Confederate attitude by saying that one Southerner expressed his readiness to resume the status of a citizen immediately, "provided the Government is properly lenient. . . . We have not as yet seen any report of the terms which Jefferson Davis is disposed to accord to the United States. But as he declared that he would rather fraternize with hyenas than Yankees, he will probably be very strict, if not severe, with us." [5]

Stark reality and not irony of statement confronted ex-Attorney General Davis, however, as he hid away in Florida while attempting to leave the country. Martial law had been established in the state by military proclamation ten days before his arrival and Confederate Governor Allison of Florida had been declared guilty of sundry acts of treason against the United States. Moreover, in order that the Confederates might understand without the slightest doubt that radical changes in social relations and government were swiftly taking place, negro soldiers were included among the Federal troops who were garrisoned throughout Florida.[6]

Determined to eliminate further possible doubt as to the changed condition of negroes, General McCook, the Federal Military Governor, announced "to those who seem to be ignorant of the fact, that the President of the United States, on the 1st day of January, 1863, issued a proclamation changing the status of persons held as slaves." [7]

General McCook's warning was echoed in an editorial directed to the approximately 5,000 former slaveowners of

Florida who, through the emancipation of the negroes, had suffered losses of some $22,000,000.[8] "There are many evils," philosophized a Tallahassee editor, "which appear greater at a distance than they really prove when brought to us. . . . The 'time is coming and now is' in which prudence will prove the highest virtue. A great change in the system of labor heretofore established among us seems to be impending, and our advice to every one likely to be affected by it is to regard it with philosophical calmness. Let us make the best arrangement possible under the circumstances to adapt ourselves to the new state of things and trust to time to compose and reduce to order what appears to so many to be only the harbinger of anarchy and suffering." [9]

That misery was actually threatening many previously wealthy Southerners who had become impoverished by their sacrifices for the "Lost Cause" is indicated by a humble appeal made to General McCook at this time. It was a plea from a plantation for commissary stores and medicine by Catherine Daingerfield Willis Murat, distinguished great-grandniece of George Washington and niece of Napoleon Bonaparte by her marriage to Prince Achille Murat.[10]

The "new state of things" to which the Tallahassee editor referred was beginning to be realized in Florida as Chief Justice Chase was welcomed to Fernandina the latter part of May, 1865, by a "thunderous volume of song" from former slaves. The correspondent of a New York newspaper described the visit as the "most notable sensation of this isolated place for some time past" and reported that the Chief

Justice "in the course of his *judicial* pilgrimage, took occasion to call upon all his political representatives sent out under patronage of the Treasury." The correspondent further reported that a Mr. Mot, "an intelligent French gentleman, formerly a tutor in Mr. Chase's family in Ohio, and who came here last Fall as the Clerk of the Tax Commission, at a municipal election, held without law and in disregard of the provisions of the act of incorporation, had been elected 'Mayor of the City of Fernandina.' The Chief Justice was invited to formally install him in office, and with great pomp the ceremony was performed, and Fernandina has now a city government recognized by the highest judicial officer in the land, though its head is not a citizen of the State and his election has no shadow of legal authority." [11]

Chase wrote to President Johnson that before Mot was elected a vote was taken to decide whether the negroes should participate in the election; inasmuch as the vote was favorable, the negroes did participate in the municipal election. Chase, therefore, "had the honor of administering the oath of office of the first Mayor of Fernandina under the new regime," he further reported. "So you see," he concluded, "that colored suffrage is practically accepted in Florida—or rather that part of it included in Amelia Island." [12]

Chase, in reporting further to President Johnson on conditions in the South, wrote: "The schools ... are composed of scholars of all ages and colors. Many of the colored soldiers attend. ... The teachers are of that army of women to whom the country owes more than it can pay." [13] These teachers had come South under the auspices of the American Freedmen's Association. Their supervisor later became Mrs. Harrison Reed, who presided over Florida's executive mansion in 1869-1873.

The Chief Justice made some amazing "discoveries" of intelligence among the ex-slaves neither previously nor since known to the human race, and on this visit to the South wrote optimistically of the future of the freedmen. These "discoveries" were of course presented for political consumption. Although the announced purpose of Chase's trip was to survey conditions and restore the courts, it was not so interpreted by James Gordon Bennett, editor of the *New York Herald,* who said "his tour through the canebrakes, cotton and rice fields of the South was only part of a grand scheme for the promulgation of ideas which he and his associates imagined would place him in the Presidential chair at the close of Mr. Johnson's term." [14] A friend of Johnson who saw something of Chase in Key West reported to the President: "I could not refrain from the conviction that the Chief Justice was looking forward to the vote of Florida one of these days." [15] Harrison Reed, later Republican Governor of Florida, had been privately informed, he reported to Washington, that Chief Justice Chase "had made sure of all the patronage necessary to control the state, including the Military Governor." [16]

Chase went from Fernandina to Jacksonville and then on to St. Augustine. There in the old Spanish plaza were

Negroes in new blue coats and fine equipage

"stalwart negroes, black as ebony, splendidly armed, and drawn up in handsome regimental lines" of a dress parade in his honor. There, also, according to Reid: "is a luxuriant garden [behind each house]; great masses of flowers hang over the walls or depend from trellis; and, through the open doors, one gets glimpses of hammocks, swinging under vine-clad trees, and huge, but airy, Sleepy-Hollow chairs. Curious little piazzas jut into the narrow streets, and dark Spanish faces, with coal-black brows and liquid eyes, look out from the windows. . . .

"The ground is covered with oranges, and the fruit is still clinging to the trees in bunches that bend down and almost break the branches . . . the deliciously dreamy, luxuriously indolent retreats one finds amid these orange groves, and in the pleasant cottages of the owners, make St. Augustine seem a town of another continent and century." [17]

One of the orange groves pointed out to Chase and his party was owned by John Hay, former private secretary to President Lincoln. Hay had purchased property in Florida when Lincoln sent him down to organize, if possible, a state government that would bring back into the Union the "smallest tadpole in the dirty pool of secession," as the *New York Herald* called Florida.[18] Hay had received letters from Unionists in Florida urging him to qualify as one of their fellow citizens and run as their representative for Congress.[19] A Union meeting had been held in Jacksonville in 1862[20] and about twelve hundred men had entered the Federal Army from Florida.[21]

Jacksonville, a town of less than twelve hundred white people during the War, was the center of Hay's activities. This present "Gateway City of Florida" did not at that time impress visitors so favorably as now. Reid described Bay Street as consisting of a few brick warehouses and stores and asserted that a "huge billiard saloon was as much of an institution as the stores. Everywhere the sand was almost bottomless, and walking, for even a square or two, was exceedingly uncomfortable." [22]   This was the setting which greeted John Hay when he landed in Florida. At once he opened an office and provided himself with oath books. There soon came to his office, Hay wrote "a dirty swarm of gray coats, and filed into the room, escorted by a negro guard. Fate had done its worst for the poor devils. Even a nigger guard didn't seem to excite a feeling of resentment. They stood for a moment in awkward attitudes along the walls. . . . I soon found they had come up in good earnest to sign their names. . . . They all stood up in line and held up their hands while I read the oath. As I concluded, the negro sergeant came up, saluted and said: 'dere's one dat didn't hole up his hand.' They began to sign,—some still stuck and asked questions, some wrote good hands, but most bad. Nearly half made their mark." [23]

Hay had explained the promise made by Lincoln in his proclamation of December 8, 1863, that when Floridians numbering one tenth of those who voted in the presidential election of 1860, took the oath "to support, protect and defend" the United States Constitution and the Union and to abide by the legislation with regard to slavery, and when those voters established a republican form of government, the State of Florida would be recognized and received back into the Union.[24]   It was generally rumored that unless Lincoln could muster some new votes for the 1864 presidential nomination he would be defeated. The *New York Herald* estimated that Florida could provide three such delegates if

Hay's plan succeeded.[25]   Many Floridians, Hay discovered, refused to sign the oath on the ground that they were not "Repentant Rebels."   It did not take him long to discover that his mission was premature.   Thus ended the efforts of the Republicans to reorganize the government in Florida until Chief Justice Chase arrived in May, 1865, while three members of the Confederate Cabinet, Benjamin, Breckinridge, and George Davis, were also in Florida attempting to escape to a foreign land.

Convinced that he must seek a refuge removed as far as possible from the "reconstruction" experiments, which Chief Justice Chase had discussed with such enthusiasm, former Attorney General Davis left Gainesville the middle of June, 1865, and spent six days near Ocala.[26]   His wisdom in going farther south was demonstrated when, shortly after his exit from the Gainesville area, Federal troops seized near there

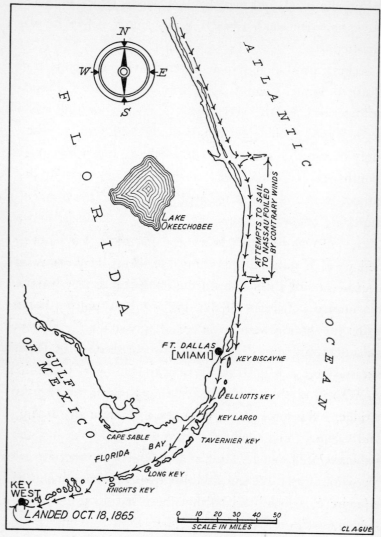

Brackets indicate settlements that did not exist in 1865

The route followed by George Davis down the coast to Key West

the private trunk and two chests of papers which President Davis had sent south from Georgia shortly before he was captured.[27]

Seeking a still more remote haven, Davis went south from Ocala to Sumter County. This west central part of Florida he described as "the very verge of civilization and clean beyond good morals and religion," where he waited seemingly in vain for a chance to get abroad. For nearly three months the ex-Confederate Attorney General, carefully disguised, went from farm to farm asking and always receiving crude but warm hospitality. Nowhere could he find a trace of Benjamin or Breckinridge. Just as he was about to despair of finding an opportunity to leave the country, he heard of a boat about to sail from New Smyrna for Nassau. He immediately went to that town and arranged passage with the captain whom he described as an Italian.[28] He had no money and since he could not reveal his identity it was necessary for him to work for his passage.[29]

"When I saw the craft in which he proposed to make the voyage, I was amazed at the rashness of the undertaking," said Davis. "The Gulf Stream between Florida and the Bahamas is notoriously the most dangerous navigation on the whole coast; and fancy the attempt to cross it during the equinox in a little boat about twenty feet long and seven feet wide, with rotten sails and a leaky hull!

"But the gentleman was determined to go, and I wouldn't be left behind . . . the calculation was that, with good luck, we could reach Nassau in five or six days."

The five or six days in which they had hoped to reach Nassau, lengthened interminably. For thirty-three days they were "beating about the coast, sometimes on the open sea and sometimes in the bays and among the reefs and keys." They suffered, said Davis, "numberless anxieties, difficulties, troubles, hardships and dangers." They were "often straitened for food," he said, and "repeatedly in such imminent peril that nothing but God's Providence saved us from destruction."

Under such conditions it was impossible for the small boat to make the oft-attempted sailing to Nassau. At length Davis learned that his small boat was far down the East Coast of Florida. It had taken him down the Indian River through which the Confederate Secretary of War, John C. Breckinridge, had escaped four months before. But Davis's captain, unable, because of equinoctial storms, to sail over to Nassau or across the Gulf Stream to Cuba, which Colonel John Taylor Wood had so successfully navigated, was forced to head for Key West. Davis landed on October 18, 1865, at this,[30] then the largest city in Florida, whose population had increased more than 20 per cent during the War, due to the fact that it had remained under Federal control throughout that period and had been of considerable value to the United States Navy. The island on which Key West was located was, according to John Hay's observation, "bathed in the quiet ripples of the pale green water, whitened by the coral, so bright green that I cannot describe the gem-like shine of the distant waters." However, Hay said he saw only one "blot of decency on the Key West escutcheon!" [31]

At Key West, George Davis learned that the former Confederate Vice President, Alexander H. Stephens, and two of his Cabinet colleagues, Judge Reagan and Mr. Trenholm, had been released. This news doubtless encouraged him to believe that the prison term awaiting him would not exceed the few months they had served. Davis thereupon determined to surrender himself to the Federal Government. While waiting in Key West for a vessel in which to take passage north and give himself up, he was arrested.[32] When the captain who had exacted menial labor of Davis in return for transporting him down the coast learned that his passenger had been the Attorney General of the Confederacy, he was most apologetic.

"I have no idea what my destination will be—probably Fort LaFayette and solitary confinement," Davis lamentingly wrote November 14, while at sea on board the United States supply ship *Memphis,* "but if they let me communicate with and see my friends, even that will be preferable to the life I have been leading." [33]

CHAPTER XII

OBLIVION

E VER a bitter foe of the Cabinet and other Confederate leaders, the *New York Times,* in discussing the possibility of their escape to foreign countries, declared in an inflammatory editorial as early as May 1, 1865:

"Expatriation would entail upon them no particular discomfort or discredit. They would take with them their booty from the Richmond banks, which alone, independently of any previous remittances they may have made abroad, would enable them to live in a far better style in Europe than they have ever maintained at home.

"They have, and always would have, a large number of sympathizers among the privileged classes of Europe, and they would have no difficulty in finding a high social position. The poverty and neglect which are usually the lot of the exile, even the worthiest, could not befall them. They would not feel their forced separation from their country to be any punishment at all. Nor in any legal sense would it be." Members of the Cabinet who fled to foreign lands did enjoy the advantages which the *Times* described, but not with the "booty from the Richmond banks."

The oracular pronouncement of the *New York Times* concerning the treatment of Confederate leaders in Europe came true when Judah P. Benjamin (1811-1884), the last Confederate Secretary of State (March, 1862 to April, 1865), reached England on August 30, 1865. Benjamin Disraeli expressed a desire to be of service to him; several members of the House of Commons and the House of Lords called to see him; and he was promised a dinner at which he would be introduced to Gladstone and Tennyson, the poet he most admired.[1] He needed this good will as he was confronted with the necessity of making a new career for himself in a foreign country.

At first without funds, he wrote that he was "lucky enough to receive a hundred bales of cotton that have escaped Yankee vigilance, and the price here is so high that it has given me nearly $20,000. . . ." In a short time, however, the greater portion of this money was lost by the failure of a bank.[2] Convinced that "nothing is more independent, nor offers a more promising future, than admission as a barrister to the bar of London," Benjamin, now without fortune, sought, with the enthusiasm and courage of a young man, such opportunity as the legal profession of England offered.[3]

"The young men who came up from Oxford and Cambridge to eat their dinners in hall that Hilary term," com-

mented the *London Times,* "saw a grizzled man, old enough
to be their father, who had, after four years of the fiercest
fights, unremitting labour, and the exercise of great power,
just escaped with his life, and now
sat quietly down to qualify himself
to earn his bread. . . ." [4]

Benjamin

The only two injuries he received
from Northerners to which Benjamin was reported to have referred
with anything like bitterness were
the burning of his law library in
New Orleans and the drinking of
his cellar of old Madeira wine.[5] His need for a law library
was filled when on January 13, 1866, he became a pupil
and law clerk in the office of Charles Pollock, later Baron
Pollock. Notwithstanding the fact that he had declined
a place on the highest court in the United States, the regulations of the English bar allowed him at first no exemption
from the customary years of study demanded of the legal
novice.[6] Later, however, he was granted a dispensation
from the usual three years of study through the insistence
of Sir George Turner, Sir George Giffard, both lords justices,
and Vice Chancellor William Page Wood (later Baron
Hatherley), and others. He then began getting briefs from
Liverpool lawyers who had heard of his extraordinary
knowledge of law and commerce. In the meantime he
supported himself by writing for a daily paper.[7]

With the expectation of extending his professional repu-

tation and gaining more clients, Benjamin wrote in 1868
A Treatise on the Law of Sale of Personal Property which,
commonly called "Benjamin on Sale," became inter-
nationally famous and still remains a standard work in
England. In time, his work so increased that he became an
acknowledged leader of the English bar, enjoyed widespread
popularity, and was one of the most highly paid lawyers of
his day.[8]

When the former Confederate Secretary of State retired
from the English bar, after seventeen years of distinguished
practice in England, he received an
unprecedented honor. His former
colleagues—those who represented
greatness, fame, and distinction at the
English bar and bench—gave him a
"collective farewell" banquet in the
Inner Temple Hall. Sir Henry James,
the Attorney General, presided and
among the speakers were Lord Cole-

Disraeli

ridge and the Earl of Selborne, who was Lord Chancellor.
Benjamin's response to the kindness and sympathy which
had been extended him in England was an affecting farewell of rhetorical beauty, spoken with a note of deep sad-
ness. He died in Paris the following year, 1884. The escape
of this member of the Confederate Cabinet, after a series
of hazardous experiences replete with privations and dangers, led to the most famous postwar career of any member
of the Cabinet and the only one that was continued in a

foreign country. Benjamin's half century of professional life constituted one of the most remarkable of modern careers, declared the *London Times,* and one as varied as an oriental tale.[9]

Benjamin's predecessor, Robert Toombs (1810-1885) of Georgia, first Confederate Secretary of State (February to July, 1861) and before the War a typical "Southern fire-eater" in the United States House of Representatives and Senate, fled into the woods as Federal officers, with orders from Secretary Stanton to arrest him, entered the Toombs mansion in Washington, Georgia, May 11, 1865, the day after Davis's capture. Accompanied by Lieutenant Charles E. Irvin, Toombs kept moving about the northern part of Georgia throughout the summer in order to avoid capture. Unable to effect a safe passage by boat from Savannah, he went by railroad and steamboat to Mobile and from there to New Orleans, from which city he was able to sail on November 4 for Havana. He remained there during the winter, safe from arrest, while certain groups in the North were fired with the resolute purpose of "crushing the rebellion and of holding the conquered sections by an army until the States are purified of treason."[10] Toombs considered locating in Mexico, but abandoning that plan, went to Europe. He remained in exile there for one and one-half years and supported himself by selling a part of a large tract of land he owned in Texas. He once amused his friends in Paris by saying that he was eating an acre of dirt a day. When, in 1867, the United States was absorbed in current problems of race relations and party politics and the fervor for punishing the Confederate leaders had passed, Toombs returned, had a satisfactory interview with President Johnson, went back to Georgia, and was never arrested. He soon resumed his position of influence in the public affairs of his state, was active in overthrowing the carpetbag rule, and maintained himself in success and wealth as a lawyer. "Unreconstructed," he never asked for the restoration of citizenship in the United States.[11]

Another predecessor of Benjamin, Robert M. T. Hunter (1809-1887) of Virginia, the second Confederate Secretary of State (July, 1861 to February, 1862), was arrested by Grant's order and, according to General H. W. Halleck's report of May 11, 1865, "is now on a gunboat in the James awaiting further instructions." Halleck had advised Grant the week before that Hunter was

Gladstone

living quietly at his home and urged Grant not to arrest him because it was understood that Hunter was advising his followers to "support the Union cause." Hunter's hostility to Jefferson Davis did much, Halleck believed, to make the Confederate President unpopular in Virginia. Halleck also reminded Grant that Lincoln had "advised against disturbing Mr. Hunter."

Stanton's policy of revenge prevailed, however, and Hunter was sent to Fort Pulaski where he was imprisoned until

August, 1865. His prewar career had included the speakership of the United States House of Representatives and a service of fourteen years in the United States Senate. After resigning from the Confederate Cabinet, he represented Virginia in the Confederate Senate. Upon his release from prison Hunter was influential in preventing many of the Reconstruction evils from devastating Virginia, which he served many years as Treasurer.[12]

Brigadier General William M. Browne (——-1884) who, while Assistant Secretary of State acted as Secretary *ad interim* in 1862, was born in England. He was a Georgian by adoption. After the War he became a planter and for years edited the *Southern Farm and Home Magazine.* He helped re-establish Democratic rule in Georgia and was Professor of History and Political Economy in the State University.

Browne's native England gave refuge not only to the last Confederate Secretary of State but to John C. Breckinridge (1821-1875) of Kentucky, the last Secretary of War, after he and his escort of five had made their way down the East Coast of Florida and crossed the Gulf Stream to Cuba, more than a month before Benjamin reached Havana. The two young soldiers, O'Toole and Russell, who had raised up from the bottom of a lake one of the *Columbine's* lifeboats, and had sailed the General up the St. Johns River, down the Indian River and over to Cuba, returned to their homes in Florida shortly after they had seen the sights of Havana. General Breckinridge wrote to Captain Dickison, from whose command they had come, that the young men would give an "account of our adventures, which may be termed both singular and perilous." [13] Their account of "singular and perilous" adventures led to their imprisonment for two months. Thomas Ferguson, the twenty-one-year-old negro servant, wanted to remain with Breckinridge but he had been so deathly seasick while crossing over from Florida to Cuba that he had neither taste nor courage for an ocean voyage to Europe. He accompanied O'Toole and Russell back to the United States, bearing a letter from his former master commending him as "honest and devoted" and expressing the hope that he would "receive such protection and advice as he may need on his journey." [14]

Colonel Wood, who was chiefly responsible for the escape of the Breckinridge party to Cuba, boarded the former blockade-runner, *Lark,* at Havana on June 23, 1865, and reached Halifax, Nova Scotia, a week later.[15] There he spent the remainder of his life, engaged in shipping and marine insurance. Colonel Wilson, aide to General Breckinridge, also took passage on a former blockade-runner to Halifax. From Canada he returned to Kentucky, where he lived quietly, and at one time, so he wrote Breckinridge, made a little money running a hotel in Henderson. "If my plan of feeding guests on the scantiest cheap fare, and charging them the most enormous bill succeeds," he wrote, "I am bound to do well until I am one day killed by some infuriated victim." [16]

As General Breckinridge, accompanied by Colonel Charles

J. Helm, was entering Southampton July 6, 1865, three weeks after he had sailed from Havana on the British West Indian Mail Steamer *Shannon,* he completed the manuscript on which a part of this narrative is based.[17] "I am not sure you can read this [manuscript]," he wrote his youngest son, "Owen,"[18] "for the weather is rough and there is much loud talking in the cabin." From England he went to Toronto, Canada, where he was joined by Mrs. Breckinridge and two of their children, Frances and "Owen." While in Toronto, Breckinridge conducted a class in law for three young Confederate refugees, Captain Thomas H. Hines and Lieutenants Bennett H. Young and George B. Easton.[19] Breckinridge's proximity to the United States border was discussed at one of President Johnson's Cabinet meetings, and instructions were issued to arrest him if he should be found within the limits of the United States.[20] Breckinridge realized this danger and wrote to a friend, "the time has not come yet when I can properly cherish the hope of returning to my country." [21]

Breckinridge

Having sailed from Quebec on the S. S. *Peruvian,* Breckinridge arrived in Liverpool August 21, 1865, and upon reaching London was accorded a hospitable welcome.

Among the notables who sought his acquaintance were the Hon. Alexander James Beresford Hope, member of Parliament for the University of Cambridge, and his wife, Lady Mildred, daughter of the Marquis of Salisbury. They became warm friends and the Breckinridges were frequently entertained by this distinguished family. "I have often . . . remarked," later wrote Mr. Hope, who had been a Confederate lobbyist in Parliament, "that out of the persons of distinction with whom, in the course of my life, I have in various ways been thrown, General Breckinridge was among those who had most irresistibly struck me with a feeling of ability and ready power." [22] Breckinridge also visited the Archbishop of Canterbury, dined with Gladstone, enjoyed the races at Ascot, and spent his period of exile not in boredom but in "visiting, dining and attending debates in the Commons." [23]

In the spring of 1867, Horace Greeley, editor of the *New York Tribune,* one of the most influential newspapers of the time, declared it was a "pity that the presence and counsel of General Breckinridge were wanting. We need him . . . in his own Kentucky, where a most unfortunate attempt to perpetuate class distinction . . . threatens to cause a feud and a struggle. . . ." [24] When Breckinridge returned to Canada in June, 1868, after a visit to the Holy Land, Greece, Egypt, and France, the *Daily Courier* of Louisville expressed the wish that "the oblivion of past differences will soon restore to our State a son so endeared to her citizens by his many shining and noble qualities." [25]

President Johnson's general amnesty proclamation on Christmas Day, 1868, made Greeley's wish about Breckinridge come true. On February 10, 1869, the *Mail* of Niagara Village on the Canadian side of Lake Ontario, carried the following note: "Last week General Breckinridge and his amiable lady, who have been resident in Niagara for a considerable time, took their departure in order to return to the South. . . . They leave this town with the sincere respect and best wishes of all classes which they deservedly won by the invariably kind and friendly manner in which they have lived among us. General Breckinridge's return to Kentucky will be hailed with delight by the people of that State who are justly proud of his talents and character which reflect luster on them all."

After an absence of almost eight years, the former Confederate Secretary of War returned March 9, 1869, to his "Old Kentucky Home" at Lexington but not to enter public service in which, before the War, he had made such phenomenally rapid advancement in a career which ability and opportunity had destined to be a remarkable one.

Early in January, 1869, William Preston Johnston, who as an aide to President Davis had shared experiences with Breckinridge in the flight of the Cabinet, wrote to Breckinridge from Virginia, where he was a member of General Lee's faculty of Washington College, indicating that if Breckinridge would join them, a law department would be established. "This college is assuming the proportions of a university, not in numbers only—a poor test—but in the character of its instruction," wrote Johnston to Breckinridge. A formal invitation was issued by the trustees[26] and President Lee wrote Breckinridge of his personal regard and esteem and expressed the hope that he would accept.[27]

Breckinridge, however, decided to remain in Kentucky. Until his premature death in 1875, at the age of fifty-four, he quietly practiced law. His memory was signally honored a decade after his passing when the Kentucky legislature, which in 1861 had branded him a traitor, appropriated $10,-000 for his statue. This memorial, which stands in the heart of Lexington, was created by Valentine and represents the General as an orator, the field of his greatest achievement.[28]

As the last Confederate Secretary of War (February to April, 1865), Breckinridge had had six predecessors, including Benjamin. Brigadier General Leroy Pope Walker (1817-1884) of Alabama, trained at the Universities of Alabama and Virginia and former member of the Alabama legislature, who became the first Confederate Secretary of War (February to September, 1861), was not imprisoned at the close of the War but resumed his popular and influential activities in the political life of Alabama. His address as President of Alabama's Constitutional Convention in 1875 was commented upon by leading journals of the North "in terms of the highest commendation, and, forgetful of past differences, recognized its wise and conservative declarations as the only standard by which the patriotism of its distinguished author must be judged today," said the *Montgomery Weekly Advertiser* of September 15, 1875.

Thomas Jefferson's grandson, George Wythe Randolph (1818-1867) of Virginia, who had risen to the rank of Brigadier General in the Confederate Army, was the second Confederate Secretary of War (March to November, 1862). Unwilling to be dominated by President Davis, he resigned eight months after assuming office and went to France to recover his health. He did not return to Virginia until after the War was over, shortly after which he died.

Major General Gustavus Woodson Smith (1822-1896) of Kentucky, the third Confederate Secretary of War (November 17-20, 1862), after holding that office three days, resigned because of presidential interference. Before the War he had taught at his alma mater, the United States Military Academy, had been cited for distinguished service in the Mexican War, and was from 1858 to 1861 Street Commissioner of New York. He held the rank of Major General in the Confederate Army throughout the War and after his release from prison, entered business in Chattanooga and later lived in New York. Smith found time, before he died, to write four books.

James A. Seddon (1815-1880) of Virginia, fourth Confederate Secretary of War, overcame the popular conception that a civilian should not direct military affairs and occupied that position from November, 1862, to February, 1865, a period longer than that of any of his colleagues who acted as head of the Department. He proved to be an able administrator but resigned when the Virginia delegation in Congress requested a reorganization of the Cabinet. Stanton had him confined in Libby Prison late in May, 1865. He was transferred to Fort Pulaski where he remained in prison until the following November. Broken and discouraged, ill in health and spirit, Seddon spent the remainder of his life at "Sabot Hill," his home in Virginia.

Stephens

When Alexander H. Stephens, former Vice President of the Confederacy, was released from Fort Warren, Boston harbor, in October, 1865, he returned to Georgia and urged the abandonment of sectional animosity. Almost at once he was elected by the Georgia legislature to the United States Senate. His Confederate disability, however, prevented his return at that time to a position of authority in the national government. He devoted much of the next decade and a half to writing. One of his works, *A Constitutional View of the Late War Between the States,* caused widespread discussion and comment. The author's purpose was to prove that secession was a legal right. It is generally regarded as one of the ablest works in defence of the Southern position. Stephens was so frail of body that he seldom if ever attained the weight of one hundred pounds. Despite his appearance as an "animated corpse," as he was once called, he remained active, entered the United States House of Representatives in 1872 and when, eleven years later, he died, "Little Ellick" had just been inaugurated Governor of Georgia.

Christopher Gustavus Memminger (1803-1888), first Confederate Secretary of the Treasury, was a native of Germany who was reared and educated in South Carolina. As Chairman of the Committee that drafted the Provisional Constitution of the Confederate Government, he was active in its permanent organization. He resigned in June, 1864, when the Confederate Congress failed to support his program, and retired to his country seat at Flat Rock, North Carolina, where, remaining after the War, he escaped arrest and imprisonment. His mansion in Charleston was seized by the Federals, however, and used as an asylum for negro orphans. Memminger's citizenship and property were restored in 1867. He resumed the practice of law in Charleston and as a pioneer in the development of the phosphate industry in South Carolina considerably hastened the restoration of prosperity in that state. He rendered noteworthy public service in the legislature, which he entered in 1877, and in the development of public schools for both races. A marble bust of Memminger by Valentine was placed in the Council Chamber of the City of Charleston in recognition of these services.[29]

Memminger's successor as Secretary of the Treasury (July, 1864 to April, 1865), George Alfred Trenholm (1806-1876), his fellow Charlestonian, advisor and friend, was removed from the Charleston jail, where he had been placed after arrest, and taken to Fort Pulaski at Savannah. Early in

October, 1865, he was paroled and allowed to return to his home at Columbia. Among those who endeavored to secure pardon for him were the Sisters of Our Lady of Mercy in Charleston, who, imploring President Johnson for executive clemency, wrote of Trenholm: "In our efforts to afford relief to the Union Soldiers, confined in the Prisons and Hospitals, we have never applied in vain for aid to this Honorable Gentleman, and we can testify to the liberality and readiness with which he always supported our works of charity." [30] Trenholm was pardoned October 25, 1866, and two years later formed G. A. Trenholm & Company, cotton brokers, at Charleston, and resumed some of the extensive business operations he had conducted before the War.

Trenholm

Trenholm was persuaded by the Democrats in 1874 to accept election to the legislature of South Carolina to build up political power with which the carpetbaggers could be overthrown. Favorable comment on his election was heard in Wall Street [31] and a contemporary report indicated that he "exerted a powerful influence" in the legislature "even with the colored Republicans," but "the price he paid was heavy. There is no room to doubt that the labor and anxiety of the session of 1874-75, coupled with the rigors of the season, hastened, if they did not directly cause, his fatal illness." [32]

Probably the most constructive postwar career that came out of the last Confederate Cabinet was that of Judge John H. Reagan (1818-1905) of Texas, the only Confederate Postmaster General and, during the last days of the Confederacy, Acting Secretary of the Treasury. He was an able builder in the Lone Star State and wrote one of its constitutions.

Reagan

His business ability, his legal acumen, his wide experience, and the forcefulness and clarity with which he advocated policies gradually regained and extended the national leadership he had enjoyed before the War. Recognition came in his election to the United States House of Representatives and later to the United States Senate. At Washington he rendered a significant service as joint author and strong advocate of the bill to establish the Interstate Commerce Commission. His death did not occur until after the beginning of the twentieth century. It marked the passing of the last member of the Confederate Cabinet.

When in November, 1861, Judah P. Benjamin was transferred from the position of Attorney General, which he had held from the preceding February, to another Cabinet post, he was succeeded by Thomas Bragg (1810-1872), brother of General Braxton Bragg. An able lawyer, Thomas Bragg had represented North Carolina in the United States Senate before the War. He remained as the second Confederate Attorney General until March, 1862. Bragg is credited with having been partly responsible for keeping North Carolina in the Confederacy at the time of the Union meetings. After the War, Bragg took a prominent part in the fight for decent government in his state.

The third Confederate Attorney General was Thomas Hill Watts (1819-1892) of Alabama, a graduate of the University of Virginia, who had been a colonel in the Confederate Army before his appointment to Richmond. He began his work in the Davis official family in March, 1862, and resigned when he was elected Governor of Alabama in December, 1863. After his release from prison he resumed the practice of law in Alabama and became active in the public welfare.

Wade Keyes (1821-1879), native of Alabama, was Assistant Attorney General of the Confederacy throughout the War and acted as Attorney General, *ad interim,* in December, 1863. While practicing law in Tallahassee in the 1840's he had established a reputation by writing two legal volumes. He resumed the practice of law in Alabama after the War and served on a commission that codified the laws of that state.

George Davis (1820-1896) of North Carolina, last Attorney
General of the Confederacy
(January, 1864 to April,
1865), who was taken to
New York after his arrest at
Key West and held in close
custody at Fort LaFayette,
was released on January 1,
1866. He then resumed the
practice of law at his home,
Wilmington, North Caro-
lina, with marked success,
in particular as counsel of
the Atlantic Coast Line

George Davis

(Railroad) during its formative period. An admirable service he rendered North Carolina was to head a commission
which brought order out of the chaotic situation of the
state debt created by the carpetbaggers. He never again
entered public life, though opportunities such as the office
of chief justice of his state were open to him. On special
occasions he displayed the oratorical powers which had con-
tributed so heavily to his political success.

"I am anxious to take the oath of allegiance and to do
what I can to evoke order from chaos, and in good faith, to
aid the administration to harmonize the country," wrote
the only Confederate Secretary of the Navy, Stephen R.
Mallory (1813-1873) of Florida, to his wife from prison at
Fort LaFayette, in June, 1865. In this letter he reviewed the

influence he had exerted as United States Senator to avert the War; in particular he recalled how he had prevented the Confederates from attacking Fort Pickens in Pensacola Harbor, an event which undoubtedly would have hastened by several months the outbreak of hostilities. This action, he wrote, had brought down on him the "thunder of denunciation" from the extremists of the South and bitter criticism in his own state of Florida.[33] Yet Mallory was the last member of the Cabinet to be released from prison, where dampness had increased his suffering from gout. When in March, 1866, he was paroled, he was without funds and without his valuable law library which had been destroyed or stolen. But he reopened his law office and resolutely began rebuilding his career and fortune in western Florida, where in happier days his father-in-law, Don Francisco Moreno, had been known as "King of Pensacola."

Mallory's strongest claim to distinction was the contribution he made to the development of naval warfare. When he became head of the Navy Department of the Confederacy, he had virtually nothing with which to start his program but his own broad knowledge of naval affairs. With the aid of John Mercer Brooke and other naval inventors and experts he helped develop two deadly weapons of warfare—the torpedo and the submarine. The privateers of his naval force were so effective that they often terrorized the Federal Navy and destroyed hundreds of merchantmen. For this, many embittered Northerners would have convicted him of piracy and had him hanged.[34]

Despite the fact that all members of the Confederate Cabinet had been paroled by March, 1866, the former President of the Confederacy was indicted for treason and was denied a trial, a right guaranteed by the constitution. "[Jefferson

Mallory

Davis] may be pronounced a traitor; but so was Washington . . . and so have been scores of others whom Americans have uniformly and consistently delighted to honor," remarked the *London Times,*[35] which periodical was, in the judgment of *Harper's Weekly,* "one of the basest and most unscrupulous defamers of this country and the most unblushing advocate of Davis. . . ." [36] The *Chicago Tribune* demanded with vengeance the hanging of Davis, the Cabinet, and other Southern leaders:

"In spite of the protestations of the English sympathizers with the rebellion, against such an act, it is as clearly the right and duty of the Government of the United States to hang Jeff. Davis and his leading and most criminal confederates, as to punish any other offenders against the peace and welfare of society. We hold that if that most guilty and infamous of men is suffered to escape the penalties he has earned, there is not a murderer, a robber, or a perjurer in all the land who may not with propriety plead the leniency that was extended to him, as a reason why all punishment should cease, and why stabbing, poisoning, arson and robbery should be considered offences no more. Davis is a thousand times guilty of every crime known to the law and to the imagination of men. . . . The number of his accomplices, and the impossibility of inflicting death on all who have been seduced into rebellion by his false and infamous persuasions, only make justice more anxious to clutch him, the head and front of the great offending. . . . We believe him to be the epitome of all human infamy—the most monstrous creation of the age. . . . The nation, despising the snivelling of English sympathizers, and the mock horror of his guilty associates at home, can afford to trust to the verdict of the ages for the vindication of its righteous act." [37]

President Johnson maintained that Davis should be hanged as an example but Chief Justice Chase contended that his capture was a mistake and that his trial would be a greater one. If the death penalty had been inflicted on Davis and the Confederate Cabinet, such action would have been taken at the risk of destroying the honor of the United States and the respect of the civilized world. This was the belief of a leading English periodical which declared the "protection which is afforded in all civilized countries to political exiles is founded on a belief that opposition to constituted authorities is not necessarily a crime. . . . Cromwell, Washington, Kossuth and Garibaldi committed treason in the same sense in which it is declared by Mr. [Andrew] Johnson to be worse than murder; but, with the exception of the greatest American patriot, not one of the number was entitled to immunity so fully as Mr. Jefferson Davis." [38]

After having remained in Fortress Monroe for two long years, Davis was finally released in May, 1867, on a $100,000 bond signed by Cornelius Vanderbilt, Horace Greeley, and others. When he arrived in Richmond he was greeted by a larger gathering of people than that which had acknowledged him the official head of the Confederacy in 1861, wrote a former member of the Cabinet, who added: "I have never seen the city in such a state of pleased excitement except upon the news of a Confederate victory." Physical and mental suffering in prison had, by the time he was released, reduced Davis to a shadow of his former self. Though he was never given a trial, the 1868 amnesty proclamation rendered him eligible for a pardon and the resumption of political activity. He was, however, unwilling to ask the United States Congress to remove his Confederate disability and remained indifferent to an opportunity to go to Washington as United States Senator from Mississippi.

Following his release from Fortress Monroe, Davis spent considerable time in Canada and England. According to one of his biographers he was much sought after by the nobility of England and was invited to the Imperial Court when he went to France, but was reported to have declined to see Napoleon III because he felt that that monarch had been false to the Confederacy.[39] A later biographer of Davis referred to this supposed incident as typical of the position the Confederate President was entirely capable of assuming.[40] Desperately in need of funds Davis twice entered upon business ventures. Failure ended each attempt.

Davis, though extraordinarily able, was never so popular as Lee. In some of his public addresses he made statements sufficiently unwise as to give occasion for such unjust criticism as that of Carl Schurz, that Davis "stimulated the brooding over the past disappointments rather than a cheerful contemplation of new opportunities. He presented the sorry spectacle of a soured man who wished everyone else to be soured too." [41] Nevertheless, the last part of his life, spent at "Beauvoir" in Mississippi on the Gulf of Mexico, halfway between New Orleans and Mobile, witnessed his general acclaim. This was partly due, no doubt, to the sympathetic desire of Southerners to compensate for the indignities to which he had been forced to submit in prison and the various manifestations of revenge visited upon him as the leader of the South, a persecution which consisted of fierce denunciations by James G. Blaine and politicians of his type. According to Dr. Robert McElroy, whose exhaustive biography of Davis now makes possible a clearer understanding of his career, the vindication of the principles for which the South fought was always uppermost in Davis's mind, heart, and actions.

The last years of Davis's life were devoted to literary pursuits, principally to the writing of *The Rise and Fall of the Confederate Government,* the concluding paragraph of which reads: "I recognize the fact that the war showed it [secession] to be impracticable, but this did not prove it to be wrong; and, now that it may not be again attempted, and that the Union may promote the general welfare, it is needful that the truth, the whole truth, should be known, so that criminations and recriminations may forever cease, and then on the basis of fraternity and faithful regard for the rights of the States, there may be written on the arch of the Union, *Esto Perpetua."* [42]

If the desire for vengeance on the Confederate Cabinet, which was expressed in the North, had been completely reflected in the policy of the United States Government, those Cabinet members who were arrested and imprisoned would have been kept there indefinitely, or possibly executed. Actually, the Confederate leaders who were punished served terms short in comparison with the charges made against them and the bitterness felt by many of their accusers. George Davis remained less than three months in prison; Reagan and Trenholm less than four months; and Mallory slightly more than ten months. But their suffering, hard as it was, constituted a minor problem compared to that which confronted them as they returned to their homes and faced the desolation left by the War and attempted to readjust their lives to the demands of a sharply changed social order. Greedy and vindictive forces were gaining the ascendancy as these statesmen resumed their careers and sought opportunities to rebuild their homes and retrieve their shattered fortunes. Having passed the half-century mark in age, bereft of fortune and power, they faced about and as a group courageously assumed leadership in their respective states. Several of them were instrumental in overthrowing the regime of the carpetbaggers. They counseled the South to recover its wasted resources and assisted it to revitalize the energy that had been so tragically dissipated in war. A certain number of ex-Confederates preferred, however, to follow the example of Judah P. Benjamin and start life anew elsewhere. At least three thousand soldiers, expecting to continue military service, crossed over the Rio Grande into Mexico. Several other thousand "unreconstructed" Confederates settled in Europe, Canada, Central America, Cuba, Jamaica, Mexico, and South America.[43]

Seventeen different men, three of whom were *ad interim* appointees, held Cabinet positions in the four years of the Confederacy. The Navy and Post Office Departments, only, remained under the administration of one man each during the entire period. Appointees in the other four departments ranged from two to seven as follows: Treasury, two; State, four; Attorney General, five; War, seven. So many substitutions in four years have been attributed to the dominant personality of the Confederate President, his inability to work co-operatively with his colleagues, and his dictatorial and overbearing attitude toward his subordinates. Proof of these assertions, however, is not available except in his relations to the War Department. On the contrary, Benjamin, Mallory, Memminger, and Reagan were given a rather free hand and occasionally successfully opposed Davis.[44]

Members of the Confederate Cabinet who retained their portfolios over a period sufficiently long to be able to produce results were: Benjamin, State; Memminger, Treasury; Mallory, Navy; Reagan, Post Office; and Seddon, War.

Four delegates to the Provisional Confederate Congress whose session extended from February 4, 1861 to February 17, 1862, namely, Reagan, Memminger, Toombs, and Hunter, were, while delegates, also for a part of the time, members of the Cabinet.[45] Jabez L. M. Curry, a member of the Provisional Congress from Alabama, wrote that the "occasional appearance of cabinet officers on the floor of Congress and participation in debates worked beneficially and showed the importance of enlarging the privilege." [46] Curry's judgment was shared by Stephens and Toombs who worked hard to provide in the permanent constitution membership in the Congress for Cabinet members. They believed the combination of the strength of Congress and Cabinet would insure for the Confederacy the effectiveness of the English system. Section 6 of Article I of the permanent constitution reads: "Congress may, by law, grant to the principal officer in each of the Executive Departments a seat upon the floor of either House, with the privilege of discussing any measure appertaining to his department." The Confederate Congress, however, never passed such a law. An explanation of why it failed to do so may or may not be found in an estimate of the Congress by Edward A. Pollard, editor of the Richmond, Virginia, *Examiner*. He described it as "remarkable in the annals of the world for its weakness and ignorance," asserted that its record was a "constant degradation of the Confederate name," and that its "composition and nature will afford to the future historian an especial study among the contradictions and curiosities of the late war." [47] Curry declared there was an "injurious lack of sympathizing intercourse between the Executive and Legislative departments [of the Confederacy], and especially between members of the Cabinet and Committees of Congress." [48]

When the last surviving member of the Confederate Cabinet, Judge John H. Reagan, passed away at the beginning of the present century, that period of American history in which the Confederacy had played a prominent part had already become remote, and in the rush of a changed order members of the Confederate Cabinet were relegated to an indistinct past. In texts and in other records, the military chieftains gradually became the heroic figures. When some one was to blame, it became easy to heap the failures on the heads of the civilians who nominally did direct the fortunes of the Confederacy.

As time has progressed, the names of the Confederate Cabinet members, which were household words before the War, have lost their significance to the public. Gladstone credited them in 1862 with having made a nation.[49] As Lord Palmerston's periodical pointed out, "to impartial minds it will always occur that the absence of that most material element of all human undertakings, success, will alone prevent" these Southern leaders from taking their places in after times by the side of recognized patriots.[50] The misfortune of the Confederate Cabinet was that the tide of war turned against its members and their flight ended in unmerited oblivion.

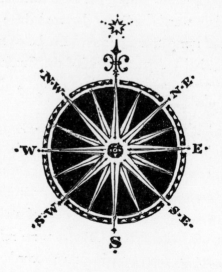

REFERENCES

Complete reference data of citations will be found in the Bibliography, pages 277-292.

CHAPTER I

1. V. H. Davis, *Jefferson Davis, ex-President of the Confederate States, a Memoir,* II, 577.

2. *The Harrisons of Skimino,* 225-227. Dr. Dallas D. Irvine, Chief of the Division of War Department Records in the National Archives at Washington, is engaged in a study revealing the fate of the Confederate Archives.

3. E. W. Weddell, *St. Paul's Church,* I, 235 ff.

4. Jefferson Davis, *The Rise and Fall of the Confederate Government,* II, 667.

5. Richmond *Evening Whig,* April 4, 1865.

6. W. H. Parker, *Recollections of a Naval Officer,* 350-351.

7. W. F. McCaleb, "The Organization of the Post Office Department of the Confederacy," *American Historical Review,* XII, 67-74.

8. J. R. Soley, *The Blockade and the Cruisers,* 182.

9. S. R. Mallory, "The Last Days of the Confederate Government," *McClure's Magazine,* XVI, 102-105.

10. *Richmond Times,* April 22, 1865.

11. *Ibid.,* April 21, 1865.

12. Mallory, *loc. cit.,* 105.

13. *Confederate Veteran,* XIX, 377.

14. Danville, Va., *Weekly Register,* April 7, 1865.

15. J. E. Walmsley, "The Last Meeting of the Confederate Cabinet," *The Mississippi Valley Historical Review,* VI, 337-338.

16. J. Davis, *op. cit.,* II, 677-678.

17. *Harper's Weekly,* April 15, 1865.

18. A. V. G. Allen, *Life and Letters of Phillips Brooks,* I, 530-531.

19. *Southern Historical Society Papers,* III, 102, cited hereafter as *S. H. S. P.*

20. J. C. Breckinridge to Jefferson Davis, April 8, 1865, Harrison Papers.

21. J. S. Wise, *The End of an Era,* 446.

22. Mallory, *loc. cit.,* 107.

23. Edward Pollock, *Sketch Book of Danville, Virginia,* (E. R. Waddill & Bro., Danville, 1885), 58, 60, and *Official Records of the Union and Confederate Armies,* Ser. I, Vol. XLVI, Pt. III, 1393-1394, cited hereafter as *O. R. (Official Records).*

24. Mallory, *loc. cit.,* 107.

25. *New York Times,* April 12, 1865.

26. *New York Tribune,* April 11 and 13, 1865.

CHAPTER II

1. *S.H.S.P.,* XXV, 270, and *O.R.,* Ser. I, Vol. XLVI, Pt. III, 1393-1394, and Robert Hunter, ed., *Sketches of War History,* III, 21.

2. *Harrisons of Skimino,* 232.

3. *O. R.,* Ser. I, Vol. LI, Pt. II, 815-816.

4. J. Davis, *op. cit.,* II, 597.

5. R. E. Yates, "Zebulon B. Vance as War Governor of North Carolina," *Journal of Southern History,* III, 43-75, (Feb., 1937).

6. Mallory, *loc. cit.,* 107. Vance maintained that North Carolina supplied more troops for the Confederacy than any other state.

7. F. R. Lubbock, *Six Decades in Texas,* 566.

8. *Harrisons of Skimino,* 232, and Mallory, *loc. cit.,* 242.

9. Diary of J. T. Wood, cited hereafter as "Wood's Diary."

10. Mallory, *loc. cit.,* 239.

11. Parker, *op. cit.,* 355.

12. *O. R.,* Ser. I, Vol. XLIX, Pt. I, 323-325.

13. V. H. Davis, *op. cit.,* II, 611.

14. Parker, *op. cit.,* 355-359, and John K. Aull in Columbia, S. C., *State,* Sept. 13, 1931.

15. *O. R.,* Ser. I, Vol. XLVII, Pt. III, 265.

16. J. Davis, *op. cit.,* II, 678-680.

17. J. E. Johnston, *Narrative of Military Operations Directed During the Late War Between the States,* 398-399.

18. J. Davis, *op. cit.,* II, 680-681.

19. Gideon Welles, "Lincoln and Johnson," *Galaxy Magazine,* XIII, 522-527.

20. *S. H. S. P.,* IX, 542-543.

21. *Harrisons of Skimino,* 236-239.

22. Mallory, *loc. cit.,* 242, and *Harrisons of Skimino,* 239.

23. Wood's Diary.

24. Clement Dowd, *Life of Zebulon B. Vance,* 485-486.

25. Alfred Roman, *The Military Operations of General Beauregard,* II, 666.

27. W. T. Sherman, *Memoirs,* II, 326.

26. Johnston, *op. cit.,* 404.

28. Dowd, *op. cit.*, 487.

29. *London Times,* April 3, 1865.

30. V. H. Davis, *op. cit.*, II, 627.

31. Dr. Paul B. Barringer to A. J. Hanna, Oct. 9, 1936.

32. *Harrisons of Skimino,* 241-242. One month later Davis's host, Lewis F. Bates, who was superintendent of the Southern Express Co. of North Carolina, was influenced to testify in the "Assassination Trial" at Washington, D. C., that when Breckinridge expressed regret over the murder of Lincoln, Davis replied: "Well, General, I don't know; if it were to be done at all it were better it were well done; and if the same were done to Andy Johnson, the beast, and to Secretary Stanton, the job would be complete." See *New York Times,* May 31, 1865.

33. *Harrisons of Skimino,* 243.

34. *The Church Intelligencer,* May 4, 1865.

35. *Ibid.*

36. *Harrisons of Skimino,* 243.

37. Wade Hampton to Jefferson Davis, April 19 and 22, 1865 (copy), Stanton Papers.

38. Walmsley, *loc. cit.,* 342.

39. Jefferson Davis to Mrs. Davis, April 23, 1865, Stanton Papers.

40. Mallory, *loc. cit.,* 244-245.

41. John H. Reagan to Jefferson Davis, April 22, 1865 (copy), Stanton Papers.

42. J. Davis, *op. cit.,* II, 696 and Lubbock, *op. cit.,* 565.

43. Mallory, *loc. cit.,* 245.

44. Walmsley, *loc. cit.,* 343-344.

45. *Boston Transcript,* May 1, 1865.

46. *Ibid.,* April 28, 1865.

CHAPTER III

1. *O. R.,* Ser. I, Vol. XLIX, Pt. I, 545-547.

2. Lubbock, *op. cit.,* 566.

3. Geo. A. Trenholm to Jefferson Davis, April 27, 1865 (copy), Stanton Papers.

4. Walmsley, *loc. cit.,* 344, and Captain Elliott White Springs (grandson of Colonel Springs and of Colonel White) to A. J. Hanna, Aug. 19, 1937.

5. Diary of Tench F. Tilghman. Subsequent references to Tilghman are made from this source. Tench Tilghman, fourth member of this distinguished Maryland family to bear the name, was the great-grandson of Lieutenant Colonel Tench Tilghman, aide-de-camp to General Washington. His family emigrated from England to Maryland in 1661. Dr. Richard Tilghman (1626-1675) settled on the Chester River in Talbot (now Queen Anne) County. His son, Richard II, was a member of the Lord Proprietor's Council and Chancellor of the Province. Of his five sons, Richard III was a member of the Council; James was a member of the Provincial Council of Pennsylvania; and Matthew was a member of the Continental Congress and President of the Constitutional Convention of Maryland. Lieutenant Colonel Tench Tilghman became a member of Washington's staff in August of 1776 and served until the end of the war. He was selected by Washington to carry to Philadelphia the official dispatches announcing the surrender of Cornwallis. Other notable members of the family were William (brother of Tench I), Chief Justice of Pennsylvania; Brigadier General Lloyd Tilghman, Confederate States Army; Edward Tilghman, member of the Stamp Act Congress of 1765.

6. John K. Aull in Columbia, S. C., *State,* Sept. 27, 1931.

7. *O. R.,* Ser. I, Vol. XLIX, Pt. I, 346 ff.

8. V. H. Davis, *op. cit.*, II, 615.

9. Parker, *op. cit.*, 361-365.

10. *Ibid.*, 351-352.

11. Dunbar Rowland, *Jefferson Davis, Constitutionalist*, VIII, 157-158.

12. John K. Aull in Columbia, S. C., *State*, May 11, 1936.

13. *Battles and Leaders of the Civil War*, IV, 764-765.

14. S. R. Mallory to Jefferson Davis, May 2, 1865 (copy), Harrison Papers.

15. Parker, *op. cit.*, 368-369.

16. John H. Reagan, *Memoirs*, 212.

17. *O. R.*, Ser. I, Vol. XLIX, Pt. I, 306.

18. Rowland, *op. cit.*, VIII, 159.

19. J. L. Orr to F. W. Pickens, April 29, 1865, quoted by John K. Aull in Columbia, S. C., *State*, Sept. 20, 1931.

20. *Confederate Veteran*, November, 1929.

21. T. W. Davis to A. J. Hanna, June 18, 1937.

22. J. M. Morgan, *Recollections of a Rebel Reefer*, 202.

23. Basil W. Duke, *Reminiscences*, 387-389.

24. Rowland, *op. cit.*, VIII, 150.

25. *New York Times*, May 1, 1865.

CHAPTER IV

1. J. Davis, *op. cit.*, II, 697, and Reagan, *op. cit.*, 211.

2. *O. R.*, Ser. I, Vol. XLVIII, Pt. II, 1284.

3. J. Davis, *op. cit.*, II, 696-697.

4. F. E. Holladay, "The Powers of the Commander of the Confederate Trans-Mississippi Department, 1863-1865," *The Southwestern Historical Quarterly*, XXI, 353, 279, 333, 281. For a different interpretation by a Confederate Senator from Texas of Kirby Smith's administration, see W. S. Oldham, "Memoirs," 334-394 (unpublished), U. of Texas, Austin.

5. Colonel Samuel H. Fisher has in preparation for publication in the *Florida Historical Quarterly* an article revealing two interesting episodes which occurred in Litchfield, Connecticut, in July, 1799 and August, 1806, which were the indirect cause of the settling in Florida of General Edmund Kirby Smith's father, Judge Joseph L. Smith.

Major Ephraim Kirby, a distinguished officer in the Revolution and the compiler of the first collection of law reports published in this country, was an outstanding Jeffersonian Democrat in a hotbed of New England Federalists. His partisanship involved him in trouble with his neighbors. Later, his son-in-law, Joseph Lee Smith, also an ardent Democrat, found himself the center of a somewhat similar political imbroglio. As a result, both men left Connecticut and emigrated south, and Florida obtained as a citizen an able and successful judge, whose son became the renowned General.

6. *Battles and Leaders of the Civil War*, IV, 374.

7. Holladay, *loc. cit.*, 334.

8. *Ibid.*, 335.

9. *Ibid.*, 352.

10. *Ibid.*, 345, 359.

11. *Ibid.*, 353, 352.

12. *Harrisons of Skimino*, 256.

13. A. H. Noll, *General Kirby-Smith*, 258.

14. *New York Times*, May 1, 1865.

15. *O. R.,* Ser. I, Vol. XLVIII, Pt. II, 1292-1293.

16. *Ibid.,* Pt. I, 1358-1359.

17. J. Fred Rippy, *The United States and Mexico,* 245.

CHAPTER V

1. John K. Aull in Columbia, S. C., *State,* Sept. 13, 1931.

2. J. D. Richardson, ed., *Messages and Papers of the Presidents,* VI, 307-308. Some writers have referred to rewards offered for the capture of members of the Cabinet, in particular for Benjamin. No record of rewards specifically offered for them has been located. Members of the Cabinet were probably, however, because of their positions, included in the general offer of rewards for "other rebels and traitors" along with Davis.

3. *Official Records of the Union and Confederate Navies,* Ser. I, Vol. XVII, 838, cited hereafter as *O. R. (Navy).*

4. *Under Both Flags,* 234.

5. J. Davis, *op. cit.,* II, 694.

6. *S. H. S. P.,* XII, 99.

7. *O. R.,* Ser. I, Vol. XLIX, Pt. II, 1278.

8. *Battles and Leaders of the Civil War,* IV, 766.

9. Reagan, *op. cit.,* 215.

10. Mallory, *loc. cit.,* 247, and Rowland, *op. cit.,* VI, 586.

11. Southern History Association *Publications,* V, 291-292 and 296-297. Where was the last meeting of the Confederate Cabinet held? There are those who maintain that the meeting in Richmond on April 2 was the last, whereas some of the inhabitants of Danville declare the last meeting occurred in that city. Another group claims it for Greensboro and still another for Charlotte. Certain citizens of Fort Mill and Abbeville in South Carolina

and of Washington, Ga., assert with surprising fervor that the last meeting was held in their respective cities. Even Shreveport, La., has lodged a claim (See San Marcos, Texas, *Free Press,* April 6, 1878.) although no member of the Cabinet was ever there! More time and interest appear to be centered in settling this unimportant question than are devoted to acquiring information about what the Cabinet was doing. Walmsley points out in *The Mississippi Valley Historical Review* (Vol. VI, 336-349) that there seems to be no definition of a Cabinet meeting by which to be guided. "As to the facts," he writes, "Davis and a small body of men were fleeing on horseback from pursuing forces; now they were all together and planning better things, now they were scattered in the woods to prevent capture. Why not 'cabinet meetings' at Yorkville, Union, Cokesbury, or even at the lunch time which Reagan describes on the banks of the Broad River? . . . Was there, then a 'last meeting'? Probably not, as a conscious, definite ending of things. By degrees the Cabinet grew smaller, pressing exigencies of personal safety took the place of public plans, and gradually meetings ceased."

12. *S. H. S. P.,* IX, 542 ff., Clark Papers, and Otis Ashmore, "The Story of the Confederate Treasure," *Georgia Historical Quarterly,* II, 119-133. For information about funds removed from the treasury train at Greensboro and attached to the President's train, see M. H. Clark to B. N. Harrison, February 20, 1865, in Harrison Papers.

13. For an account of the disposition of the funds belonging to the Richmond banks see Otis Ashmore, "The Story of the Virginia Banks Funds," *Georgia Historical Quarterly,* II, 171-197. Captain Clark was under the impression that these funds amounted to about $230,000, whereas an 1886 report of Congress referred to them as about $450,000. Ashmore relates that the United States Court of Claims in 1893 awarded $16,987.88 to the Bank of Virginia and ruled that the balance of $78,276.49 was the property of the United States and that the bulk of the funds

were stolen in a raid by stragglers on the bank officials as they endeavored to transport their funds back to Virginia.

14. Robert McElroy, *Jefferson Davis, the Unreal and the Real,* II, 502.

15. *Sketches of War History,* III, 37.

16. *S. H. S. P.,* IX, 542 ff. and Clark Papers.

17. *Harrisons of Skimino,* 253-255.

18. *O. R.,* Ser. I, Vol. XLIX, Pt. I, 515 ff.

19. *O. R., (Navy)* Ser. I, Vol. IV, 555 and Vol. IX, 275-277.

20. *Harrisons of Skimino,* 263, and G. L. Colburn to A. J. Hanna, Oct. 7, 1936.

21. *O. R., (Navy)* Ser. I, Vol. I, 818, Vol. VI, 59 and 684, and Morgan *op. cit.,* 100.

22. *O. R., (Navy)* Ser. I, Vol. XIII, 288.

23. *New York Herald,* May 27, 1865.

24. E. C. Long, *Florida Breezes,* 380.

25. *O. R.,* Ser. I, Vol. XLIX, Pt. II, 556, 665.

26. *Ibid.,* Pt. I, 530-532.

27. J. Davis, *op. cit.,* II, 701-702.

28. *New York Herald,* May 15, 1865.

29. M. L. Avary, ed., *Recollections of Alexander H. Stephens,* 112-114.

30. *Harper's Weekly,* June 24 and May 27, 1865.

31. *London Saturday Review,* May 20, 1865.

32. Wood's Diary. Subsequent quotations attributed to Wood and facts relating to his escape are drawn from his diary unless otherwise cited.

33. E. A. Pollard, *Lee and His Lieutenants,* 619.

34. Lord Charnwood, *Abraham Lincoln,* 159. Davis described Breckinridge in the presidential campaign of 1860 as "the best representative of the interests and avowed policy of the South, as well as the best hope of the preservation of our Constitutional Union." See McElroy, *op. cit.,* I, 221.

35. *O. R.,* Ser. I, Vol. XLIX, Pt. II, 719.

36. E. J. Vann, "Reminiscences" (privately printed, Madison, Florida, 1937). Judge Vann was a son-in-law of D. G. Livingston.

CHAPTER VI

1. Long, *op. cit.,* 381.

2. M. H. Clark to B. N. Harrison, Feb. 20, 1866, Harrison Papers.

3. Diary of Tench F. Tilghman. Unless otherwise cited quotations and facts in this chapter are drawn from this source.

4. *O. R.,* Ser. I, Vol. XLVII, Pt. III, 653-654. David Levy Yulee (1810-1886), cousin of Judah P. Benjamin, who occupied a place of unique prominence in national affairs during the twenty years preceding the War, was born in St. Thomas in the West Indies. Early in the last century his family moved to Florida and when the peninsula, passing out of Spanish control in 1821, became a territory of the United States, Yulee's father automatically became an American citizen.

He was educated privately in Norfolk, Va., and studied law at St. Augustine with Judge Robert R. Reid, later governor of the state. His political career started in the Territorial Legislative Council and became established nationally when he represented Florida in Congress during the Seminole Indian War. There he was usually an opponent of John Quincy Adams. His strong advocacy of Florida's admission to statehood began when, as a member of the Constitutional Convention at St. Joseph, 1838-1839, he helped frame the constitution of the state.

In the United States Senate Yulee was one of the earliest champions of the building of ironclad vessels. His wealth made possible many Florida developments, notably a railroad from the Gulf of Mexico to the Atlantic Ocean, which he hoped would connect commercial activities of the lower South with New York. His line of steamers, which had been built to carry the products of Florida and Georgia to the North and to return with immigrants and tourists, was seized by the Federals and used for conveying troops. Mrs. Yulee and her sister, the latter the wife of Joseph Holt, Judge Advocate General of the United States Army, were noted for their beauty. See Leon Hühner, *David L. Yulee, Florida's First Senator* (privately printed, New York, 1917); also family papers of Hon. Samuel Yulee Way, Mayor (1938) of Orlando, Fla., whose grandfather, Captain Elias Yulee, was a brother of D. L. Yulee; and family papers in the possession of Mrs. Wallace Neff, Washington, D. C., sole surviving child of D. L. Yulee.

Mr. Mills M. Lord, Jr., of Oviedo, Florida, has been working for the past four years on a biography of David L. Yulee, as partial fulfillment of the degree of Master of Arts at the University of Florida.

5. Clark to Harrison, cited above, and Clark Papers.

6. M. H. Clark to B. N. Harrison, Aug. 26, 1867, and B. N. Harrison Memorandum, August 20, 1867, Harrison Papers.

7. "I have lately been informed," wrote Jefferson Davis to Watson Van Benthuysen from Montreal, July 5, 1867, "that you had expressed your readiness to pay the sum of money left in your hands whenever a written order for it from me was presented. . . . I have therefore drawn an order. . . . Incidental expenses had been already incurred and others of a like necessary character will accrue when I again appear before the court as required by the trial bond."

Davis's order read: "Watson Van Benthuysen of New Orleans, La., will pay to my attorney, Henry J. Leovy, the five thousand dollars in gold coins, more or less, left in his hands in May, 1865, by the party of gentlemen consisting of Messrs. Van Benthuysen, Clark, Dickinson, Tilghman, Scott and others, in trust to be used to pay expenses of my defense against a charge of treason, etc., before the United States Court, and for the benefit of my wife and children."

According to memoranda left by Burton N. Harrison, former secretary to Davis, he received from Watson Van Benthuysen in New York on Aug. 20, 1867, a certificate of deposit of $1,500 "on account of and to be transmitted to Jefferson Davis" and gave Van Benthuysen a statement that he was "entirely satisfied by your integrity and good faith in the transaction." On September 4, 1867, however, Davis requested Harrison not to "give Mr. V. Benthuysen any exonerating statement or receipt unless his settlement be first accepted by Mr. Clarke [last Acting Treasurer of the Confederacy] and such others as are involved with him." See Harrison Papers.

8. C. W. Yulee, "Senator Yulee of Florida," *Florida Historical Society Quarterly,* II, 10, and Rowland, *op. cit.,* IX, 450.

9. Clark to Harrison, Feb. 20, 1866, Harrison Papers.

10. *O. R.,* Ser. I, Vol. XLVII, Pt. III, 652-656.

11. *Ibid.*

12. *Ibid.*

13. *Ibid.*

14. *Ibid.*

15. Jefferson Davis to P. Phillips, Sept. 26, 1864, Davis Collection.

CHAPTER VII

1. *O. R.,* Ser. I, Vol. XLIX, Pt. II, 405, 715-717 and Ser. I, Vol. XLVII, Pt. III, 444-445.

2. *O. R.,* (*Navy*), Ser. I, Vol. XVII, and *New York Herald,* May 27, 28, 29, and 30, 1865.

3. *O. R.,* Ser. I, Vol. XXV, Pt. I, 338 and 324-333.

4. Facts about Breckinridge's escape through Florida and quotations subsequently attributed to him are drawn from his own account, the original of which is in the possession of Mrs. Lee Breckinridge Thomas.

5. M. E. Dickison, *Dickison and His Men,* 225.

6. Whitelaw Reid, *After the War: A Southern Tour,* 163-164.

7. W. W. Davis, *The Civil War and Reconstruction in Florida,* 53. In 1860 there were 61,700 slaves in Florida.

8. *O. R.,* Ser. II, Vol. VIII, 844 and Ser. I, Vol. XLIX, Pt. II, 902.

9. W. W. Davis, *op. cit.,* 324.

10. A. M. Murray, *Letters from the United States, Cuba and Canada,* (G. P. Putnam and Co., New York, 1857) 230-233.

11. Thaddeus Oliver to Mrs. Oliver, May 8, 1864, Rollins College Library.

12. Reid, *op. cit.,* 181.

13. *O. R.,* Ser. I, Vol. XLVII, Pt. III, 580.

14. *New York Herald,* May 27, 1865.

15. S. H. A. *Publications,* VI, 132-142, 210-219.

16. Inquiry about the character of George Sauls indicates that Breckinridge was not accurate in this estimate. Sauls was probably not unlike the unique type of Floridian so ably described by Marjorie Kinnan Rawlings in *The Yearling.*

CHAPTER VIII

1. W. D. Harville, "The Confederate Service of John Taylor Wood," 7, 54, 60.

2. The map used by Breckinridge was given by R. H. Russell to W. H. Toombs, who in turn gave it to W. L. Wittich. Wittich presented it to the Confederate Museum at Richmond.

3. Lloyd Lewis, *Sherman, Fighting Prophet*, 67.

4. "How the Seminole ever managed to discover the value of koonti starch as a food is . . . a problem. In its raw state this plant is deadly poisonous and yet for many years it has been the mainstay of these people and of the early white settlers. It is a beautiful fern-like plant of the sago family. It grows in the highland sand and rocks, in spite of fire and other drawbacks.

"Its turnip-like root is full of starch but also of poison. The root is pounded in a trough made from a log. The starch settles to the bottom and is washed to free it from fibre and poison. If an animal drinks the water from these washings he soon swells up and dies in agony. . . .

"Its leaves are valuable for decorative purposes and in many other ways it is one of the most interesting of all the tropical or semi-tropical plants which grow in South Florida."—John C. Gifford, *Billy Bowlegs and the Seminole War*, (The Triangle Co., Coconut Grove, Fla., 1925), 62-63.

5. *O. R.*, (*Navy*), Ser. I, Vol. V, 346.

6. The Dry Tortugas, a group of small, barren, isolated coral islands extending ten miles from east to west and forming the outermost tip of the reef from the end of the Florida peninsula about sixty-five miles west of Key West in the Gulf of Mexico, were discovered in 1513 by Juan Ponce de León and were so named by him because large loggerhead turtles lay their eggs there. These islands were the last lair of buccaneers, pirates, and wreckers during the early part of the nineteenth century. On Garden Key, in the center of the group, is Fort Jefferson, an irregular hexagonal structure, the construction of which was begun in 1846 when its site was regarded as the key to the defence of the United States in the Gulf. Though never completed it was

used as a prison during the period immediately following the War. Dr. Samuel A. Mudd, who was accused of complicity in the assassination of Lincoln, was perhaps the Fort's most famous prisoner. He rendered heroic service in the yellow fever epidemic. Fort Jefferson has recently been rehabilitated after having been abandoned many years and is now a national monument.

The proximity of the Gulf Stream with its abundant marine life, the presence of the richest coral reefs of Florida, and the absence of local fisheries led the Carnegie Institution to establish on Loggerhead Key in 1904 a marine biological laboratory for the study of the tropical ocean.

Since 1908 these islands have served as a Federal bird reservation in view of the fact that there is to be found here, as Audubon observed as early as 1832, the largest of the few nesting colonies of noddy and sooty terns in North America.

7. J. T. Wood, "Escape of the Confederate Secretary of War," *Century Magazine,* XLVII, 115, and *Harrisons of Skimino,* 262.

CHAPTER IX

1. Charles Vignoles, *Observations upon the Floridas,* (E. Bliss & E. White, New York, 1823), 118.

2. Lieut. L. M. Powell, U. S. N., built a temporary stockade at the mouth of the Miami River in the summer of 1836 to prevent Spanish filibustering expeditions of Cuba from selling arms and ammunition to the Seminole Indians in their warfare against the United States Government. This stockade was named, probably, in honor of Commodore James Dallas, then in command of the U. S. Naval forces in West Indian waters. Two years later Capt. L. B. Webster established a temporary post which continued the name of Fort Dallas and which was probably on the site of the former stockade. The fort was occupied from time to time until the close of the Seminole War in 1842. Between 1848-1850 Wil-

liam F. English, a South Carolina planter, built out of coral rock several structures which he later abandoned and which were occupied by U. S. troops in 1855 to quell an outbreak of the Indians near Lake Okeechobee. These buildings were moved in 1925 to a city park located at N. W. 2nd Ave., east of the River.

3. Wood, *loc. cit.,* 116-118.

4. *Harrisons of Skimino,* 262-263.

5. "Well, gentlemen, this is what is left of me," General Breckinridge is quoted as having announced to a group of Federal prisoners, who, after the Battle of Chickamauga, asked if they might see the famous Kentuckian. Whereupon one of them exclaimed: "Yes, and a damn fine specimen of humanity you are, too! There is not another such a hunk of humanity in our land! I voted for you once, and I want this cursed war over with so that I may vote for you again for president." John L. McKinnon, *The History of Walton County,* [Florida] (Byrd Printing Co., Atlanta, Ga., 1911), 289.

6. Statement of General Carlos M. de Rojas, Cardenas, May 19, 1936.

7. *New York Herald,* June 22 and 27, 1865.

8. U. S. Consul General at Havana to U. S. Acting Secretary of State, June 15, 1865.

9. *O. R.,* Ser. I, Vol. XLVII, Pt. III, 647-648 and Ser. II, Vol. VIII, 664.

10. *Boston Transcript,* April 18 and 21, 1865.

CHAPTER X

1. See p. 85.

2. Reagan, *op. cit.,* 211.

3. Louis Gruss, "Judah Philip Benjamin," *Louisiana Historical Quarterly,* XIX, 965. See also Reagan, *op. cit.,* 211.

4. Pierce Butler, *Judah P. Benjamin*, 365.

5. Wood's Diary.

6. Wood, *loc. cit.*, 110.

7. Reagan, *op. cit.*, 211.

8. Wood's Diary.

9. Butler, *op. cit.*, 363.

10. See Lillie B. McDuffee, *The Lures of Manatee*, 158, for aid given by the Lesley family, and Woodward, "Romantic Adventure of a Confederate Statesman," *Atlanta Journal*, March 10, 1935, for aid given by the McKay family.

11. Because of its impressiveness and its historic associations the Gamble mansion is one of the most interesting houses in this country. The charm of the mansion is expressed in high ceilings, thick walls, and deep-seated embrasures, sufficiently spacious for lounging seats. The mansion and gardens were purchased in 1924 by the Judah P. Benjamin Chapter of the United Daughters of the Confederacy and deeded to the State of Florida, whose Legislature has so far made two appropriations of $10,000 each for restoration and maintenance.

12. McDuffee, *op. cit.*, 160-161.

13. Rev. W. B. Tresca, son of the Captain, in McDuffee, *op. cit.*, 162.

14. *Ibid.*

15. *Ibid.*, 163, and Butler, *op. cit.*, 364.

16. H. A. McLeod, *The Escape of Judah P. Benjamin*, 3-4, and McLeod interview in Galveston *Daily News*, May 27, 1894. For a romantic account of the arrogant sea lord, José Gaspar (or Gasparilla) and his freebooters, see Edwin D. Lambright, *The Life and Exploits of Gasparilla, Last of the Buccaneers* (Hillsborough Printing Co., Tampa, Fla., 1936).

17. T. F. Davis, "Juan Ponce de León's Voyage to Florida," *Florida Historical Society Quarterly*, XIV, 41. (July, 1935.)

18. McLeod, *op. cit.*, 3-4.

19. One of the victims of this tragedy was Dr. Henry Perrine who had devoted a decade while U. S. Consul at Campeche, Yucatan, to collecting valuable plants and seeds of the tropics. At the time of his death he had ready for introduction into Florida approximately two hundred species and varieties of tropical economic plants and seeds. These were lost when the Indians burned his house. His family, after remaining concealed for many hours under a wharf, escaped. The former Mrs. Grover Cleveland in writing an account of the Indian Key Massacre hailed Dr. Perrine, her step-grandfather, as a "hero of horticulture."

20. McLeod, *op. cit.*, 4.

21. Tresca, in McDuffee, *op. cit.*, 163.

22. McLeod, *op. cit.*, 5.

23. Butler, *op. cit.*, 364 and *New York World*, Aug. 3, 1865.

24. Butler, *op. cit.*, 365-366.

25. New Orleans *Times-Democrat*, May 13, 1900.

CHAPTER XI

1. T. F. Davis (a nephew of George Davis), *A Genealogical Record of the Davis, Swann and Cabell Families*, (Pepper Printing Co., Gainesville, Fla., 1934), 9-10.

2. T. W. Davis to A. J. Hanna, June 18, 1937.

3. George Davis to his son, Junius, Nov. 14, 1865, in possession of T. W. Davis, Wilmington, N. C.

4. *O. R.*, Ser. I, Vol. XLVII, Pt. III, 597.

5. *Harper's Weekly*, June 3, 1865.

6. *O. R.,* Ser. I, Vol. XLVII, Pt. III, 322, 498, 581. Allison's career was unique. He had started out as an Indian trader, became a merchant, held the rank of captain in the state militia, practiced law and had been a judge. Finally he was elected Speaker of the House in the Florida Legislature, was a member of the Committee which drew up Florida's ordinance of secession, at the close of the War succeeded John Milton as Governor, and was then imprisoned.

7. *Tallahassee Floridian and Journal,* May 20, 1865.

8. W. W. Davis, *op. cit.,* 53.

9. *Tallahassee Floridian and Journal,* May 20, 1865.

10. C. D. W. Murat to E. M. McCook, May 19, 1865, Rollins College Library.

11. *New York Times,* July 2, 1865.

12. S. P. Chase to the President, May 21, 1865, Johnson Papers.

13. J. W. Schuckers, *The Life and Public Services of Salmon Portland Chase,* 524.

14. *New York Herald,* June 1, 1865.

15. J. G. Harris to the President, June 9, 1865, Johnson Papers.

16. W. W. Davis, *op. cit.,* 351-352.

17. Reid, *op. cit.,* 169-171.

18. Long, *op. cit.,* 303. The author of these spirited lines probably did not know how important Florida's contributions of salt and beef had been to the Confederacy.

19. W. R. Thayer, *The Life and Letters of John Hay,* I, 155.

20. *O. R.,* Ser. I, Vol. VI, 251-252.

21. W. W. Davis, *op. cit.,* 322-323.

22. Reid, *op. cit.,* 162.

23. Thayer, *op. cit.,* I, 161-162.

24. *Messages and Papers,* VI, 213-215.

25. *New York Herald,* Feb. 23, 1864.

26. George Davis to Junius Davis, *loc. cit.*

27. *O. R.,* Ser. I, Vol. XLVII, Pt. III, 652-653.

28. This captain was probably Ramon Canova or Adolphus Pacetty, descendants of early Florida colonists who helped found New Smyrna when in 1763-83 Florida was the "fourteenth" English colony. This unique settlement was established by Dr. Andrew Turnbull, Sir William Duncan, and Sir Richard Temple, who in 1768 brought over about fifteen hundred Minorcans, Greeks, and Italians to engage in an ambitious agricultural development on six grants totaling 101,400 acres. See Carita Doggett, *Dr. Andrew Turnbull and the New Smyrna Colony, Florida,* ('The Drew Press, Jacksonville, 1919).

29. Statement of Mrs. George Rountree, only surviving child of George Davis, to A. J. Hanna in Wilmington, N. C., Sept. 21, 1937.

30. George Davis to Junius Davis, *loc. cit.*

31. Thayer, *op. cit.,* I, 165-166. Hay and Nicolay wrote a part of their monumental ten-volume work on Lincoln while guests at the old Seminole Hotel, Winter Park, Florida, according to *Lochmede,* a tourist paper, of March 2, 1888.

32. Lieutenant Commander Edward Conroy, U.S.N., to the Secretary of the Navy, Nov. 15, 1865.

33. George Davis to Junius Davis, *loc. cit.*

CHAPTER XII

1. Butler, *op. cit.,* 372-373.

2. H. H. Hagan, "Judah P. Benjamin," *American Law Review,* XLVIII, 381-382.

3. Butler, *op. cit.,* 372.

4. *London Times,* May 9, 1884.

5. *The Green Bag,* X, 398.

6. Hagan, *loc. cit.,* 382.

7. *The Green Bag,* X, 396; Butler, *op. cit.,* 379-380, 383; and *Georgetown Law Journal,* I, 146-151.

8. Gruss, *loc. cit.,* 1062.

9. *London Times,* May 9, 1884. Prof. Robert D. Meade of Randolph-Macon Woman's College, Lynchburg, Va., has recently made an intensive study of Benjamin, both in this country and in Europe and expects to publish a biography of the Confederate Secretary of State in 1939.

10. Philadelphia *Press,* April 24, 1865.

11. Phillips, *op. cit.,* 236-237, 252-258, and P. A. Stovall, *Robert Toombs* (Cassell Pub. Co., New York, 1892), 286, 314.

12. *O. R.,* Ser. II, Vol. VIII, 534, 550.

13. Dickison, *op. cit.,* 227.

14. This letter is in the possession of Mrs. Wm. C. Goodloe, Lexington, Ky., a granddaughter of General Breckinridge.

15. Wood's Diary.

16. James Wilson to J. C. Breckinridge, Aug. 1, 1868, Breckinridge Collection.

17. See p. 266, reference number 4.

18. John Witherspoon Breckinridge, born in 1850, was called "Owen" in appreciation of the heavy vote given his father by the people of Owen County, Ky., that year in his re-election to Congress. He was at one time a member of the California Senate. One of his daughters is Lady Fermor-Hesketh.

19. Frankfort, Ky., *Yeoman,* Dec. 21, 1865, and J. W. Headley, *Confederate Operations in Canada and New York,* 449.

20. *O. R.,* Ser. II, Vol. VIII, 747.

21. J. C. Breckinridge to G. M. Bruce, Oct. 26, 1865, in possession of Mrs. Mary Breckinridge, Wendover, Ky., a granddaughter of General Breckinridge.

22. Louisville, Ky., *Courier-Journal,* Nov. 13, 1875.

23. Diary of J. C. Breckinridge, 1866-68, in possession of Mrs. Mary Breckinridge.

24. Horace Greeley to George Shaw, April 17, 1867, Breckinridge Collection.

25. Frankfort, Ky., *Yeoman,* Sept. 18, 1875.

26. W. P. Johnston to J. C. Breckinridge, Jan. 8 and 25, 1869, Breckinridge Collection.

27. Robert E. Lee to J. C. Breckinridge, Jan. 28, 1869, Breckinridge Collection.

28. When asked for proof of his editorial observation in J. B. Jones, *A Rebel War Clerk's Diary* that Breckinridge's brilliance and promise came to naught, Howard Swiggett, author of *The Rebel Raider: A Life of John Hunt Morgan,* quoted a letter of Bragg to Davis in Don C. Seitz, *Braxton Bragg,* 401, which, according to Mr. Swiggett, "sums up the general verdict against Breckinridge." For Breckinridge's reply to Bragg, see *S. H. S. P.,* XIV, 475-477.

29. H. D. Capers, *The Life and Times of C. G. Memminger,* 372 ff.

30. Sisters of Mercy to the President, Nov. 23, 1865, Trenholm Collection.

31. F. G. de Fontaine, Financial Editor of the *New York Herald* to G. A. Trenholm, Nov. 19, 1874, Trenholm Papers.

32. Charleston, S. C., *News and Courier,* Dec. 11, 1876.

33. S. R. Mallory to Mrs. Mallory, June 17, 1865, in possession of Mrs. William Fisher, Jr., Pensacola, a granddaughter of Mallory.

34. Occie Clubbs, "Stephen Russell Mallory, The Elder," A. M. thesis (unpublished), University of Florida, Gainesville, 1936.

35. *London Times,* May 29, 1865.

36. *Harper's Weekly,* June 24, 1865.

37. *Chicago Tribune,* June 7, 1865.

38. *London Saturday Review,* May 20, 1865.

39. W. E. Dodd, *Jefferson Davis,* 372.

40. McElroy, *op. cit.,* II, 614.

41. *Ibid.,* 625, 617.

42. J. Davis, *op. cit.,* II, 764.

43. L. F. Hill, "The Confederate Exodus to Latin America," *Southwestern Historical Quarterly,* XXXIX, 100-134, 161-199, 309-326.

44. Mr. Rembert W. Patrick is working in the University of North Carolina at Chapel Hill on a doctoral dissertation, "Jefferson Davis and his Cabinet," treating the relations between the chief executive and his official advisers and making a study of the administration of the six departments.

45. *O. R.,* Ser. IV, Vol. III, 1184.

46. J. L. M. Curry, *Civil History of the Government of the Confederate States,* 83.

47. E. A. Pollard, "The Confederate Congress," *Galaxy Magazine,* VI, 758. For a favorable description of the Confederate Congress see John Goode, "The Confederate Congress," *The Conservative Review,* IV, 97-113.

48. Curry, *op. cit.,* 81-82.

49. *London Times,* Oct. 9, 1862.

50. *London Morning Post,* May 27, 1865.

BIBLIOGRAPHY

The assembling of material for this volume has been an adventure almost as varied and as exciting as the episode described. Facts of the narrative have been drawn from the writings of the Confederate President and Cabinet and those who accompanied them, from supplementary manuscripts, from official and unofficial reports and records, from English and American magazines and newspapers, and from other contemporary sources. Two members of the Cabinet wrote their accounts on the high seas while escaping to Europe. Others set down their recollections in prison. Neither group had access to notes and official records nor the use of maps and other reference materials essential to accuracy. Their articles appeared in such magazines as the *Century* and *McClure's* from four to six decades ago. While the retreat of the Confederate Government has been described in general and while particulars relating to parts of it have been printed, it has been surprising to discover that no one has previously pieced together the entire narrative and treated it with an adequate background.

The writing of this book has, therefore, involved the organization of available facts from widely scattered sources, their amplification with related materials, and the correction of errors inadvertently made in previous accounts. This undertaking, which was begun four years ago, has necessitated visits to localities from Richmond to Havana where one or more members of the Cabinet found a refuge for a night or more. Consultations with families involved in the flight and a long and careful checking of sources still leave many facts to be gathered to complete the story. It is hoped that the publication of this book will assist in uncovering much relevant new material.

Participants in tragic experiences are sometimes disinclined to reveal their part in them afterwards. Several members of the Confederate Cabinet declined ever to discuss this episode. Their withdrawal from national politics lessened public interest in their lives and work. Year by year their names have become less known and while a few of them have been subjects of biographies, such studies with but one, possibly two exceptions, have been neither complete nor critical. Of the seventeen members of the official Davis family, fourteen (Benjamin, Bragg, Breckinridge, Davis, Hunter, Mallory, Memminger, Randolph, Reagan, Seddon, Smith, Toombs, Walker, and Watts) are included in the *Dictionary of American Biography.*

No endeavor has been made to include in this bibliography other than the essential manuscripts, publications, and references.

I. MANUSCRIPTS

Breckinridge MSS. Collection, Library of Congress. The John C. Breckinridge part of this collection pertains almost exclusively to the period beginning with Breckinridge's return to Kentucky in 1869.

Breckinridge, John C., letter to his son, "Owen." In possession of Mrs. Lee Breckinridge Thomas, 1404 LeRoy Ave., Berkeley, Calif. Written on the British West Indian Mail Steamer, *Shannon,* en route from Havana to Southampton, dated July 6, 1865, this detailed account of his escape from Madison, Fla., to Cardenas, Cuba, with the diary of Col. Wood, forms the basis for Chapters VII, VIII, and IX.

Breckinridge, John C., Diary, 1866-1868. In possession of Mrs. Mary Breckinridge, Wendover, Ky. It contains interesting information about Breckinridge's exile in Europe.

Clark, Micajah H., Papers, Library of Congress. Receipts covering the disbursement of the last funds of the Confederacy.

Davis, Jefferson, Collection, Library of Congress.

Harrison, Family Papers, Library of Congress. Letters of Jefferson Davis and M. H. Clark with memoranda by Burton N. Harrison constitute material indispensable to a study of this subject.

Johnson, Andrew, Papers, Library of Congress. The year 1865 contains letters pertaining to this subject.

Stanton, Edwin M., Papers, Library of Congress.

Tilghman, Tench Francis, Diary, April and May, 1865. In possession of his grandson, Dr. Tench Francis Tilghman, St. Johns College, Annapolis, Md. Chapter VI is largely based on this diary.

Trenholm, George A., Collection, Library of Congress. With a few notable exceptions, these letters begin with the Reconstruction period.

II. ARTICLES IN PERIODICALS

Abbeville, S. C., *Press and Banner,* Feb. 21, 1917.

Ashmore, Otis, "The Story of the Virginia Banks Funds," *Georgia Historical Quarterly,* II, 171-179, (December, 1918).

Aull, John K., in Columbia, S. C., *State,* September 13, 20, and 27, 1931.

Boston Transcript, Daniel Noyes Haskell, Editor. Republican. April 18, 21, 28, and May 1, 1865. Editorials demanding severe punishment for the Confederate leaders.

Charleston, S. C., *News and Courier,* December 11, 1876.

Chicago Tribune, Joseph Medill, Editor, who was credited with having been the foremost organizer of the Republican Party. May 2, June 7, and 21, 1865. Editorials bitterly denouncing Davis and his associates.

Church Intelligencer, May 4, 1865. Founded at Raleigh, N. C., 1860. It was moved to Charlotte in 1864, when F. M. Hubbard and George M. Everhart became editors. Account of the service held in St. Peters Church, Charlotte, April 23, 1865, attended by President Davis and the Cabinet and an editorial based on the sermon Everhart preached that day.

Confederate Veteran. Published monthly from January, 1893 through December, 1932, 40 vols., in the interests of veterans of the Confederate military forces. Articles cover a wide variety of subjects, are valuable in parts but not uniformly accurate.

"Confederate Naval Cadets," XII, 170-171, (April, 1904).

"Survivor of President Davis's Escort," XXXIV, 368-369, (October, 1926).

"The Last of the C. S. Ordnance Department," XXXIV, 450-452, (December, 1926) and XXXV, 15-16, (January, 1927).

"The Confederate Treasure Train," XXV, 257-259, (June, 1917).

"Last of the Confederate Treasury Department," XXXVII, 423-425, (November, 1929).

Danville, Va., *Weekly Register,* April 7, 1865, and May 17, 1914, and April 13, 1919.

Folk, Winston, "A Treasure Hunt in Reverse," United States Naval Institute *Proceedings,* LXIII, 380-387, (March, 1937).

Frankfort, Ky., *Yeoman,* December 21, 1865, and September 18, 1875.

Galveston, Tex., *Daily News,* May 27, 1894. Account of Benjamin's escape by the Confederate sailor, H. A. McLeod, who accompanied him. This account, enlarged and edited, was published as an eight-page pamphlet at an undetermined date by the Tribune Publishing Co., Tampa.

Georgetown Law Journal, I, 146-151 (March, 1913). Published quarterly since 1911 by the students of the School of Law, Georgetown University. Benjamin's Farewell Address to the English Bar.

Goode, John, "The Confederate Congress," *The Conservative Review,* IV, 97-113, (September, 1900). A quarterly publication of five volumes, 1899-1901. Goode was a member of the Confederate House of Representatives from 1862-65.

Green Bag, The, X, 396-401, (September, 1898). "An entertaining magazine for lawyers," published in Boston, 1889-1914.

Gruss, Louis, "Judah Philip Benjamin," *The Louisiana Historical Quarterly,* XIX, 964-1068, (October, 1936).

Hagan, H. H., "Judah P. Benjamin," *American Law Review,* (Later, *United States Law Review*), XLVIII, (May-June, 1914) 365-389.

Harper's Weekly, Fletcher Harper, Editor. March 11, April 15, May 27, June 6, and 24, 1865. The four Harper brothers, publishers of this influential illustrated magazine changed from Democrats to War Republicans after the firing of Fort Sumter. The average circulation of the magazine in 1865 was 160,000.

Harrison, Burton, N., "The Capture of Jefferson Davis," *Century Magazine,* XXVII, 130-145, (November, 1883).

Henderson, Dr. Archibald, in Greensboro, N. C. *Daily News,* September 1, 1935. An excellent summary of the Confederate Cabinet.

Hill, Lawrence F., "The Confederate Exodus to Latin America," *Southwestern Historical Quarterly,* XXXIX, 100-134, 161-199, 309-326, (October, 1935 and January and April, 1936).

Holladay, Florence Elizabeth, "The Powers of the Commander of the Confederate Trans-Mississippi Department, 1863-1865," *Southwestern Historical Quarterly,* XXI, 279-298 and 333-359, (January and April, 1918).

London *Morning Post,* May 27, 1865.

London *Saturday Review,* May 20, 1865.

London *Times,* April 3, 25, and May 29, 1865; May 9, 1884. Perhaps the most reliable exponent of British public opinion. It had strong sympathies for the South.

Louisville, Ky., *Courier-Journal,* November 13, 1875, and January 13, 1882.

Mallory, Stephen R., "The Last Days of the Confederate Government," *McClure's Magazine,* XVI, 99-107 (December, 1900) and 239-248, (January, 1901). Written in Fort LaFayette Prison.

McCaleb, W. F., "The Organization of the Post Office Department of the Confederacy," *The American Historical Review*, XII, 67-74, (October, 1906).

New York *Daily News*, Benjamin Wood, Editor. Pro-Confederate. April 6, 1865, an editorial urging Lincoln to invite the Southern people to return to the Union. The *Chicago Tribune*, June 21, 1865, in denouncing the policy of the *News* said: "Never did dog serve master more faithfully and affectionately than the New York *News* licked the wounds of the rebellion."

New York Herald, James Gordon Bennett, Editor. Republican. February 23, 1864; May 15, 27, 28, 29, 30; June 1, 22, 27; July 4, 23, 30, 31, and August 20, 1865. In the last five issues named are detailed descriptions of scenes and incidents connected with the flight of the Cabinet, written by an unidentified member of the escaping party.

New York Post, William Cullen Bryant, Editor. Republican. May 2, 1865, an editorial proposing that the more prominent Confederate leaders be permanently disfranchised.

New York Times, Henry J. Raymond, Editor. Probably the most orthodox of the Republican Party press, this newspaper devoted much space during April, May, and June, 1865, to arguments for hanging Davis and insulting Lee.

April 12, May 1 and 28, and June 1, 1865, and January 6, 1882, accounts of the movements of the Confederate treasure train by Walter Philbrook, Chief Teller of the Confederate Treasury Department and others.

New York Tribune, Horace Greeley, Editor. Republican. Aspired to an advanced position. Occasionally radical.

April 11 and 13, 1865, editorials opposing the demand of the *Times* that Davis be hanged.

New York World, Manton Marble, Editor. Democratic.

June 12, 1865, an editorial advocating forbearance rather than severity in punishing Confederate leaders.

June 22, 1865, account of the escape of John C. Breckinridge.

August 3, 1865, account of the escape of Judah P. Benjamin.

Philadelphia *Press,* April 24, 1865.

Pollard, E. A., "The Confederate Congress," *Galaxy,* VI, 749-758, (December, 1868). Editor of the Richmond, Va., *Examiner,* 1861-67, Pollard was an able and prolific though prejudiced writer.

Richmond, Va., *Evening Whig,* April 4 and 25, 1865. Issued as an Union paper.

Richmond, Va., *Times,* P. H. Aylett, Editor. April 21 and 22, 1865. This paper supported Johnson's reconstruction policy.

Southern Historical Society Papers, Richmond, Va., 47 volumes extending from 1876 to 1930. Uniformly reliable. Much valuable information not available elsewhere.

"Resources of the Confederacy in 1865," III, 97-111, (March, 1877).

"The True Story of the Capture of Jefferson Davis," V, 97-126, (March, 1878).

"The Confederate States Navy Yard at Charlotte, N. C., 1862-1865," XL, 183-194, (September, 1915).

"The Last Days of the Confederate Treasury," IX, 542-556, (December, 1881).

"The Confederate Treasure," X, 137-141, (March, 1882).

"Last Letters and Telegrams of the Confederacy," XII, 97-105, (March, 1884).

"The Evacuation of Richmond," XXV, 267-273, (January-December, 1897).

"Retreat of the Cabinet," XXVI, 96-101, (January-December, 1898).

"Cabinet Meeting at Charlotte," XLI, 61-67, (September, 1916).

Southern History Association *Publications*

"President Davis's Last Official Meeting," V, 291-299, (July, 1901).

"History of the Confederate Treasury," V, 1-34, 95-150, 188-227, (January, March and May, 1901).

"Hon. John H. Reagan's Letter to President Johnson," VI, 132-142, 210-219, (March and May, 1902).

Swallow, W. H., "Retreat of the Confederate Government from Richmond to the Gulf," *Magazine of American History,* XV, 596-608, (June, 1886). The author accompanied Breckinridge through Georgia.

Tallahassee, Fla., *Floridian and Journal,* May 20, 1865.

Yulee, C. Wickliffe, "Senator Yulee of Florida," *Florida Historical Society Quarterly,* II, 26-43, 3-22, (April and July, 1909).

Walmsley, J. E., "The Last Meeting of the Confederate Cabinet," *Mississippi Valley Historical Review,* VI, 336-349, (December, 1919). A careful study of Cabinet meetings held while the Government was retreating.

Welles, Gideon, "Lincoln and Johnson," *Galaxy Magazine,* XIII, 525-537. An account of Lincoln's last Cabinet meeting, April 14, 1865.

Wood, John Taylor, "Escape of the Confederate Secretary of War," *Century Magazine,* XLVII, 110-123, (November, 1893). Colonel Wood's colorful account was edited for juveniles and included in a volume containing similarly thrilling adventures entitled *Famous Adventures and Prison Escapes of the Civil War,* (D. Appleton-Century Co., New York, 1893). Since then it has been through thirteen printings.

Woodward, Margaret Almeria, "Romantic Adventure of a Confederate Statesman," *Atlanta Journal,* March 10, 1935.

III. BIOGRAPHIES AND MEMOIRS

Allen, Alexander V. G., *Life and Letters of Phillips Brooks,* E. P. Dutton & Co., New York, 1901, 3 vols.

Ashe, S. A., *George Davis,* Edwards & Broughton Printing Co., Raleigh, N. C., 1916.

Avary, Myrta L., ed., *Recollections of Alexander H. Stephens,* Doubleday, Page & Co., New York, 1910.

Butler, Pierce, *Judah P. Benjamin,* [American Crisis Biographies] George W. Jacobs & Co., Philadelphia, Pa., 1907.
Contains letters written by Benjamin to his family describing his escape from Georgia to England.

Capers, Henry D., *The Life and Times of C. G. Memminger,* Everett Waddey Co., Richmond, Va., 1893.
The author was for a short time Chief Clerk and Disbursing Officer under Secretary of the Treasury Memminger. The appendix contains valuable documents relating to the finances of the Confederacy.

Charnwood, Lord, *Abraham Lincoln,* [Makers of the 19th Century] Henry Holt & Co., New York, 1917.

Clubbs, Occie, "Stephen Russell Mallory, The Elder," Unpublished A. M. thesis, University of Florida, Gainesville, 1936. An excellent study.

[Davis, Varina Howell] *Jefferson Davis, ex-President of the Confederate States, A Memoir,* by his Wife, Belford Co., New York, 1890, 2 vols.
Contains a vivid description of the flight of her husband and herself, and a bitter arraignment of Northern officials.

Dickison, Mary Elizabeth, *Dickison and His Men,* Courier-Journal Job Printing Co., Louisville, Ky., 1890. Eulogistic.

Dodd, W. E., *Jefferson Davis,* [American Crisis Biographies] Geo. W. Jacobs & Co., Philadelphia, 1907.

Dowd, Clement, *Life of Zebulon B. Vance,* Observer Printing & Publishing House, Charlotte, N. C., 1897.

Duke, Basil W., *Reminiscences,* Doubleday, Page & Co., New York, 1911.

Harville, W. D., "Confederate Service of John Taylor Wood," Unpublished A. M. thesis, Southern Methodist University, Dallas, Texas, 1935. Incomplete.

Hunter, Martha T., *A Memoir of Robert M. T. Hunter,* Neale Publishing Co., Washington, D. C., 1903.

Lewis, Lloyd, *Sherman, Fighting Prophet,* Harcourt, Brace & Co., New York, *ca.* 1932.

Lubbock, F. R., *Six Decades in Texas,* Ben C. Jones & Co., Austin, Tex., 1900.

McElroy, Robert, *Jefferson Davis, The Unreal and the Real,* Harper & Bros., New York, 1937. 2 vols.

Morgan, James Morris, *Recollections of a Rebel Reefer,* Houghton Mifflin Co., Boston, 1917. The recollections of this son-in-law of George A. Trenholm are part fact and part imagination but always interesting.

Noll, Arthur Howard, *Life of General Edmund Kirby-Smith,* The University of the South Press, Sewannee, Tenn., 1907. Neither adequate nor critical.

Phillips, U. B., *Life of Robert Toombs,* The Macmillan Company, New York, 1913.

Pollard, E. A., *Lee and His Lieutenants,* E. B. Treat & Co., 1867. Over-sentimental.

Reagan, J. H., *Memoirs, with Special Reference to Secession and the Civil War,* Neale Pub. Co., New York, 1906. Edited by W. F. McCaleb, this volume treats Reagan's early life, his political career prior to 1861, the organization of the Confederacy, the War period, and Reconstruction.

Rowland, Dunbar, *Jefferson Davis, Constitutionalist,* Miss. Dept. of Archives and History, Jackson, 1923, 10 vols. Contains statements about the flight of the Cabinet from principal participants.

Schuckers, J. W., *The Life and Public Services of Salmon Portland Chase,* D. Appleton & Co., New York, 1874.

Sherman, W. T., *Memoirs,* D. Appleton & Co., New York, 1875. 2 vols.

Simms, Henry Harrison, *Life of Robert M. T. Hunter,* William Byrd Press, Richmond, 1935.

Stillwell, Lucille, *John Cabell Breckinridge,* The Caxton Printers, Caldwell, Idaho, 1936. A brief, non-critical work.

Thayer, W. R., *The Life and Letters of John Hay,* Houghton Mifflin Co., Boston, Mass., 1915.

IV. GENERAL WORKS

Andrews, Eliza F., *The War-Time Journal of a Georgia Girl,* D. Appleton Co., New York, 1908. Valuable for its description of conditions in Washington, Ga., during the last days of the Confederacy.

Battles and Leaders of the Civil War, The Century Co., New York, *ca.* 1887-89, 4 vols. A valuable collection of war papers by Union and Confederate officers, many of which were originally published in the *Century Magazine,* ably edited by Robert Underwood Johnson and C. C. Buel.

Bullock, James D., *Secret Service of the Confederate States in Europe,* Richard Bentley & Son, London, 1883, 2 vols. Captain Bullock was the naval representative of the Confederacy in Europe and its agent in building and fitting out cruisers.

Confederate Soldier in the Civil War, The, The Prentice Press, Louisville, Ky., 1897. Published as a "companion volume" to Harper's *Pictorial History of the Civil War, The Pictorial Battles of the Civil War,* and Frank Leslie's *Soldier in the Civil War* the purpose of this volume was to present, from the Confederate standpoint a compilation of official Confederate records, reports of officers, and articles from many authors. It was edited by Ben La Bree and contains valuable, though occasionally inaccurate, information about the organization of the Confederate Government with lists of civil and military officials.

Curry, J. L. M., *Civil History of the Government of the Confederate States,* Johnson Publishing Co., Richmond, Va., 1901.

The author represented Alabama in the House of Representatives before the War and in that body of the Confederacy during a part of the War. His treatment of the civil history of the Confederacy, in particular the Constitution, is valuable.

Dana, C. A., *Recollections of the Civil War*, D. Appleton & Co., New York, 1898. Observations included in this book were made by the author when he was Stanton's Assistant Secretary of War with a roving commission to visit battlefronts. He later became famous as Editor of the *New York Sun*.

Davis, Jefferson, *The Rise and Fall of the Confederate Government*, D. Appleton & Co., New York, 1881, 2 vols. Contains an account of the retreat of the Confederate Government by the President of the Confederacy. The evident purpose of the author is to justify his actions. It is unfortunately more controversial than descriptive.

Davis, W. W., *Civil War and Reconstruction in Florida*, (Columbia University *Studies in History, Economics and Public Law*, LIII) Longmans, Green & Co., New York, 1913.

Harrisons of Skimino, The, privately printed, New York, 1910. This memoir of the Harrison family was edited by Fairfax Harrison from material collected by Francis Burton Harrison. It contains an account of the retreat of the Confederate Cabinet written by Burton N. Harrison, Secretary to President Jefferson Davis, and first printed in the *Century Magazine*, November, 1883. When he received the proof sheets from the *Century*, Harrison submitted them to Davis and invited his comments. Davis made a number of suggestions, not all of which were adopted by Harrison. The Davis notes are included in full in *The Harrisons of Skimino*.

Richard Watson Gilder, Editor of the *Century* at the time Harrison's article was published, wrote of it to Mrs. Harrison: "It is of absorbing interest, told with evident frankness and truthfulness, and with a refreshing sense of humor giving the comedy along with the tragedy of the events. It . . . [will] be one of the most interesting and important contributions to history that the *Century* has published. . . ." See her *Recollections, Grave and Gay,* 220.

Headley, John W., *Confederate Operations in Canada and New York,* Neale Publishing Co., New York, 1906. The author accompanied the Cabinet during a part of the flight.

Hunter, Robert, ed., *Sketches of War History, 1861-65,* Robert Clarke & Co., Cincinnati, Ohio, 1890. A series of twenty papers prepared for the Ohio Commandery of the Military Order of the Loyal Legion. In Volume III is an account of Stoneman's last campaign and a description of the pursuit of Davis and the Cabinet. Written from a patriotic point of view.

Johnston, Joseph E., *Narrative of Military Operations Directed During the Late War Between the States,* D. Appleton & Co., New York, 1874.

Kirk, Charles H., ed., *History of the 15th Pennsylvania Volunteer Cavalry,* Philadelphia, 1906, 2 vols. Volume II includes an account of the pursuit of Davis and the Cabinet.

Long, Ellen Call, *Florida Breezes,* Ashmead Bros., Jacksonville, Fla., 1883. This rare book presents an authentic description of Florida conditions before and during the War. Mrs. Long lived her entire life (1825-1905) in Tallahassee where as a daughter of General R. K. Call, twice Territorial Governor and Congressional Representative, she enjoyed unusual opportunities for observation.

McDuffee, Lillie B., *The Lures of Manatee,* Marshall & Bruce Co., Nashville, Tenn., 1933. Contains letters and statements possessing valuable information about Benjamin's stay in and near the Gamble mansion.

Parker, William H. *Recollections of a Naval Officer,* Chas. Scribner's Sons, New York, 1883. A straightforward, heroic account of the movements of the Confederate treasure train, written by the commanding officer of the midshipmen who guarded it. Honor graduate of the U. S. Naval Academy at

Annapolis, Parker organized and was Superintendent of the Confederate States Naval Academy. After the War he served as U. S. Minister to Korea and as President of the Maryland Agricultural College (University of Maryland). Commodore Foxhall Alexander Parker, U. S. N., was his brother.

Reid, Whitelaw, *After the War: A Southern Tour,* Moore, Wilstack & Baldwin, New York, 1866. Consists of observations made by the author while accompanying Chief Justice S. P. Chase on an extensive tour of the South. Originally published as letters to newspapers. Reid was later editor of the *New York Tribune.*

Richardson, James D., ed., *A Compilation of the Messages and Papers of the Confederacy, Including Diplomatic Correspondence, 1861-65,* U. S. Publishing Co., Nashville, Tenn., 1906, 2 vols.

Rippy, J. Fred, *United States and Mexico,* Alfred A. Knopf, New York, 1926.

Roman, Alfred, *The Military Operations of General Beauregard,* Harper & Bros., New York, 1884, 2 vols. Official and other documents included in the appendix constitute the chief value of this work.

Scharf, J. Thomas, *History of the Confederate States Navy,* Rogers and Sherwood, New York, 1887. The author was one of the midshipmen who guarded the Confederate treasure.

Soley, J. R., *The Blockade and the Cruisers,* [The Navy in the Civil War] Chas. Scribner's Sons, New York, 1903. Describes the blockade of Southern ports, the operations of the blockade-runners and commerce destroyers, and stirring episodes in which the latter were involved.

Taylor, Richard, *Destruction and Reconstruction,* D. Appleton & Co., New York, 1879. Contains an account of the surrender of the Confederate forces in Alabama and Mississippi by the son of General Zachary Taylor.

Under Both Flags, J. S. Round & Co., Boston, 1896.

Wise, John S., *The End of an Era,* Houghton Mifflin Co., Boston, 1902. Valuable for its description of conditions surrounding Lee's army immediately preceding the surrender. Wise reported these conditions to President Davis at Danville April 8, 1865.

V. GOVERNMENT PUBLICATIONS

Official Records of the Union and Confederate Armies, Washington, D. C., 1881-1901, 70 vols. The compilation and publication of these records by the United States Government was projected near the close of the first administration of President Lincoln, but not much progress was made until 1874. Shortly after the evacuation of Richmond, many boxes of Confederate Archives were shipped to Washington from various southern points. Later a division was organized in the Adjutant General's Office in the War Department for the collection and safekeeping of official papers of the Confederacy. Many papers of great historical value were destroyed by the Confederate Cabinet and other leaders before and during their flight from Richmond. Other records were accidentally burned, destroyed, or hidden. The cost involved in the publication of the 128 books, an index, and an atlas which made these invaluable historical records available was approximately $3,000,000.

Official Records of the Union and Confederate Navies. Washington, D. C., 1894, 1921, 30 vols., illustrations. Published by the Naval War Records Office under authority of Congress. The records of the Confederate Navy are incomplete because so many of the papers were burned at the close of the War.

Richardson, James D., ed., *A Compilation of the Messages and Papers of the Presidents, 1789-1897,* 10 vols., Government Printing Office, Washington, 1896-1900.

VI. MAPS

Map of the State of Florida compiled in the Bureau of Topogl. Engrs. from the most recent authorities and prepared by order of the Honorable Jeff. Davis, Secretary of War, in conformity with a resolution of the Senate of the 11th Feby. 1856, calling for "a general map of the Peninsula of Florida, illustrative of the recent surveys for a canal, executed by virtue of the appropriations made for that purpose." 1856. Reproduced in 1875.

Miscellaneous maps of the Southern States and the Caribbean Sea.

The Trans-Mississippi Department of the Confederacy, June 30, 1863, in the *Atlas* accompanying the *Official Records of the Union and Confederate Armies.*

United States Coast and Geodetic Survey *Charts,* Numbers 162, 163, 1248-1257.

United States Coast and Geodetic Survey Progress *Reports.*

ACKNOWLEDGMENTS

The flight of the Confederate Cabinet is a subject which apparently holds a widespread and strong grip on the public. Judged by the unusual interest expressed in this undertaking, its varied appeal extends to the North as well as to the South, to the young as well as to the elderly. Evidence of this exists in the help given by a large number of people in all parts of this country and even abroad in assembling and checking the facts in this volume.

Acknowledgment is gratefully made of the uniform courtesy extended and assistance rendered by those in charge of records in the State, War, Navy, and Treasury Departments at Washington and the staffs of the various libraries and historical and other organizations and individuals consulted; in particular the Library of Congress, the National Archives, the American Antiquarian Society, the Boston Athenaeum, the New York Public Library, the Department of Archives and History of the State of Mississippi, the Mississippi Valley Historical Association, the Rollins College Library, the search room of the London *Times,* the Virginia State Library, the Confederate Museum at Richmond, and the Howard Memorial Library of New Orleans.

Without the assistance of Carl Gillette Alvord and John Rae this volume would have lacked much. Mr. Rae's spirited illustrations clarify the narrative and stir the imagination to a clearer understanding of conditions. Mr. Alvord's maps, ably executed by Mr. Allen Clague, are the result of a scientific study and personal exploration by him, not only throughout the length of the Indian River but along almost the entire coast line of Florida. Mr. William Lytle created the end papers.

The generous advice, criticism, and suggestions of Dr. Rhea Marsh Smith of Rollins College, of Mr. Watt Marchman, Librarian of the Florida Historical Society, of Mr. Julien C. Yonge, Editor of the *Florida Historical Quarterly*, Dr. Charles W. Ramsdell of the University of Texas, and of Dr. Dallas D. Irvine, Chief of the Division of War Department Records in the National Archives, Washington, D. C., cannot be adequately acknowledged. Mr. Marchman is responsible for some of the new data and has helped in numerous other ways. Mr. Herbert Hopkins has assisted with the research and index. Dr. Irvine extended aid with the bibliography out of his study of the history of the Confederate Archives, to be published under the title, "Notes on the Fate of the Confederate Archives."

Mrs. Lee Breckinridge Thomas and Mrs. Mary Breckinridge have generously made available the diary and other unpublished papers of their grandfather, General Breckinridge. Without the use of the diary of Colonel John Taylor Wood, graciously lent by his daughter, Miss Lola Wood, it would have been impossible to identify plantations and other sites. Some valuable and colorful facts have been gleaned also from the diary of Tench Francis Tilghman, which was lent by his grandson, Dr. Tench Francis Tilghman, whose interest in the work has prompted him to extend invaluable aid.

Among many others who have helped are:

ALABAMA
Montevallo, Dr. Hallie Farmer. *Montgomery,* Dr. Peter A. Brannon.

CONNECTICUT
Scotland, Mrs. Beatrice Holt Chadbourne.

DISTRICT OF COLUMBIA
Washington, Mrs. Kate Trenholm Abrams, Dr. Philip M. Hamer, Mr. F. Eberhart Haynes, Mr. Frank J. Metcalf, Mrs. Florida Yulee Neff, Mr. Robert Wickliffe Woolley.

FLORIDA
Boca Grande, Mr. Benjamin W. Crowninshield, Mrs. Louise

du Pont Crowninshield, Mr. J. E. Riley. *De Funiak Springs,* J. L. McKinnon. *De Land,* Mr. I. Walter Hawkins. *Fort Pierce,* Mr. William I. Fee. *Jacksonville,* Mr. T. Frederick Davis, Dr. Dorothy Dodd, Mrs. Robert Gamble, Sr., Dr. J. Lee Kirby-Smith, Mrs. Sue Alderman Mahorner. *Lake City,* Mr. George L. Colburn. *Lake Wales,* Miss Rebecca Caldwell. *Leesburg,* Rev. R. F. Blackford, Mrs. F. L. Ezell. *Madison,* Mr. Carlton Smith. *Manatee,* Mrs. T. M. McDuffee. *Miami,* Mr. Edward C. Romfh, Mr. Gaines R. Wilson, Mr. Agnew Welsh. *New Smyrna,* Mrs. Zelia Wilson Sweett. *Ocala,* Mrs. Mary Waldo Harriss, Mr. and Mrs. R. V. Ott. *Orlando,* Mr. H. J. Chaffer, Mrs. Walter W. Rose, Mrs. Veronica Taylor. *Osteen,* Mr. K. B. Osteen. *Oviedo,* Mr. Mills M. Lord, Jr. *Oxford,* Mr. W. M. O'Dell. *Pensacola,* Miss Occie Clubbs. *Sanford,* Mr. Sydney O. Chase. *St. Augustine,* Mr. Leon J. Canova, Mr. Albert C. Manucy, Mrs. E. M. McCook, Mr. X. L. Pellicer. *St. Petersburg,* Mr. Leon D. Lewis. *Tallahassee,* Dr. Kathryn T. Abbey, Mrs. Esther B. Ferguson, Mr. Albert Hubbard Roberts. *Tampa,* Mrs. Geraldine McGregor Caldwell, Miss Lena E. Jackson, Mr. Theodore Lesley, III, Colonel D. B. McKay, Mrs. M. F. McKay, Mrs. Amos H. Norris. *Titusville,* Mr. H. C. Conkling, Mr. J. M. Osban, Mr. L. C. Stewart. *Webster,* Mr. Robert Hayes. *Winter Park,* Mr. Joshua Coffin Chase, Dr. C. W. Dabney, Prof. Edwin P. Granberry, Mr. Joe D. Hanna, Jr., Mr. and Mrs. George C. Holt, Dr. Hamilton Holt, Miss Dorothy Lockhart, Miss Mary E. Marchman, Mr. Harold Mutispaugh, Mrs. Rose Mills Powers, Mrs. Mary M. Price, Miss Jessie B. Rittenhouse, Mr. Frederic H. Ward.

GEORGIA

Atlanta, Dr. Butler Toombs. *Lagrange,* Mrs. Nell Blalock Lester. *Valdosta,* Mr. A. W. Varnedoe.

ILLINOIS

Chicago, Miss Barbara Donaldson.

KENTUCKY

Frankfort, Ex-Governor J. C. B. Beckham, Mrs. Elgin Morison. *Henderson,* Miss Susan Starling Towles. *Lexington,* Mrs. William C. Goodloe, Mr. J. M. Roche, Miss Lucille Stillwell, Mr. John Wilson Townsend. *Louisville,* Miss Edna J. Grauman, Mr. D. W. Potter.

LOUISIANA

New Orleans, Miss Elsie Bing, Miss Grace Johnston Connor, Mr. Victor Leovy, Mr. Albert Louis Lieutaud, Mr. Robert J. Usher, Mr. Walter Van Benthuysen.

MARYLAND

Annapolis, Mr. Richard J. Duval, Dr. James A. Robertson. *Chevy Chase,* Mrs. Jeter R. Horton. *Easton,* Col. Harrison Tilghman.

MISSOURI

St. Louis, Mr. John G. Lonsdale, Mr. John G. Lonsdale, Jr.

NEW YORK

New York, Mr. John C. Breckinridge, Dr. Frederick M. Dearborn, Mr. Louis H. Fox, Mr. Joe H. Gill, Mrs. Marjorie Daingerfield Holmes, Mr. Leon Hühner, Miss Alice P. McCarthy, Mr. Charles Magruder, Mr. Charles B. Reynolds, Mr. Julian T. Trenholm.

NORTH CAROLINA

Chapel Hill, Dr. Archibald Henderson, Mr. R. W. Patrick, Mr. J. Maryon Saunders. *Charlotte,* Rev. Willis G. Clark, Miss Nan Weller. *Greensboro,* Mr. R. D. Douglas, Mr. Charles B. Gault, Miss Mary Ellen Hall. *Raleigh,* the late Captain Samuel A'Court Ashe. *Wilmington,* Mr. Platt W. Davis, Mr. Thomas W. Davis, Judge George Rountree, Mrs. Meta Davis Rountree, Mr. Lindsay Russell.

PENNSYLVANIA
Philadelphia, Miss Gladys May Vogdes. *Rosemont,* Mrs. E. Waring Wilson.

SOUTH CAROLINA
Abbeville, Major Robert B. Cheatham, Miss Kate Marshall, Miss Nettie Russell. *Camden,* Mr. Frank H. Heath. *Charleston,* Prof. J. H. Easterby, Mr. Thomas E. Haile. *Columbia,* Mr. John K. Aull. *Fort Mill,* Captain Elliott Springs.

TEXAS
Dallas, Dr. Herbert Gambrell. *Palestine,* Mr. Jefferson D. Reagan.

VIRGINIA
Danville, Mrs. J. L. Hagan, Rev. N. E. Wicker, Jr. *Lynchburg,* Dr. Robert D. Meade. *Quantico,* Major General James C. Breckinridge. *Richmond,* Mr. Mallory Freeman, Miss Susan B. Harrison, Dr. Margaret Johnson, Dr. Robert A. Stewart.

CANADA
Niagara-on-the-Lake, Miss Catherine Creed.

CUBA
Havana, Mr. Ellis O. Briggs, Señor Augusto Pacetti. *Matanzas,* Mr. Edward S. Benét.

ENGLAND
Kent: *Breckinham,* Mrs. Frank Hall.

Appreciation is also expressed to the following authors and publishers for use of quotations from their publications:

To Prof. Jerome Dowd for *Life of Zebulon B. Vance* by Clement Dowd; to the author for *Billy Bowlegs and the Seminole War* by John C. Gifford, published by The Triangle Company; to Houghton Mifflin Company for *The End of an Era* by J. S. Wise, and *Life and Letters of John Hay* by W. R. Thayer; to John K. Aull for articles which appeared in *The State,* Columbia, South Carolina; to the *Galveston Daily News* for *The Escape of Judah P. Benjamin* by H. A. McLeod, May 27, 1894; to W. W. Davis for *Civil War and Reconstruction in Florida;* to Harper & Brothers for *Jefferson Davis, the Unreal and Real* by Robert McElroy, and *Military Operations of General Beauregard* by Alfred Roman; to E. P. Dutton & Co. Inc., for *Life and Letters of Phillips Brooks* by A. V. G. Allen, 1901; to Dr. Robert G. Stephens, Judge Alexander W. Stephens, and Mr. Robert L. Avary for *Recollections and Letters of Alexander H. Stephens* published by Doubleday, Doran & Company, Inc., 1910; to Henry Holt and Company for *Abraham Lincoln* by Lord Charnwood; to *McClure's* Magazine for "The Last Days of the Confederate Government" by S. R. Mallory; to D. Appleton-Century Company for *Battles and Leaders of the Civil War* edited by Underwood Johnson and C. C. Buel; "The Escape of the Confederate Secretary of War" by John Taylor Wood, *Century* Magazine, November, 1898; "The Capture of Jefferson Davis" by Burton N. Harrison, *Century* Magazine, November, 1883; and *The Rise and Fall of the Confederate Government* by Jefferson Davis; to *American Law Review* (now *United States Law Review*) for *Judah P. Benjamin* by H. H. Hagan; to Dr. Pierce Butler for *Judah P. Benjamin;* to Francis Burton Harrison for *Recollections Grave and Gay* and *The Harrisons of Skimino;* to The Times-Picayune Publishing Company, New Orleans, for excerpt from an article which appeared in the *Times-Democrat* May 13, 1900.

INDEX

302

High Point, N. C., Cabinet passes through, 40-41
Hill, Benjamin H., 136
Hillsboro, N. C., 43
Hilton Head, S. C., 124, 133
Hobe Sound, 159
Holden's Landing, Fla., 146
Hollis, J. J., ordered to Cape Sable, 98; arrested Harris and party, 127
Hope, Alexander James Beresford, 233
Houston, John C., 155
Howell, Miss, sister of Mrs. Davis, 4
Hunter, Robert M. T., 229, 230

— I —

Indian Key, 203; massacre at, 271
Indian River, Fla.; boat at, mentioned, 97; mosquitoes on, 156; nature of, 153; route followed on, by Breckinridge party, 154
Indian River Inlet, blockade camp at, 156
Interstate Commerce Commission, 240
Irwin, Charles E., 228
Irwinville, Ga., Davis camps near, 99; Thorburn leaves, 96
Isabella II, 188

— J —

Jacksonville, described, 217; Union meeting held in, 217
Jacksonville & Cedar Keys Railroad, 119
Jamestown, N. C., Cabinet passes through, 40
Johnson, Andrew; appeal to by Reagan, 146; disapproves Johnston-Sherman Agreement, 52; General Amnesty Proclamation of, 234; maintains Jefferson Davis should hang, 245; mentioned, 46, 229, 232, 239; offers reward for capture of Davis, 84
Johnston-Sherman agreement, 52
Johnston, Joseph E.; advises cessation of hostilities, 36; conferences with Sherman, 44, 50; empowered to negotiate with Sherman, 37; terms of surrender of, 52
Johnston, William Preston; aids government removal from Richmond, 11; captured with Davis, 100; member of Washington College faculty, 234; offers professorship to Breckinridge, 234; receives $1,510, 92, 94

— K —

Kanapaha Plantation, 121
Key West, Fla.; S. P. Chase visits, 140; George Davis arrested at, 223; Mallory, early life at, 9; supported

by wrecking, 174; to Indian Key, picketed, 127
Keyes, Wade, 241
"King of Pensacola," 243
Kirby, Ephraim, 259
Kirby-Smithdom, 79, 80
Knights Key, 203
Koonti, 267

— L —

Lagrange, Ga., 87, 136
Lake City, Fla., arrangements made at, for escape of Cabinet, 97
Lane, Mrs. Thomas Hill, 210
Lanier, Sidney, 147
Last meetings of Confederate Cabinet, 260-261
Lee, Robert Edward; mentioned, 23, 152, 188, 197, 211, 247; offers professorship to Breckinridge, 234; pursued by Grant, 19; surrenders to Grant, 20; telegraphs Richmond must be evacuated, 4; telegraphs withdrawal from Petersburg, 4; writes to Breckinridge, 235
Leovy, Henry J.; accompanies Benjamin, 195; quoted on Benjamin, 207, 208
Leovy, Mrs. Henry J., 68, 117
Lexington, Ky., Breckinridge returns to, 234
Lexington, N. C., Cabinet passes near, 41
Libby Prison, 237
Lincoln, Abraham; assassination of, announced, 44; effect of death of, on North, 79; honored in North with day of prayer, 154; in Richmond, 18; mentioned, 217, 219; policy of conciliation of, 37, 79
Litchfield, Conn., 74
Lubbock, Francis Richard; aids removal of government, 11; boasts of South Carolina hospitality, 29; destroys official papers, 68; promise of hospitality justified, 57; receives $1,510, 92, 94

— M —

Madison, Fla., haven for Confederate refugees, 107
Mallory, Stephen R., Secretary of the Navy; arrested at Lagrange, Ga., 136; biographical sketch of, 8, 9; criticizes North Carolinians, 29; developed two deadly weapons, 243; feeling of North toward, 243; last Cabinet member released from prison, 243; last years of, 242; paroled, 243; quoted, 14, 20, 21;

303

304

305